The

OXFORD MAP COMPANION

The

OXFORD MAP COMPANION

One Hundred Sources in World History

Patricia Seed

New York   Oxford
OXFORD UNIVERSITY PRESS

Oxford University Press is a department of the University of Oxford.
It furthers the University's objective of excellence in research,
scholarship, and education by publishing worldwide.

Oxford New York

Auckland   Cape Town   Dar es Salaam   Hong Kong   Karachi
Kuala Lumpur   Madrid   Melbourne   Mexico City   Nairobi
New Delhi   Shanghai   Taipei   Toronto

With offices in

Argentina   Austria   Brazil   Chile   Czech   Republic   France   Greece
Guatemala   Hungary   Italy   Japan   Poland   Portugal   Singapore
South Korea   Switzerland   Thailand   Turkey   Ukraine   Vietnam

For titles covered by Section 112 of the US Higher Education Opportunity Act,
please visit www.oup.com/us/he for the latest information about pricing and
alternate formats.

Published by Oxford University Press
198 Madison Avenue, New York, New York 10016
http://www.oup.com

Library of Congress Cataloging-in-Publication Data

Seed, Patricia.
The oxford map companion : one hundred sources in world history / Patricia Seed.
p. cm.
ISBN 978-0-19-976563-8
1. Historical geography—Maps. 2. World history—Maps. 3. World maps. 4. Atlases. I. Title.
G1030.S363   2014
911—dc23

2013000189

Printing number: 9 8 7 6 5 4 3 2 1

Printed in the United States of America on acid-free paper

For CC and TZ

Thanks for the wonderful journey

Table of contents

Preface

I first became fascinated with maps while writing *Ceremonies of Possession in Europe's Conquest of the New World*, when I discovered that political leaders in the Netherlands in the seventeenth century often based their legal claims in the Americas upon the accuracy of their newly drawn maps. How Dutch authorities had acquired such certainty was a mystery. Uncovering the origins of their confidence drew me into the history of mapping in the Americas, to its origins in fifteenth-century maps of West Africa, and from there back to Mediterranean precursors centuries earlier. As I delved even deeper into the past and moved further around the world, I became ever more intrigued by the immense artistic and cultural diversity of maps. Courtiers to kings, adherents of many different religions, members of minority groups, and people without written language had drawn incredible maps.

Maps contained remarkable visual images of the whole Earth or whole sky, as well as parts of both. They varied widely over time and space, diverging significantly in both their methods and materials: carved into wood and clay, painted on cave walls and tree bark, or simply drawn in the sand. When Charles Cavaliere of Oxford University Press invited me to write a book on maps in world history he created the perfect excuse for exploring the historical and cultural diversity of maps and presenting readers with a brief snapshot of an astonishing visual world.

In creating this work, I wanted to avoid reproducing maps that appear in virtually every coffee table book. Hence, I deliberately sought out unusual maps in far-flung locations. During a trip along the Silk Road in western China in 2009, I came across an eighth-century map of constellations only known through an outline created decades earlier. A rare copy of the second oldest road map of France, complete with images of automobiles from 1902, turned up in a collection in California, and a retired Marine colonel furnished me with rarely glimpsed British aviation maps for bombing Germany during the Second World War. HRH Princess Maha Chakri Sirindhorn of Thailand graciously allowed me to include one of a recently discovered cache containing her country's oldest surviving maps. The immense generosity of those who agreed to share with me their unusual or little-known maps made creating this book a rewarding experience.

However, not all of the maps will be unknown. Some will be familiar because they are unique—the oldest surviving maps of their kind, such as the Babylonian clay world map; or the earliest map of a certain area, such as the well-known Cantino map of the New World.

Readers familiar with world history will notice that the way I organized this book diverges from standard world history chronologies. Following a strictly sequential approach would have entailed constantly jerking the reader back and forth between different subjects, and losing sight of evolving trends in mapmaking. For example, maps of the heavens, often ignored in most world histories, constitute the oldest and culturally most varied approaches to mapping. During the period between the tenth and sixteenth centuries, a single Persian astronomer's drawings of the constellations remained the template for astronomers across Europe, the Middle East, and Central Asia. Splitting the maps according to time periods would have hidden

the remarkable continuities in these maps. Regionally compartmentalizing them in the usual world history fashion would also have effectively hidden the similarities across religious faiths and over vast reaches of territory. Even land survey maps, which became widely popular during the seventeenth and eighteenth centuries, first appeared in Japan during the eighth century. Making mapping secondary to world history effaces the resemblances as easily as it does the dissimilarities among maps and their makers. Maps have their own history and rhythms of development, and this brief history of the world through its maps tries to see that world through these changes.

In order to share this historical and cultural wealth of maps with many people, Charles Cavaliere, my former student Tsvetelina Zdraveva, and I devised several means of making the book accessible to those with little or no knowledge of geography in addition to those whose only familiarity with maps comes from their cell phones or computers equipped with images from Google, Bing, or Mapquest.

In order to make maps from remote, obscure, or even vanished places more understandable, many of the historical maps are accompanied by an explanatory diagram and/or small locator map. Of additional use, and appearing on the left side of each map layout, is a QR code that can be read by any smart phone, iPad, or computer with a webcam. (QR readers are free for all of these devices). The code will automatically take readers to a Google Map outlining where locations on the historical map can be found today. Alternatively, the same Google Maps can be found at www.mapcompanion.org. Using the zoom feature, readers can dive in to see details of a location or zoom out to see its surrounding areas. Using the cursor to pan around the world, any reader can understand the relation of the historical map's location to any other place around the globe.

In addition to learning where the map was made or the area that it depicts, the QR links to Google Maps also allow anyone who wishes to see more of the area as it appears today, through one of two methods. For many inhabited areas of the world,

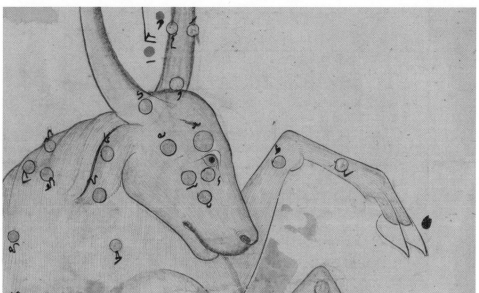

one can click on the human icon for "street view" and Google will show photographs of a place as it appears today. For remote historical monuments, archeological sites, abandoned cities, or panoramic views of inaccessible mountains or plains, typing "Panoramio" (or another photo aggregation site) into the search bar above the map will automatically place small images or place markers across the map. Each thumbnail or place marker contains clear, often professional, photographs of the area. While the pictures from Panoramio are copyrighted, they allow anyone to see remote or deserted sites without undertaking difficult or dangerous journeys.

Two other devices included in the *Oxford Map Companion* are designed to enrich the reader's experience. The first section, "Types of Maps Included in the Volume," uses a coding system to organize the maps into six different categories. Using the coding system, readers can focus on particular types of maps across parts. The second section, "Locations for Maps in the Volume," uses a global locator map to show the place (or places) associated with each map. Readers interested in a particular region can use the locator to identify the geographical distribution of maps in the book. Both of these pedagogical aids are located at the end of the volume.

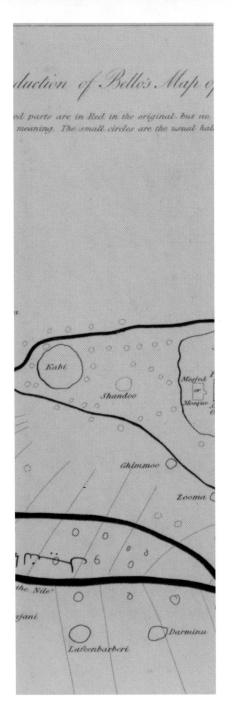

Acknowledgments

So many people contributed in bringing this volume together that I feel fortunate in being able to thank them, even in this small fashion, for their kind assistance. The biggest thanks go to Charles Cavaliere and Tsvetelina Zdraveda, who worked with me on this project from the beginning. Through hours of Skype conferencing, thousands of emails, and face-to-face meetings in Irvine, Houston, New York, and London, Charles and Tsevti never wavered in their support—indeed, I owe them countless thanks for the wealth of ideas and good advice they offered at each of the project's many turns. With great pleasure and deep gratitude, I dedicate my book to Charles and Tsveti. Francelle Carapetyan, the project's picture researcher, went above and beyond her normal brief to acquire previously unpublished images in remote collections and to retrieve images even during her own personal travels overseas. Lauren Aylward kept excellent track of the constant flow of images of maps as they arrived in seemingly haphazard fashion. Susan Lee, Kim Howie, and the entire production and design team at Oxford demonstrated excellence at each and every stage of the book's journey from manuscript to bound volume. Nick Millea, Map Curator of Oxford University's Bodelian Library, facilitated access to rare maps and provided helpful counsel on map selection. David Helliwell provided an image of the newly restored Selden Map of China and Southeast Asia.

Moving out from the circle of Oxford-related assistance, I wish to thank many people around the world. In China, the biggest thanks go to Gao Bingzhong head of the Center for Civil Society Studies at Peking University who facilitated access to so many places and sources in China. Sun Xiaochun of the Chinese Academy of Natural Sciences, Li Xia of the Commercial Press, Man Ke, Wen Hua, Xu Lili who showed us Kublai Khan's palace, and Tsetseg Ulh, of the Beijing Ancient Observatory, and Zhang Shaozeng, for responding to endless queries. For Korea, Jae Chung's assistance was invaluable. In Japan, the Imperial Household Museum was especially helpful in providing previously unpublished maps from their collection. In Thailand, I would first like to express my profound gratitude to HRH Princess Maha Chakri Sirndhorn for allowing us to publish maps from her collection. Coeli Barry, Dawn Rooney, Komkrich Chongbunwatana, Khunying Aaraya Pibulnakarin,and Jeff Petri were also helpful in guiding me in Thai-related matters. For Bali, Steve Lansing provided results of his own research on the availability of historical maps. For Australia, Fred Myers and Peter Sutton provided helpful assistance, as did the South Australian Museum.. In Russia, Alexei Elfimoff worked hard to secure maps from his country. For Iran, Massumeh Farhad of the Smithsonian provided helpful historical information on Persian clothing. R. H. von Gent supplied information on Mesopotamian star maps. From Saudi Arabia, former Rice undergraduate Mohammed Aljishi transliterated historical Arabic place names, allowing me to create original maps in Arabic. For the nation of Georgia, special thanks are due to Natia Chakvetadze and Nelli Pertia, for translating and interpreting an historical map of their homeland. In Turkey, Erkan Saka and Ebru Kayallap, located Istanbul's best-regarded map dealers and willingly trekked across Istanbul with me in search of Ottoman maps. Tzvi Langermann of Hebrew University in Israel helped locate unpublished color images constellations and provided excellent guidance regarding their interpretation.

In Egypt, despite the recent turmoil, a great many people demonstrated the generosity for which the country is justly famous. The Egyptian Museum of Antiquities provided a beautiful photograph of a Middle Kingdom coffin. Yasmin El-Shazly, head of Documentation at the Museum was especially helpful and Lisa Sabbahay, Hannan Sabea, and Julia Elychar helped me find the way. The South African Astronomical Observatory supplied their own excellent drawings and graciously answered questions about their origins and history.

The National Library of Austria's well-hidden Map Library contains many great treasures, including the Peutinger Table, for which it supplied outstanding images. Peter Prokop of the same library was also extremely helpful in locating Austro-Hungarian maps. Piero Falchetta of the Marciana Library in Venice was extremely generous with his time. In Rome, Andrea Aureli arranged for a rare photograph from the Superintendent of Archeology. The French National Library in Paris and Royal Netherlands Library in the Hague responded to requests with their customary speed and efficiency. Herik Dupont of the Royal Library in Copenhagen was an excellent source of advice. In Illulissat, Greenland, a local ship captain provided copies of his own nautical charts and the Danish Geodetic Society kindly consented to the publication of its historical charts. Special thanks are due to Francis Hebert and Jamie Owen of the Royal Geographic Society in London for their time and assistance in locating maps from their collection. In Britain, the British Museum and the British Library's imaging department both provided outstanding scans, the latter from previously unphotographed maps.

In Canada, the National Archives undertook new photography in order to better demonstrate the quality of one of its maps. The University of British Columbia Library contributed maps from its famous collection of Tokugawa Era Japanese maps. In the United States, the Library of Congress's policy of allowing free use of its images allowed me to include incredible maps from its collection—including the sealskin map of Disko Bay, Greenland, a cloth map of Srinagar in Kashmir, and its own construction of the Waldseemüller world map. Marty Baldessari, picture researcher, navigated the Library's many collections like an old sea captain. Christian Kelleher of the Nettie Lee Benson Latin American Collection at the University of Texas supplied an outstanding image from its collection of sixteenth-century Mexican maps. In California, the Earth Science Collection allowed me to borrow a valuable map from its collection. At UCLA, Polly Robertson provided the Luba mapping device and provided advice on the text.

I wish to thank my colleagues at the University of California-Irvine, for their support and encouragement during this process. Retired airline captain Charles Quilter—who holds a PhD from Irvine—supplied me with aeronautical charts collected during his forty-year career flying all over the world. Undergraduates Narbeh Abdalian, Adriana Aden, Vincent Ahn, Diana Audish, Mindy Bui, Norma Eng, Pierre Fragoso, Perrie Garcia, Patrick Hara, Lawrence Ho, Soon-Won Hong, Shandell Jordan, Joel Karahadian, Sabeen Khanmohamed, Husam Khoudari, Lev Kulyashov, Jeffrey La Motte, Darren Lee, Faris Madha, John Mcdonough, Stephanie Mckenna, Colin Moberly, Evan Nagayama, Mehrdad Nourikalouri, Danh Phan, Raymond Ramzi, Jonathan Roth, Roxana Sorooshian-Tafti, Christie Sosa, Nicole Tolman, and Sara Zarate Garcia, provided helpful commentaries and critiques of the manuscript. So too did Kirsten Alonso, Kathleen Douglas, Catherine Doyle, Sonny Duong, Katherine Ewing, Imran Faruqui, Christine Feghali, Sif Goodale, Emily Guild, Arielle Hinojosa, Patric Huynh, Adam Jerro, Caitlyn Koby, Lotfullah Sohaib, Triya Wei Sum Leong, Alex Martenka, Jason Payag Mateo, Vincent Minter, Theodore Motu, Andrew Ortiz, Chris Jason Padeo, Matthew Perez, Daisy Ramirez, Chad Toshiki Rutherford, Aleczander Scott, David Liu Singer, and Alexander Edwin Valdez

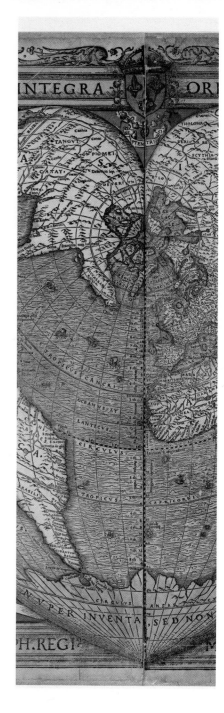

with special thanks to the Final Eight: Kirsten Alonso, Kathleen Douglas, Catherine Doyle, Sonny Duong, Imran Faruqui, Arielle Hinojosa, Jason Mateo, and Vincent Minter who gave extra time on these chapters.

I want to especially thank Kim Ricker and Jean Niswonger of the GIS Data Center of Fondren Library, who helped locate data sets of unusual places, and handled data incompatibilities and other software malfunctions usually caused by my attempt to do something they had specifically cautioned against doing. Together they made it possible to create, with great precision, the original locator maps and schematic diagrams for this book. Tsvetelina Zdraveda then cast her critical design eye over the end result and made the maps more legible. Sarah Lyons, also an architecture student at Rice University, contributed several of the diagrams appearing in this book.

Numerous people not named above also provided encouragement and helpful advice over the course of creating this book, reading either the entire manuscript or portions thereof: Jerry Brotton, Felipe Fernández-Armesto, and Martin Lewis, as well as the following: Peter Dykema, Arkansas Tech University; Trevor Getz, San Francisco State University; Maxim Matusevich, Seton Hall University; Robert Scott Moore, Indiana University of Pennsylvania; Stephen Morillo, Wabash College; Luke A. Nichter, Texas A&M University-Central Texas; Hollie Schilig, California State University Long Beach; William K. Storey, Millsaps College; Kate Transchel, California State University, Chico. Any errors are of course my own.

Finally, I thank my family: Rachel, Avery, and George Marcus. Without them, I could never find my way home, even with the best map.

About the author

Patricia Seed is Professor of History at the University of California, Irvine. Her scholarly career has followed a fascinating trajectory of achievements: from Latin American colonial history, culminating in *To Love Honor and Obey in Colonial Mexico* (Bolton Prize, 1989), to the comparative history of European colonialism in the New World, marked by *American Pentimento* (Atlantic History Prize, 2003), and the highly influential *Ceremonies of Possession in Europe's Conquest of the New World*, (1995). The insights she gained into the techno-scientific basis of Dutch and Portuguese colonialism led to research on the history of the oceans and the design and launch (since 1999) of a much consulted website on the history of navigation (www.rice.edu/ latitude). In recent years, she has been most intensively involved in research on old and new questions in cartography. To this she has brought to bear her skills in the use of digital imaging technologies (GIS and graphic design software) not only to reformulate the questions of the history of map making but to offer historical and comparative scholarship both new tools of analysis and new ways of representing the knowledge that it produces.

Introduction: maps and mapmaking in history

History books can tell when, why, and how things happened in the past, but they answer the question of "where" with words. They might name one of the places where ancient Egyptians quarried gold, or tell that Louis XVI and Marie Antoinette were executed in Paris in 1793 during the French Revolution. But these books simply provide the names of the places—they do not *show* where history happened.

Maps, however, answer the question "where" visually. Since they are visual, maps show where a volcano erupted, a village flooded, or a deadly battle was fought. Equally important, maps depict these locations in relation to surrounding geographic areas. For example, a map of the ancient Egyptian quarries shows its location along the main route from the ancient capital of Thebes to the Red Sea. For the unfortunate French monarchs, a map completed four years before their deaths shows where they were imprisoned in relation to where they would be executed at the Place de la Concorde, not far from the Louvre.

In both of these examples, the maps were made by individuals who lived close to the time that the events happened (see maps 15 and 64). While historians have long understood the importance of contemporaneous primary source documents

(such as eyewitness accounts, letters, journals, and transcripts) in reconstructing the past, they less frequently have utilized images showing how people in the past visually represented the space in which they ordered their lives.

Maps thus offer an important yet different primary source for the study of history. They provide a window into the visual world of people in the past, the spaces they inhabited and how they imagined them.

In this respect, the history of mapmaking differs significantly from historical atlases. The latter employ contemporary maps that display geographic and political information about past societies. But as useful as these maps can be, they lack the vantage point of the mapmakers of the past. They are not informed by the materials and visual conventions that were employed, or by how bygone cartographers envisioned and represented the space around them.

Maps created near the time of events can provide clues to the places that people once knew or recognized, but that have since disappeared. Through the centuries maps have related information of local importance—they identified rivers, mountains, caves, and canyons. They depicted features that dominated a landscape or a way of life—a giant mountain range looming over a valley, a wide swift-moving river such as the Amazon, or a sluggish waterway like the Euphrates that annually overflows its banks, bathing the crops in life-giving water. Some of these places that appear on historical maps were destroyed long ago, or have since been overgrown by jungle (such as the roads of eighteenth-century Thailand; see Map 66) or buried under desert sands (like the quarries of ancient Egypt).

Above all, maps provide insight into the visual cultures of the past. Because mapmakers operated in a fundamentally visual idiom, they employed distinct and sometimes elaborate symbols and colors to indicate geographical features, or they sketched routes to destinations that they considered important using symbols, colors, and shapes whose significance they understood. In this way, maps provide an opportunity to discern the visual vocabularies of societies long extinct.

Colors or shapes on maps create a link to the physical world, but they also convey something about the importance of that space at the time of the map's creation. The Tien Shen mountains in western China appeared as a series of bright red straight lines in an eleventh-century map by a native of the region. Nearby mountains to the north, in Mongolia, were depicted by their inhabitants a few centuries later as unattractive, inverted brown "L" shapes. This is not surprising, because in the eleventh century, the Tien Shen mountains were of great significance to travelers along the Silk Road, while to Mongols several centuries later the mountains north of the now-defunct Silk Road corridor were perceived simply as seasonal grazing pastures (see maps 27 and 70).

Sometimes makers of maps from distant cultures and remote times employed similar symbols for historically very different purposes. For example, hills and mountains appear in abstract circular shapes in both ancient Mesopotamian and current

British aviation maps. Ancient Mesopotamian clay tablets represented hills and mountains with circles; today's British Civil Aviation Authority employs similar shapes. But the relative size and color of these symbols tells us about the importance of elevations to makers and readers of each map. Babylonian mapmakers used small circles for mountains relative to rivers, indicating that hills and mountains held little interest since their society relied entirely upon fertile, flat river valleys. British aviation maps, on the other hand, have large, brightly colored, rounded contours indicating even relatively low heights so that pilots approaching a runway will stay sufficiently above these areas to avoid crashing. Rivers are barely visible. In both cases, variations in color and size are employed to indicate elevation. In each example, the distinct size and color of similar abstract shapes tell us something about the function of the map and the context in which it was made (see maps 13 and 99).

The earliest maps sought to locate humans in the universe. For millennia, humans have tried to define where they fit in the immense cosmos and to depict their own perceptions of their place in a broader social, spiritual, or celestial universe. The oldest known maps are, therefore, maps of the heavens. Past societies employed maps of the heavens to indicate a time for action. In this respect, the skies became the giant clock of human time, with the appearance of certain stars indicating when hunting season should begin, or when crops could be planted. Depictions of the heavens, and what humans should do when they saw patterns in the sky, underline the first maps.

Another impulse that has long motivated humans is the desire to map the relationships among various societies, to visually represent people in relationship to their fellow humans or, as it might be called today, the spatial representation

of social networks. Social network mapping is often motivated by commercial or religious reasons to find other humans. Such maps seek to answer such questions as: Where can I go to find my fellows—both friend and foe alike? Where are their towns, houses, and markets? Where can I go to exchange my goods? Where can I go to worship with them? Where can I go to find animals and plants for food, clothing, and shelter? What are the best routes to travel? The opposite of friendship—enmities and hatreds—constitute equally powerful motives for mapping. If there are rival groups, or invaders, where might they be found? What paths or routes might they travel on their way to attack?

Now as in the past, people often sketched the places and spatial relationships that were most important to them. In an agricultural society, the layouts of fields and allocation of water frequently made their way onto maps. In similar fashion, in cities the arrangement of streets, plazas, and public institutions were featured on maps. Often maps were drawn up at the urging of leaders of a society, seeking knowledge for political glory or social change.

For individuals on the move, other kinds of maps were created. Cartographers traced routes based upon information they collected from merchants and pilgrims, often indicating both hospitable and inhospitable areas as well as natural obstacles, such as mountain passes, and manmade ones, such as walls.

Humans have also sought to locate themselves within the natural world—asking where they are with respect to rivers, hills, and volcanoes, natural objects that we might know of but not be able to see. Maps thus place humans in relationship to nature and landscape.

Over the centuries, people have used whatever materials they have had at hand in order to draw. Maps have been painted on cave walls, animal skins, and artists' canvasses, carved into pieces of clay or wood, sewn onto fabric, and woven into tapestries. In contemporary times, maps may even appear as pixels on a computer screen or a hiker's handheld locator device (GPS). But regardless of the material upon which they have been produced, maps have always illustrated spatial information.

Despite the immensely diverse materials used to create them, maps provide a vantage point that is different from other kinds of historical sources—namely, a visual perspective on space. Traditionally there have been five crucial aspects of spatial relationships that appear on maps: direction, distance, area, shape, and scale. Historically, however, these five spatial aspects of a map have been expressed in a wide variety of forms including figures, texts, shapes, colors, and sometimes a combination of the above. All these choices reveal something about the visual culture of the mapmaker and his times.

However, for historical maps such as the ones included in this book, a sixth category is required—orientation, or the direction in which the viewer is looking as she examines the map. In the present day it has become customary to place north at the top—but this custom, like all others, has its own distinct historical and cultural evolution (see pages 84–85). Historical maps have been aligned north, south, east, west, or somewhere in between. Furthermore, the symbol most commonly employed today for north (an arrow) is the product of a distinct cultural and historical period.

Some of these maps will appear odd to modern eyes. Without standardization, and lacking scientific equipment to survey and measure, people in the past had very imperfect ideas about locations, distances, the heights of mountains, the width of rivers, or the lengths of coastlines. What matters, however, is how people chose to represent their world and what that representation tells us about how they saw their world.

Not all societies created maps, even ones with distinguished pictorial traditions. India, for example, has a long and distinguished artistic tradition but, as many historians of cartography have noted, it produced few, if any, maps before the nineteenth century. Since it was the birthplace of the Buddha, India frequently appeared on maps made by Buddhists from elsewhere in Asia but not on maps made by Indians themselves.

The individuals who produced maps in the past were not necessarily literate. Many of the earliest maps were created by people who could draw, but not necessarily those who could read, write, or who even possessed an alphabet. As millennia passed, and maps began to include the names of places, at least one person involved in creating the map had to be able to write the names in the appropriate spaces. When large-scale maps came into existence, a primary cartographer would direct the enterprise, reading various accounts of journeys and places and writing out the names and approximate locations.

But those who drew the maps and created the artwork did not need to be literate.

Instead, many mapmakers were skilled painters or artists. In compositions such as the map from Hereford Cathedral in England (see Map 28), a wide range of anonymous artists participated in the project—the style in which human figures and animals are drawn changes dramatically as one pans across the map. Artists such as the ones who created the Hereford map were skilled at painting and sketching, but they did not need to know how to write.

Historical maps are also almost always collaborative endeavors. Even when maps were directed or paid for by elites, the act of creating a map involved a variety of different skilled artisans who could represent spaces and distances. Traces of their perspectives and their work can be discerned by today's viewers. Kings, aristocrats, or knights may have commissioned maps for taxation, land surveys, or military planning, but they left the task to specialized artists who knew how to represent space and the world around them.

The maps are organized into 9 Parts. Each map is numbered and given a title and the year or approximate date it was created. Source information provides data concerning the dimensions of the map, the material used in its making, and the museum, library, or archive where it currently can be found.

Each map is accompanied by an essay that sets the map in its historical context, explains the map's cartographic significance, and points out details that may not be obvious to the reader. Technical terms are set in boldface type and defined in the Glossary at the end of the book.

Each map includes a QR code that takes readers to a Google Map that outlines where locations on the historical map are found.

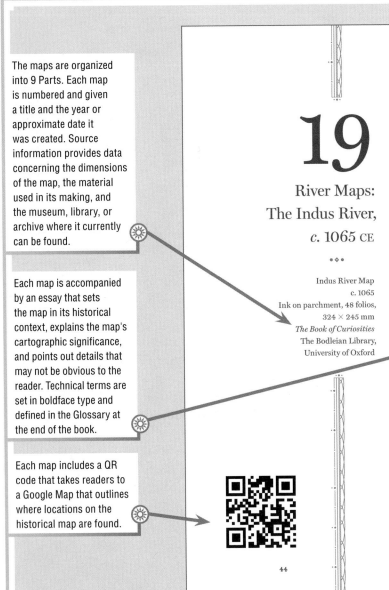

19

River Maps:
The Indus River,
c. 1065 CE

• • •

Indus River Map
c. 1065
Ink on parchment, 48 folios,
324 × 245 mm
The Book of Curiosities
The Bodleian Library,
University of Oxford

44

India is named for the Indus River, which today flows mostly through neighboring Pakistan. The river originates high in the Tibetan plateau and slowly wends its way southward to the Indian Ocean. In the map on the right, Tibet appears in red at the upper left while the Indian Ocean appears at the opposite corner in green. The map presents a mirror image of the actual river, which flows from the northeast (upper right) down to the southwest (lower left).

Alexander the Great (356–323 BCE) reached the northern Indus River after crossing the Iranian plateau and defeating the Persians. He crossed the Indus south of Rawalpindi, reaching the Jhelum River (known as the Hydaspes to the Greeks), the eastern limit of his conquests, in 326 BCE. His return trip took him southward along the Jhelum and then the Chenab River to Multan, shown at the bottom of the map.

When Alexander withdrew, the northern Indus became absorbed by the Mauryan Empire from 321–185 BCE. The founder's grandson, Ashoka (304–232 BCE), converted to Buddhism and fostered its spread throughout India. Nine hundred years later, yet another group of conquerors came to the Indus Valley. At the bottom of the map, part of an 11th century medieval Islamic cosmography, the text explains that the Muslim conqueror Muhammad bin Qasim Al-Thaqafi invaded the rich city of Multan on the Indus River around 710 CE.

To the right of Multan on the map is the city of Mansurah (whose original name was Brahmanabad). Like Multan, Mansurah was conquered by Muslim forces early in the eighth century CE. As this map indicates, Mansurah lay along the banks of the Indus River, with a river channel on the other side, making it appear as an island. From the eighth to the eleventh centuries, Mansurah functioned as a prosperous market town set in a fertile agricultural area. However, sometime after this map was made the Indus River changed course, stranding the city in

the center of a sandy plain miles from water of any kind, This is not the first time the Indus river had been cruel to those who lived along its banks. Around 1500 BCE, the great civilization of Harappa had collapsed due to similar environmental changes.

Although the central focus of this map is the Indus River, it also contains information about a land route to China. To the right of the backwards S-shaped river are two very long straight black lines of text with red dots. The dots are the names of towns along the route from the Muslim town of Multan to the strategically situated city of Kannauj in northeastern India, and from Kannauj onward to China.

In terms of the map these two lines are oddly placed, almost as an afterthought. In fact, a route between Multan and Kannauj and then down the Ganges River would have been in a single direction, nearly directly east and slightly south. But such a single straight line would not have fit on the paper, which perhaps explains the unusual shift in direction.

For centuries, Kannauj (now in the state of Uttar Pradesh in modern India) was the crossroads of commerce for the subcontinent. Three lines of text on the map describe the city as the capital of India, with many markets and different parts of the city. The ruler was said to own 2,500 elephants. From Kannauj, a second straight line of text continues at a right angle toward the top of the paper. It says "the road to China from …" Only the first three of the twelve names of places along the road to China can be linked to modern names. All three are cities along the Ganges in eastern India: the first is Fraypan or Prayag (modern Allahabad), followed by Benares, and then Paliputra (modern Patna). The remainder of the names remain unidentifiable, suggesting that they, like Mansurah, may have fallen into decline. At the very top of the row of dots, curving backwards toward the mountain of Tibet, is the "The Gate of China." There the map ends.

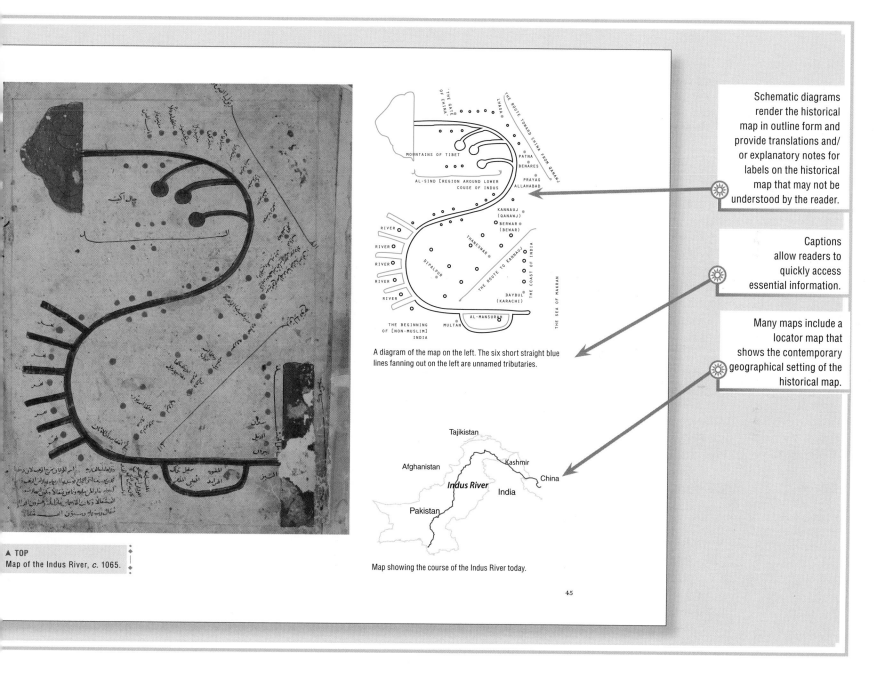

THE GATE OF CHINA

LHASA

THE ROUTE TOWARD CHINA FROM QANAWJ

MOUNTAINS OF TIBET

PATNA
BENARES

AL-SIND [REGION AROUND LOWER COUSE OF INDUS]

PRAYAG
ALLAHABAD

KANNAUJ
(QANAWJ)

BERWAR
(BEWAR)

RIVER

THANESWAR

RIVER

DIPALPUR

RIVER

THE ROUTE TO KANNAUJ

THE COAST OF INDIA

RIVER

RIVER

DAYBUL
(KARACHI)

THE SEA OF MAKRAN

AL-MANSURAH

THE BEGINNING OF [NON-MUSLIM] INDIA

MULTAN

Schematic diagrams render the historical map in outline form and provide translations and/or explanatory notes for labels on the historical map that may not be understood by the reader.

Captions allow readers to quickly access essential information.

Many maps include a locator map that shows the contemporary geographical setting of the historical map.

A diagram of the map on the left. The six short straight blue lines fanning out on the left are unnamed tributaries.

Tajikistan

Afghanistan

Kashmir

China

Indus River

India

Pakistan

Map showing the course of the Indus River today.

▲ **TOP**
Map of the Indus River, *c.* 1065.

45

Timeline of world history

160,000 to 20,000 years ago:	Most recent Ice Age
since at least 100,000 years ago:	Art, ritual, religion; *homo sapiens* migrations out of Africa
60,000 years ago:	Colonization of Australia
since 5000 BCE:	Intensive agriculture: Tigris-Euphrates, Nile, Indus, Yellow rivers
c. 3000 BCE:	Rise of Sumerian civilization; earliest use of celestial directions in East Asia
c. 3000 BCE:	Earliest writing (Sumer)
c. 2300 BCE:	earliest known road map (Mesopotamia)
c. 2000 BCE:	Beginning of Bantu expansion (Africa)
c. 1800 BCE:	Spread of iron technology
c. 1600 BCE:	Beginning of Polynesian migrations
c. 1130 BCE:	Earliest surviving map of the zodiac
since 800 BCE:	Trans-Mediterranean trade
c. 600 BCE:	Earliest surviving world map (Babylon)
c. 550–334 BCE:	Persian Empire
since 300 BCE:	Silk Roads; Monsoon-driven Indian Ocean trade
334–323 BCE:	Alexander's Empire
c. 321–185 BCE:	Mauryan Empire, India
240 BCE–476s CE:	Roman Empire
c. 239 BCE:	Earliest surviving Chinese map
221 BCE–220s CE:	Han Empire
since 100 BCE:	Mediterranean-Atlantic trade
c. 60:	First T-O maps
c. 150 CE:	Ptolemy, *The Almagest*
200s and on:	Spread of Buddhism to East Asia
220 CE:	Breakup of the Han Empire
c. 350 CE:	Earliest surviving Roman road map
300s and on:	Spread of Christianity
476 CE:	End of Roman Empire in the West

c. 500 CE:	Teotihuacán (Mexico) one of the largest cities in the world
600–800 CE:	Growing trans-Saharan trade
618:	Beginning of the Tang Dynasty, China
630 CE on:	Rise and spread of Islam
c. 750 CE:	First land surveys, Japan
960–1279:	Song dynasty, China
c. 964 CE:	First maps of the Greek constellations (Persia)
1040s–1090:	Turkish migrations into Middle East
c. 1072 CE:	Earliest surviving Turkish world map
1098:	First Crusade
1000–1200:	Spread of Islam to West Africa
c. 1100:	Compass introduced to the Mediterranean from China
c. 1200:	First Buddhist world maps, Japan
c. 1200:	First portolan charts
1206–1360s:	Mongol hegemony
c. 1300:	First Gyoki maps, Japan; earliest surviving Ptolemaic world map
1300–1800:	Little Ice Age
1300s–mid-1400s:	Plague in Eurasia
from 1350s:	Rise of the Ottomans
1360:	Earliest surviving road map of Britain
1368–1644:	Ming dynasty, China
1392–1910:	Choson dynasty, Korea
since mid-1400s:	Growth of Atlantic navigation
from mid-1400s:	Rise of Incas, Aztecs. Beginnings of oceanic imperialism
c. 1450–1650:	Expansion of the Ottoman, Mughal, and Safavid empires
since 1492:	Columbian exchange
1497:	Vasco da Gama reaches India; nautical astrolabe invented

c. 1500:	Development of Sikhism (India)
1502:	First European map to include the Americas
since 1513:	Atlantic navigation; discovery of Gulf Stream
1502:	First map to include lines of latitude
1519–1522:	Magellan's circumnavigation of the globe
1549:	First Jesuit missionaries arrive in China
1550–1700:	Scientific Revolution in the West
1569:	Mercator's world map
1570:	First atlas, published by Abraham Ortelius
1640:	Closing of Japan
1644:	Beginning of Qing dynasty, China
since early 1700s:	Decline of Asian empires
since 1720s:	Rise of global horticulture
c. 1720–1790:	European Enlightenment
1754–1763:	French and Indian War (North America)
1756–1757:	British conquest of Bengal (India)
c. 1760:	British industrialization begins
1768–1779:	Pacific voyages of Captain James Cook
1776–1783:	American Revolution
1780–1800:	Peak of Atlantic slave trade
1789–1797:	French Revolution
1791:	Creation of Ordnance Survey, England
1800–1880:	Decline of slavery
since c. 1800:	Coal and steam power
1803:	First Ottoman maps to use Mercator projection
1809:	Founding of Sokoto Caliphate (Africa)
1815:	First geological map
c. 1850:	Peak of whaling industry in the United States
c. 1825:	First railroads
1840s–1860s:	Opium Wars, China
c. 1850:	Electricity

1860s–1910:	Mass migrations
1875–1914:	Height of European imperialism
1863:	First underground railway, London
1870–1900:	Famine and drought worldwide
1884:	First gasoline powered automobile
1884–1885:	Berlin Conference, Scramble for Africa
1893:	First patent for a radio
1894–1895:	First Sino-Japanese War
1903:	First successful airplane flight
1905:	Korea becomes a protectorate of Japan
since 1905, 1918, 1930:	Relativity—quantum mechanics
1910–1912:	First expedition to reach the South Pole
1914–1918:	World War I
1920:	Ottoman Empire abolished
c. 1920:	Development of international air travel
1922:	Soviet Union established
1929–1939:	Great Depression
1937–1945:	Second Sino-Japanese War
1939–1945:	World War II in Europe and the Middle East
1945–1989:	Cold War, Decolonization
1950:	Apartheid legislation passed in South Africa
since 1950s:	Tectonic plate theory widely accepted
since 1960s:	Development of GIS
since 1960s:	Global warming accelerates
1983:	Aborigines receive full voting rights, Australia
1991:	Breakup of the Soviet Union
1994:	First free elections in South Africa
since mid-1990s:	Widespread use of Internet, GPS
since mid 2000s:	Google Maps, Google Earth

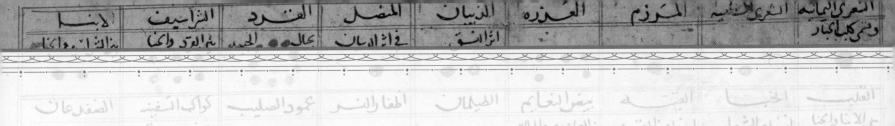

Part **1**

Mapping the Skies: Prehistory – 1515 CE

Mapping the sky is the oldest and most widespread type of cartography. From the earliest times, humans looked to the heavens to understand when to plant or hunt and where to travel.

When certain stars appeared in the sky they signalled the change of seasons, marking the time for planting or harvesting. Other stars indicated the direction in which to travel on foot, camel, or horseback. The movement of stars across the nighttime sky also functioned as a kind of clock, the passage of time marked by the apparent movement of the moon and groups of stars across the sky. Since the stars told of approaching changes, humans began to use them to foretell other aspects of their lives as well.

Celestial mapping differs from all other kinds of mapping. It does not depict a physical reality that can be touched, smelled, or even altered. The skies can only be seen. Humans on Earth merely observe, sketch, catalog, and measure that distant and ever-changing display.

Views of the sky have been painted or drawn for most of human history. Only the media have changed. Ochre and charcoal used by early humans gave way to colors distilled from plants and animals, to photography in the nineteenth century, and digital streams of data in the twentieth and twenty-first. Given that so many of these renderings take the form of art, the question arises whether images of the sky constitute maps?

Many illustrations of the constellations are indeed works of art. Renaissance painter Albrecht Durer's drawings of the nighttime sky are clearly art (Map 12). So too are the drawings by ninth-century Persian Al-Sufi in his *The Book of the Fixed Stars*

(Map 7). But these works of art also represent the relations of objects (stars and planets) to each other in space. Thus drawings of constellations and lunar mansions can be characterized as maps since they establish the spatial relationship of stars and planets to each other.

Mapping the sky differs from mapping the Earth in yet another way. For most of history, the connections that humans have portrayed among the stars in the sky have been imaginary associations. In this regard, humans have imposed their own realities upon the heavens. But the concepts that any group of people attach to the skies depends upon their own perceptions and understandings. Thus seafaring Polynesians detected the backbone of fish and fish hooks (Map 2), ancient peoples of Southern Africa identified giraffes and zebras (Map 3), while aborigines in Australia recognized giant emus (Map 4).

Modern astronomers understand the actual gravitational forces, magnetic fields, and pulsing beams of light from exploding supernova that factually establish the physical bonds of stars to one another. Today, instead of animals, or giants, or gods, astronomers most often see the sky as a giant card catalog and its sections numbered like books on a library shelf. However, even today the latest images of the skies created by giant telescopes and satellites are often created with the help of an artist.

The most ancient drawing of a constellation dates back to the late Stone Age, or Paleolithic era. We begin with the oldest known depiction of the heavens, found on the walls of a cave in France.

Timeline of world history

160,000 to 20,000 years ago
Most recent Ice Age

since ca. 150,000 years ago
Homo sapiens

since at least 100,000 years ago
Art, ritual, religion; *homo sapiens* migrations out of Africa

60,000 years ago
Colonization of Australia

since 20,000 years ago
Global warming

since ca. 10,000 BCE
Agriculture

since 5000 BCE
Intensive agriculture: Tigris-Euphrates, Nile, Indus, Yellow Rivers

since 3500 BCE
Complex hierarchical societies and states

ca. 3000 BCE
Rise of Sumerian civilization; earliest use of celestial directions in East Asia

ca. 2000 BCE
Beginning of Bantu expansion (Africa)

ca. 1600 BCE
Beginning of Polynesian migrations

ca. 1130 BCE
Earliest surviving map of the zodiac

ca. 150 CE
Ptolemy, *The Almagest*

ca. 964 CE
First maps of the Greek constellations (Persia)

1

Lascaux, France: Pleiades, *c.* 17,000 BCE

• ◆ •

Rock painting of a
bull with long horns,
the Hall of Bulls
c. 17,000 BCE
Caves of Lascaux,
Dordogne, France

In southwestern France, 180 kilometers from the bustling city of Bordeaux, lies a quiet river valley whose waters flow into the Dordogne and eventually past Bordeaux and into the Atlantic. Under hills surrounding the peaceful Vézère River lie 37 grottos, the greatest concentration in Western Europe of the remains of human settlement from the Paleolithic era (45,000–10,000 years ago).

Discovered accidentally in 1940 by four teenagers following their dog down a narrow entrance into a cavern in 1940, the Lascaux caves contain an astounding collection of Paleolithic art. Over 2,000 drawings, nearly half of animals, cover the walls. The vibrant colors owe their enduring brilliance to unusually sophisticated paints. Where most cave painters employed simple charcoal and earth, the Lascaux muralists used longer-lasting minerals, including differing iron oxides that produce yellows and reds, and manganese dioxide for black.

The artistry displayed at Lascaux is extraordinary. Horses, deer, bison, and horned aurochs (ancestors of modern cattle) gallop and soar across the walls as if in perpetual movement. Variations appear among the individual horses and deer, in recognition of the distinctiveness of each animal. Like other drawings from the late Stone Age, human figures are virtually absent, leaving only a world of fleeing animals and abstract lines and dots.

In 2002 German scholar Michael Rappenglück suggested that a small group of dots above the head of a horned animal were, in fact, the constellation Pleiades. He argued that the Pleiades would have come into view at the start of the hunting season, noting the constellation's appearance next to an auroch (the horned animal). Unlike other representations of astronomical phenomena that can be identified precisely, the categorization of these dots as the Pleiades can never be established beyond a doubt. However, the explanation remains reasonable, and so these drawings are often called the earliest map of the stars.

Map of France showing location of Lascaux.

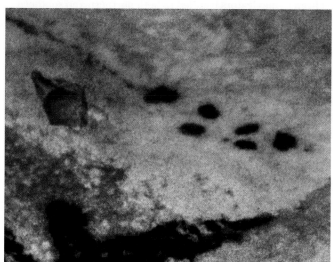

5

2

Polynesian Constellations, 300–1200 CE

• ◆ •

'Imiloa Astronomy Center
The Backbone and
Fishhook Constellations
Hilo, Hawaii

Around 300 BCE, people in the western Pacific islands of Tonga and Samoa journeyed across a thousand miles of the open Pacific to settle the Cook Islands. While Europeans were still sailing within sight of the Mediterranean coast, Polynesians were traveling over a thousand miles in canoes built with tools of stone, bone, and coral, guided by their observations of the ocean and sky. By 700 CE, Polynesians had traveled 3,500 nautical miles east to Easter Island (Rapa Nui). Over the next 500 years, they settled Hawaii (700 CE) and New Zealand (1200 CE).

While knowledge of winds and currents were crucial to their successful voyages, Polynesians also employed constellations as their guides. Two constellations appeared in many Polynesian societies: Maui's Fishhook and The Backbone. The first constellation is linked to a story of how the Pacific Islands came into existence. In one Hawaiian version, the demigod Maui had a magic fishhook that he cast into the waters. With his brothers paddling the canoe, Maui slowly pulled the fishhook out of the water, dragging up great mountains from the depths of the ocean. As the peaks broke the surface of the ocean, Maui yelled to his brothers to paddle faster, and not to look back. But one of his brothers could not resist the temptation, and turned around, dropping his paddle in awe of the sight of the great mountains. With the paddle lost, Maui's line grew slack, and most of the great landmasses fell back into the sea. All that remained behind were the pieces of land making up Hawaii. In another version, Maui and his brothers are trying to bring the islands closer together, and when the one brother looks back they separate. Similar tales are told about the origin of Mangareva (Gambier Islands), Mangaia (Cook Islands) Tonga, and New Zealand (Aotearoa).

In New Zealand, the tale is slightly different. The North Island is the giant fish that Maui pulled up from the sea (Te Ika-a-Maui), while the South Island is his canoe. Several modern commentators believe that the legend of Maui reflects events that may have occurred the other way around; namely, the fishermen originally found the islands and, in that sense, fished them out of the sea.

While the constellation Maui's Fishhook retells a story of the creation of the islands of Polynesia, in several island groups the fishhook had a second function as well. In Tahiti, Hawaii, Mangareva, and New Zealand, the giant fishhook was fashioned from a jawbone that Maui had used to capture the sun to make it move slower so that people would have more hours of daylight to work.

The Polynesian constellation called "The Backbone" (Ka Iwikuamo'o) is the longest constellation in the world, stretching from the north to the south celestial poles. Since Polynesian navigators traveled in both northern and southern hemispheres, it is not surprising that they would find a single constellation to become the backbone of their navigation.

Several stars along the "backbone" appear directly overhead specific island groups in Polynesia. The brightest star in the northern celestial hemisphere that appears directly above the Hawaiian Islands is Arcturus. It is called Hokulea, "star of joy," in Hawaiian, because it points the way to Hawaii. Spica, which appears 10 degrees south of the celestial equator, appears directly overhead in Samoa and hence points the way to Samoa.

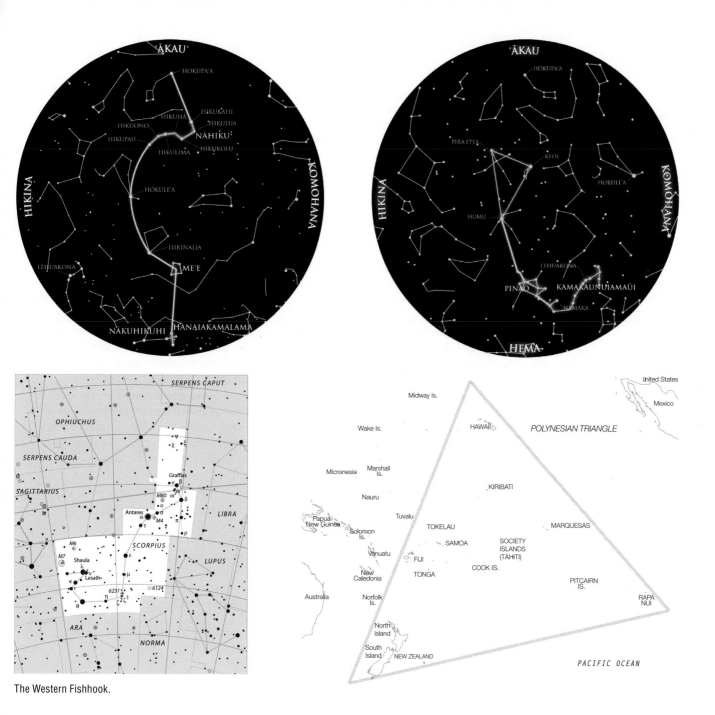

The Western Fishhook.

Map of Polynesia.

7

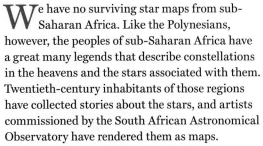

3

African Star Lore

●◆●

The Starlore poster
1998
South African
Astronomical Observatory
Cape Town, South Africa

We have no surviving star maps from sub-Saharan Africa. Like the Polynesians, however, the peoples of sub-Saharan Africa have a great many legends that describe constellations in the heavens and the stars associated with them. Twentieth-century inhabitants of those regions have collected stories about the stars, and artists commissioned by the South African Astronomical Observatory have rendered them as maps.

The Milky Way dominates the night sky of the Southern Hemisphere much more than it does in the north. In the north the pole star faces away from the center of the Milky Way, making the galaxy appear less bright. But the Milky Way dramatically crosses southern skies, which makes not surprising that it features much more prominently in stories from that hemisphere. Several stories from the San and Khoikhoi communities of South Africa describe the creation of the Milky Way in a tale of a young girl and fire.

In one version of the story, a young girl became angry when her mother refused to give her the roots that were roasting in a fire. So the girl picked up the roots and threw them into the sky, where they became the red and white stars of the Milky Way. Because the roots were covered with ashes, the ashes too were thrown into the sky producing the great hazy areas of the galaxy.

A similar version of the same story takes a more charitable view of the young girl. Instead of throwing the fire in a fit of temper, she tossed the fire and ashes into the sky in order to create a path of light through the darkness.

Other South African people had different stories. The Xhosas, from what is now the Eastern Cape Province of South Africa, thought the Milky Way looked like raised bristles on the back of an angry dog. Sotho and Tswana people of the interior of South Africa told stories of it being the resting place of lightning and a support to keep the sky from collapsing.

The three stars that in Western societies are known as the Belt of Orion were three zebras to the Namaquas (a pastoral Khoikhoi group). But for the northern Tswana, the three stars were warthogs, who tended to give birth in litters of three just as the constellation rose in the sky in the spring.

Several South African groups saw the constellations near the south celestial pole as giraffes. For the Venda, when the stars came close to the horizon in October the giraffes appeared to be skimming above the trees in the evening. The appearance of the giraffes signaled the time to finish planting.

◄ TOP LEFT
The Khoikhoi and San constellation of the Milky Way, coming into existence when a girl tosses ashes and fire into the sky.

◄ TOP RIGHT
The giraffes at the southern celestial pole.

▼ BOTTOM LEFT
The three zebras, according to the Khokhoi of South Africa. The same stars represented warthogs to the Tswana.

Map of South Africa.

4

The Emu, Australia

• • •

Voie lactée 5100 mètres altitude V2
Photograph, Serge Brunier

Another ancient tradition of mapping the heavens comes from a stone engraving in a park near Sydney, Australia. Dating the engraving is difficult, since there are no other clues in the surrounding area that help to determine its age. Aboriginal occupation of Australia dates back to Paleolithic times, the same era as the cave paintings at Lascaux, but the age of the rock drawing can never be ascertained. Nonetheless, the drawing illustrates an entirely different approach to mapping the heavens.

Unlike most other societies from antiquity, who looked for the bright points of light in the sky and drew lines through them, the aboriginal people of Australia looked to both stars and dark spaces. As in South Africa, the Milky Way dominates the skies.

However, unlike South Africans who saw a girl near fire, or an angry animal, the indigenous inhabitants of southeast Australia saw the cloudlike Milky Way as an emu, a large flightless bird that left its claw prints at the place in the sky known as the Southern Cross. While the Milky Way remains visible throughout the year in this part of Australia, when it appears at this particular angle it signals the time to begin egg hunting.

The galaxy reaches this position beginning in late autumn or early winter, just as giant emus begin settling down to lay their eggs during late afternoon or early evening. To aboriginal people that meant it was time to begin to raid emu nests at night, just after the eggs were laid. A single giant blue emu egg can feed a dozen people.

Cairns

Northern Territory

Queensland

Alice Springs

Western Australia

AUSTRALIA

Brisbane

Perth

South Australia

New South Wales

Garigal Aboriginal Park

Adelaide

Sydney

Victoria

Melbourne

Tasmania

◄ **LEFT**
The Milky Way galaxy.

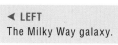

An emu.

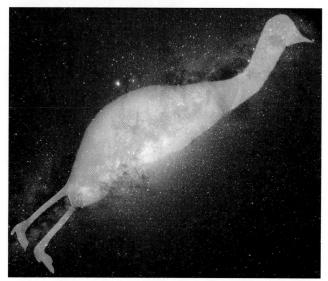

The Milky Way galaxy seen in
the shape of an emu.

5

The Origin of the Zodiac: Ancient Mesopotamia, 1130 BCE

• ◆ •

Drawings of the Babylonian Zodiac
1913
Ink on paper
Alfred Jeremias, *Handbuch der altorientalischen Geisteskultur*
Leipzig, Germany

The oldest maps of the constellations we know today come from Mesopotamia. More than a third of all modern constellations were mapped for the first time on ancient clay tablets from the Tigris and Euphrates river valley. While ancient Mesopotamians produced other maps, their most important and enduring legacy lay in the identification of the group of stars that came to be called the **zodiac**.

The word *zodiac* is Greek, but the discovery of most of the constellations originated many centuries before classical Greek civilization. The residents of Babylon began observing that the sun took a slightly different path across the sky every day throughout the year. They noticed that certain groups of stars came into view in the sky and remained visible as the sun's path changed over the course of many days. Certain groups of stars remained conspicuous for about four weeks as the sun's daily path changed, until another group of stars became visible. The Babylonians decided to group approximately 30 days of the sun's path through the sky into twelve distinct segments according to groups of discernible stars. Looking a little above and a little below the position of the sun, they identified stars that they grouped into twelve patterns, which have come to be known as the constellations of the zodiac: Aries (The Ram), Taurus (The Bull), Gemini (The Twins), Cancer (The Crab), Leo (The Lion), Virgo (The Virgin), Libra, (The Scales), Scorpio (The Scorpion), Sagittarius (Centaur, The Archer), Capricorn (Goat-Horned, or The Sea-Goat), Aquarius (The Water Bearer), and Pisces (The Fish). With two or perhaps three exceptions, these names for the constellations of the zodiac remain the same as those first ascribed by the people of ancient Mesopotamia more than 3,000 years ago.

In 1130 BCE, at the height of the Assyrian Empire in Mesopotamia, an unknown individual or group in Mesopotamia compiled a star catalog containing 66 known stars and constellations, including the timings of the rising and setting of the stars. That list is called MUL.APIN, and includes the earliest drawings of the signs of the zodiac. Three tablets (shown at right) survive, each containing at least one of the signs of the zodiac as they were first depicted.

The people of ancient Mesopotamia identified other constellations apart from the zodiac that are still recognized today. Some of these star groups would be renamed in later centuries, principally by the Greeks. For example, one group of stars that the Mesopotamians identified as an ordinary agricultural feature, "the field," was renamed as the legendary winged horse, Pegasus. In all, the Greeks renamed a total of fourteen Mesopotamian constellations and kept both the names and constellations for another twenty.

The Babylonian constellations would spread far and wide, being adopted in ancient Egypt and India. Of the great ancient empires, only China followed a different pattern, but, eventually, it too would adopt the Mesopotamian pattern in the seventeenth century.

Even though Babylonians first developed the zodiac, they did not associate the zodiac with the lives of individuals or predictions of the future. That connection would be made by the Greeks.

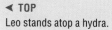

◀ **TOP**
Leo stands atop a hydra.

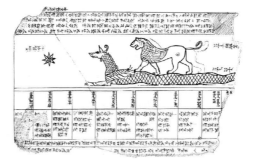

◀ **MIDDLE**
Virgo (carrying a stalk of barley in her hands) faces a crouching vulture.

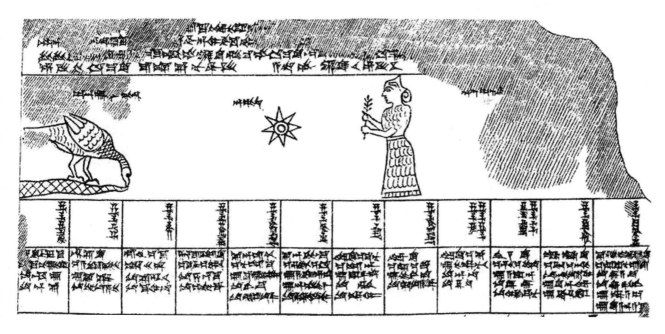

◀ **BOTTOM**
Taurus (The Bull) confronts The Archer (Sagittarius), with the Pleiades to the left.

13

6

Greek Constellations and Arabic Stars: The *Almagest* (150 CE) and Arabic Star Lists (1065 CE)

• ◆ •

Arabic Star Lists
c. 1065 CE
Ink on parchment, 48 folios,
324 × 245 mm
The Book of Curiosities
The Bodleian Library,
University of Oxford

Sometime during the early fourth century BCE, a young man named Eudoxus (*c.* 390/395–342/347 BCE) traveled west from present-day Turkey to study at Plato's academy in Athens. He soon abandoned philosophy for astronomy and mathematics and created a reputation for himself by compiling a list of all 49 known constellations. To this index, Eudoxus added the positions of some of their component stars. However, scholars have recently discovered that the stars appeared at different positions in the sky during Eudoxus' lifetime than those he recorded. Most of the locations he recorded actually correspond to the stars' positions 700 years earlier, when the constellations now known in the West were first being compiled in Mesopotamia. Hence most of Eudoxus' file was not original, but a copy of a now-lost Mesopotamian catalog. Eudoxus' inventory, however, became part of *Phaenomena*, a popular work by the Greek didactic poet Aratus (*c.* 310–240 BCE), which was used by the earliest Greek astronomers as the starting point for their own work.

Most of the constellations that are in use today come from the list of 48 (rather than the original 49) recompiled by second-century astronomer Claudius Ptolemy (*c.* 90–168 CE). In assembling his inventory, however, Ptolemy primarily drew upon Aratus' poem that had transcribed Eudoxus' list. Thus Ptolemy inadvertently copied much of a thousand-year-old Mesopotamian list, reducing Eudoxus' number of constellations by one.

Ptolemy lived during the height of the Roman Empire. He spent his entire working life in Alexandria, never traveling outside his native Egypt. Of Greek descent, Ptolemy wrote in Greek rather than Latin, which was the dominant language of the empire in which he lived. In addition to his interest in geography (see Map 30), Ptolemy was also an avid supporter of astrology, the belief that events on earth are dictated by the position of the stars and planets in the heavens. His major work on astrology, *Tetrabiblos*, would become widely popular in the Islamic and medieval European world. Around 150 CE, Ptolemy composed his greatest work, which he called the *Mathematical Treatise*, in which he made several original contributions. He described the risings and settings of stars and the length of a day, and estimated the length of a year. He also defined what would become for centuries the most popular version of the geocentric universe, with a round Earth lying motionless at the center and the stars and planets revolving around it. However, his most enduring contribution from the treatise would be his list of stars.

Ptolemy took the 48 largely Mesopotamian constellations and divided a large number of individual stars (1,025) among them, while renaming some constellations according to Greek mythology. The names he bestowed upon them have remained the standard groupings to this day. The 48 names are Andromeda, Aquarius, Aquila, Ara, Argo Navis (now subdivided into Carina, Puppis, and Vela), Aries, Auriga, Boötes, Cancer, Canis Major, Canis Minor, Capricornus, Cassiopeia, Centaurus, Cepheus, Cetus, Corona Australis, Corona Borealis, Corvus, Crater, Cygnus, Delphinus, Draco, Equuleus, Eridanus, Gemini, Hercules, Hydra, Leo, Lepus, Libra, Lupus, Lyra, Ophiuchus, Orion, Pegasus, Perseus, Pisces, Piscis Austrinus, Sagitta, Sagittarius, Scorpius, Serpens, Taurus, Triangulum, Ursa Major, Ursa Minor, and Virgo.

Two important facts stand out about this list. First, Ptolemy drew no pictures of any of the constellations, leaving us only with names. Second, Ptolemy's original manuscript with its list of over a thousand stars and their constellations vanished; only a single copy from the ninth century remains. But it was not the Greek version of Ptolemy's work that would become influential. The compilation of constellations became codified only in the ninth century CE, after it was published in Arabic as part of the immense Muslim project of translating the philosophical and scientific wisdom of the Greco-Roman civilization.

The star lists and constellations originally appeared in sections VII and VIII of Ptolemy's *Mathematical Treatise*, which Arab scholars renamed "The Greatest" or "The Greatest Compilation" (in Arabic *al-kitabu-al-mijisti*). In the twelfth century, the Spanish king of Castile sponsored a similar effort in reverse–but this time translating Arabic *al-kitabu-al-mijisti* into Castilian. "Al-mijisti" was difficult to transliterate into European languages; hence the book came to be known in the Western world by an approximation of *al-mijisti*, namely "the *Almagest*."

Ptolemy drew no images of the constellations; neither did the many astronomers who expanded his work. In some Arabic works, stars and constellations appeared as simple arrangements of dots without any figures. The image on the right, from about 1065 CE, is from a North African Arabic source and contains a mixture of stars and constellations from the Greek/Mesopotamian traditions as well as those native to the Bedouins, the region's indigenous inhabitants.

Sometimes the constellations are the same in both the Greek-Mesopotamian and Bedouin traditions, while others were slightly altered. Hercules became "the kneeling man" and Capricorn "the little goat." Others were altered still further. In the Bedouin tradition, two Greek mythological figures (Cassiopeia and Andromeda) became the head of a female camel. New constellations also appeared, such as the donkey's rear end.

Ptolemy had followed an extremely awkward and inconsistent naming system. With the translation of the *Mathematical Treatise* into Arabic,

astronomers throughout the Muslim world began resurveying the sky, re-measuring the brightness of stars and, most importantly, renaming them. The box at the bottom left shows a big red dot, which represents the brightest star in the constellation Ophiuchus, named *ra's al-hawwa* in Arabic and known today in its Latinized form as Ras Alhague (see Map 7). Today, 165 of these Arabic star names remain in use among professional astronomers.

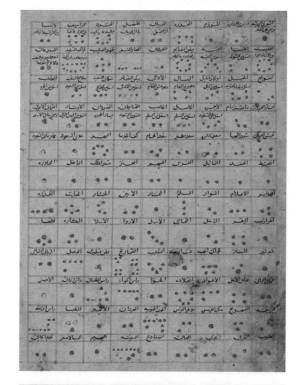

◄ **TOP IMAGE**
108 stars and constellations from North Africa from approximately 1065 CE. The positions of the stars are only approximate, missing both their relative sizes and the exact shapes they formed.

◄ **BOTTOM IMAGE LEFT**
The head of the constellation Ophiuchus (serpent bearer).

◄ **BOTTOM IMAGE MIDDLE**
The "head of a female camel."

◄ **BOTTOM IMAGE RIGHT**
The unmistakable "donkey's rear end."

7

First Maps of the Greek Constellations, Persia, 964 CE

• ◆ •

First Maps of the Greek
Constellations, Persia
1730 copy of the original
10th century CE map
Ink on parchment
'Abd al-Rahman ibn 'Umar al-Sufi
(d. 986), *Suwar al-Kawakib* (*The Depiction
of Celestial Constellations*)
The Library of Congress

The constellations were first accurately mapped onto a globe in Greece sometime in the second century BCE. While the Greek original has perished, a largely intact copy has survived in a slightly unusual Roman reproduction. A white marble statue depicts the Greek god Atlas as if he has just grasped the globe of the heavens as it fell from behind toward his left shoulder, with its weight forcing him down on one knee. Forty-one constellations appear in relief upon the globe, their positions reflecting the observations of either Ptolemy's famous predecessor Hipparchus (c. 190–120 BCE) or another, as yet unknown, astronomer of the same era. This depiction, however well rendered, was never widely disseminated since its manner and style of execution were expensive and difficult to reproduce.

Instead, for centuries the best known and most widely imitated star map of the Greek constellations came from a manuscript produced by neither a Greek nor a Roman, but rather a Persian scholar who belonged to a mystical branch of Islam known as Sufism. Abd al-Rahman al-Sufi (903–986 CE) produced his masterwork, *Book of the Fixed Stars*, in Isfahan, Persia, where he worked at the court of 'Adud al-Dawla, ruler of much of present-day Iraq and Iran during the tenth and eleventh centuries.

A gifted astronomer and a careful reader of the Arabic translation of Ptolemy's *Almagest*, al-Sufi closely examined its description of the position of the stars. In creating his star map he followed Ptolemy's assignment of stars to constellations, but included in the accompanying text his own independent measurements of the stars' brightness. His care in positioning the stars, together with the text's brilliant drawings, turned his *Book of Fixed Stars* (964 CE) into the most widely admired and imitated catalog of star maps of the Middle Ages. Composed in Arabic, it was translated into Hebrew, Latin, and Persian. When the Arabic version of Ptolemy's *Almagest* was translated into Spanish around 1250 CE, al-Sufi's star maps were included as if they had formed part of the original.

In the *Book of Fixed Stars*, al-Sufi also tried to integrate two diverse traditions—the traditional star names in Arabic, and the older Arabic constellations—into Ptolemy's register of constellations. The names of constellations had thus come full circle, from their largely Mesopotamian origins (present-day Iraq) through their Greek interpreters, and then back to an astronomer in a region just east of Mesopotamia.

Even though he was Persian, al-Sufi composed his scientific texts in Arabic. During the Middle Ages, Arabic was the international language of science in much the same way English has become today. In al-Sufi's day, all of the major discoveries and advances in science were composed in Arabic. If new ideas were to circulate among the scientific community, they needed to be written in Arabic.

Al-Sufi's name (meaning literally "the Sufi" or adherent of mystical Islam) sounded strange to ears trained in European languages, and when his work was later translated into those languages the name "al-Sufi" became "Azophi." Three of al-Sufi's constellation drawings (copied from a 1417 manuscript) are shown on the right: his depiction of Sagittarius the Archer, Taurus the Bull, and Ophiuchus the Serpent Bearer (also sometimes known as the Serpent Charmer). Al-Sufi's basic outlines of the constellation drawings remained the template for all such illustrations until the Renaissance.

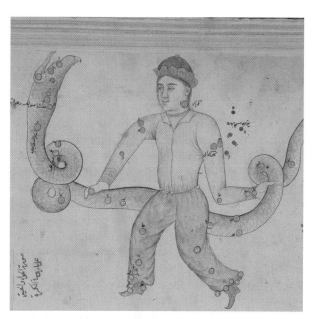

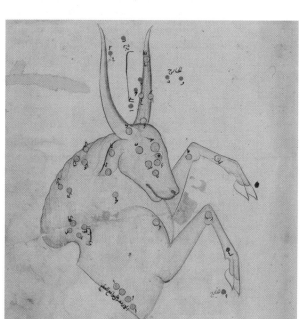

8

Hebrew Zodiac,
1361 CE

• • •

Sefer Hafmivcharim (Book of Selection)
Catalonia (perhaps Barcelona),
Spain, ca. 1361–62
Schoenberg Center, University of
Pennsylvania Library

First Maps of the Greek
Constellations, Persia
1730 copy of the original
10th century CE map
Ink on parchment
'Abd al-Rahman ibn 'Umar al-Sufi
(d. 986), *Suwar al-Kawakib* (*The Depiction
of Celestial Constellations*)
The Library of Congress

During the Middle Ages, Jewish astronomical research flourished in Spain, Portugal, and the Provence region of southern France. Many Hebrew scientists read Arabic and were conversant with the leading Arabic scientific writings of the day. Both Hebrew and Arabic scientists shared a common interest in improving instruments for observing and measuring the stars, since both religions placed a high value on keeping the correct date or time of day for beginning religious holidays. (By contrast, Christian authorities were long aware of the increasingly incorrect date of Easter but waited until 1583 to fix it.) This greater importance of proper timing meant that celestial observation played an important role in both religious cultures.

Both Muslim and Jewish scientists were concerned with astronomical tables that calculated the setting and rising of the sun and the moon, monthly or daily positions of planets, and lunar or solar eclipses. Because measuring the skies mattered to both religions, both Jews and Muslims continually improved instruments such as the quadrant and astrolabe. Jacob ben Machir ibn Tibbon (1236–1312) and Levi ben Gerson (1288–1344), both Jews, created an improved version of the quadrant and invented the backstaff, respectively.

Scientists from both religions shared a common interest in classifying the stars and constellations, including the Jewish scientists Abraham bar Hiya (*fl.* 1104 CE) and Ibn Ezra (*fl.* 1146 CE) However, few of their astronomical drawings have survived. In 1361, an unnamed Jewish astronomer from Iberia drew the constellations and their component stars in the examples shown at right. The names of the stars and constellations are treated in a miscellaneous fashion: sometimes they are transliterated from the Arabic; in other instances, they are combinations of Hebrew and Arabic or simply in Hebrew.

The most unusual features of this manuscript are the drawings of the constellations. Some are sketched along the traditional lines established by Abd al-Rahman al-Sufi in the tenth century CE (Map 7). However, two images in particular reflect societal and economic changes in the Mediterranean. The Water Carrier (Aquarius), on the bottom left, appears clothed in garments more typical of medieval Iberia than of tenth-century Persia. An even more striking change is the way the constellation Argos is depicted. Instead of a series of geometric shapes roughly indicating an oared ship, the Hebrew manuscript shows a highly detailed, three-masted, late-medieval sailing vessel complete with rigging and flying pennants, reflecting the expanding maritime economy of the late-medieval world. Beneath the drawings of the constellations are the names in Hebrew of the stars and their relative brightness.

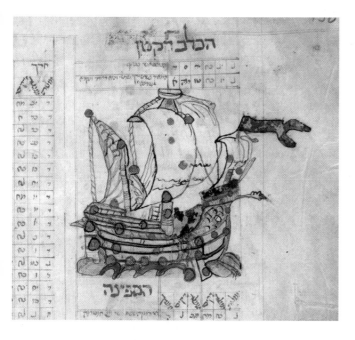

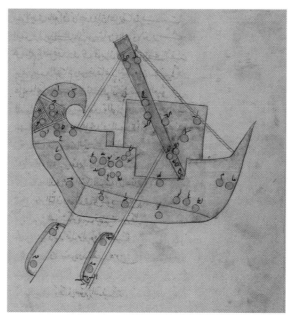

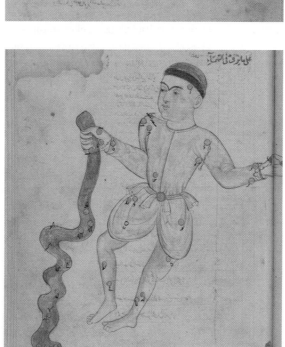

◄ **TOP LEFT**
The constellation of
The Ship (Argos) as it
appeared in a Hebrew
star map of 1361 CE.

◄ **TOP RIGHT**
The constellation of
The Ship (Argos) as it
appeared in an 964 CE
star map by al-Sufi.

◄ **BOTTOM LEFT**
The water carrier
Aquarius pictured in
fourteenth-century
Iberian dress.

◄ **BOTTOM RIGHT**
al-Sufi's depiction
of Aquarius.

9

Dunhuang Star Map (Tang Dynasty), 618–907 CE

• ◆ •

Photograph: Patricia Seed
Dunhuang County Museum, Dunhuang
Or.8210/S.3326
Dunhuang Star Atlas
The British Library, London

In a dry and dusty region of northwest China lies long range of sand-covered hills dotted with small dark spots barely visible from the road. Upon closer inspection, the dark spots on the hills reveal themselves as arched entrances to caves carved into the hillsides. In this strange and desolate landscape the wind blows through the nearby dunes at night, making sounds that resemble music. This land was once immensely fertile, supporting hundreds of Buddhist monks who worshiped and carved massive statues of the Buddha between the third and ninth centuries CE. Their long-forgotten and abandoned caves at Dunhuang preserve the earliest star map from the Tang Dynasty (618–907 CE). The map fragment shown on the opposite page top left is from one of the caves and is exhibited in the nearby Museum of Dunhuang County, Gansu Province, China.

This fragment depicts the region around the North Pole and shows a view to the sky that is very different from that which developed out of the Mesopotamian tradition. From the Han dynasty (206 BCE – 220 CE) onward, Chinese star maps differed from those that evolved everywhere else in the world. They were centered on the brightest star near the North Pole, which represented the emperor. The Big Dipper was the emperor's chariot pulling both the emperor and the entire sky.

Since the nighttime stars all appear to rotate around the pole star, the pattern mirrored life on the ground where the kingdom revolved around the emperor, reflecting both Daoist and Confucian philosophies that upheld the belief that a harmonious relationship existed between heavenly and human worlds. China (represented in Chinese pictograms by a symbol literally meaning "the middle") lay at the center of the flat Earth, ruled by the emperor just as the mighty god Shangdi ruled heaven. The emperor was the Son of Heaven, whose rule was mandated by the God of Heaven. Furthermore, the emperor had to maintain harmony between heaven and earth partly by means of a calendar announced at the start of the new year. Astronomy thus played a more central role in China than it did in other societies. Only 10 inches high, the entire map represented by the section shown on the opposite page top right is over two yards long (25 by 210 centimeters, or 10 by 82 inches). The entire Dunhuang map illustrates 12 months, in addition to the polar region shown in the fragment. In total, the map contains 1,345 stars grouped in 257 non-constellation patterns.

Over seven hundred years before this star map, Chinese astronomers had begun to make lists of stars and measure their positions in the skies. The oldest and most famous of these, although named for Warring States' astronomer Shi Shen (fourth century BCE), actually reflects carefully measured positions of the stars in the sky around 100 BCE. Two other astronomers working during the Han era also compiled star lists, which were brought together in a single catalog by Chen Zhuo, an astronomer from the Three Kingdom period (220–280 CE). This catalog became the basis for the Dunhuang map, in which the stars were colored according to the astronomer who had contributed them. Thus the colors yellow, white, and black do not reflect anything about the stars but rather identify the astronomer who described their position in the sky.

Because of the belief in the fundamental harmony of heaven and earth, stars were organized into a heavenly human society that included the emperor, queen, and princes, and depicted the royal court, palaces, imperial bureaucracy, military installations, and weapons. Constellations and stars also represented rituals, ceremonies, traffic, transportation, and geographic features.

The Chinese also filled the heavens with far more mundane objects. The constellation Baijiu represented a tub for waste disposal and the constellation Ping was a screen for the privacy of people using the toilet, while the constellation Ce was a toilet and the constellation Tianshi was excrement from that toilet. Nowhere else in the world did a heavenly toilet make an appearance.

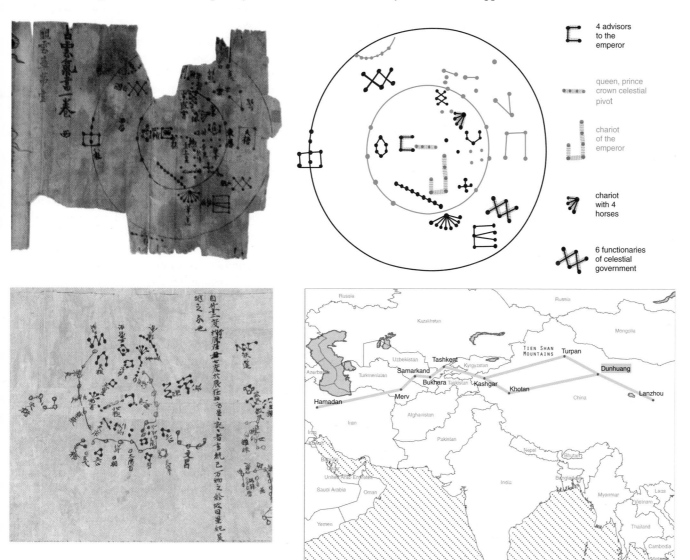

4 advisors to the emperor

queen, prince crown celestial pivot

chariot of the emperor

chariot with 4 horses

6 functionaries of celestial government

◄ TOP LEFT
The region around the Pole as depicted in the Dunhuang star chart. The image on the right shows an outline from the star chart.

▼ BOTTOM LEFT
A section of the long star chart roll in the possession of the British Library.

Location of Dunhuang along the Silk Road.

10

Chinese Constellations (Song Dynasty),

1193 CE

• ◆ •

Photograph by Patricia Seed
Beijing Ancient Observatory

The map at right is perhaps the best-known Chinese star map, reflecting traditional perspectives on the sky. It was created in 1193 during the Song Dynasty by a little-known Chinese astronomer named Huang Shang, based on observations made as early as 1052. It was later engraved on a stone inside a Confucian temple in Suzhou in 1247. Its presence inside a temple in which students prepared for imperial examinations suggests that it was an object of study.

While the Song-era map seems to depict far more stars than the earlier Dunhuang map (see Map 9), in fact it contains only about 120 more stars than this earlier representation. The biggest difference between the two maps lies in the manner in which the stars are represented. The Dunhuang map divides the sky into many different sections and places each of the sections of the sky next to one another on a long scroll. The Song map, in contrast, transfers the stars onto a single plane, called a **planisphere**, showing nearly all the stars and constellations visible from within China. The polar stars that appear in the fragment from Dunhuang occur in the innermost circle of the planisphere.

This Song star map beautifully illustrates two unique features of Chinese astronomy: the system of **lunar mansions**, and the distinctive relationship that existed between terrestrial phenomena and directions in the sky. Both of these features were present in Chinese astronomy for centuries, but they were brilliantly illustrated for the first time during the Song era.

By about 2400 BCE, the Chinese had divided the sky into four cardinal points, each identified with one of the seasons. Approximately 2000 years later, around 433 BCE, we have the first evidence of the Chinese dividing the visible sky into 28 zones. If you imagine the sky as the top half of an orange with the pole star at the top, the sectors are the individual sections within the orange, joined together at the top and broadening out as they extend down toward the horizon. Each of these divisions ("mansions" or "houses") was separated by a star that marked the boundary. An imaginary line drawn from this boundary star to the pole defined the edges of each region. Their names appear in black characters on the white band that encircles the planisphere on the right.

China also developed a unique system for measuring the positions of stars in the sky. Instead of measuring from the equator, Chinese astronomers measured the distance between the star and the pole star, and the distance between the star and the starting point of the lunar mansion in which it was located (its westernmost part). Given the importance of astronomical phenomena for legitimizing imperial rule, the measurements of the positions of the stars in the sky during the Song era reached a level of accuracy not attained by the West for several more centuries.

Another characteristic of Chinese star maps is the way in which constellations within a lunar mansion frequently relate to the name of the mansion. The lunar house "Jing" means *water well*, and the house is located in the south, just to the east of the Milky Way. The Milky way itself was referred to as the "Celestial River"; hence the constellations near the river and in the house of the Water Well all concern water affairs. One constellation in this group is called "South River," another "North River," and another "Four Rivers." In addition, "Stored Water," "Water Level," and "Water Palace" all appear under this grouping.

The planisphere from the Confucian temple in Suzhou, China. The image shown here is the copy made by the Beijing Astronomical Observatory.

11

From Sky to Land: Directions in China, 3000 BCE–Present

• ◆ •

Drawings by Tsvetelina
Zdraveva based on
Photographs by Patricia Seed
Beijing Ancient Observatory

Another system for organizing directions originated in China several thousand years ago, perhaps as early as 3000 BCE. While the abstract names of north, south, east, and west were commonly used on maps of the Earth, the Chinese developed a unique scheme to designate these same four basic directions in the sky. Principal directions in the heavens were designated by mythical creatures and animals as well as by colors. In the heavens, north was identified with a dark blue-black color, west with white, south with red, and east with blue-green. Each was also identified with an animal guarding the four principal directions. A tortoise embellished with the head and tail of a serpent embodied north, a white tiger exemplified the west, a red phoenix designated the south, and a blue-green dragon represented the east. Despite appearing on maps of the heavens, these symbols did not constitute constellations but rather directions. In Chinese mythology they took on the additional role of being protectors or guardians of the four corners of the sky.

The blue-green dragon (east) and white tiger (west) were the oldest of the four celestial directions, first appearing on a tomb from the Neolithic era around 3000 BCE. The heart of the blue-green dragon was Antares, the brightest star in the western constellation Scorpio, and the sixteenth brightest star in the sky when Antares appeared above the eastern horizon at sunset. Between 1600–1046 BCE, it indicated the arrival of spring. The intertwined tortoise and serpent (north) were sometimes referred to as the "Black Warrior" because the shell of the giant river turtle symbolized a suit of armor. The origin of the tortoise-serpent remains uncertain, although it might be connected to a numerological image of "river writing" on the turtle's back.

In their guise as protectors, these originally celestial creatures and colors began to appear on tombs from the second century BCE as a way of warding off evil. Since the characters in Chinese for tomb represent "house of the dead" and the characters for residence represent "house of the living," the use of these names for directions soon extended to another popular practice. *Feng shui* refers to the practice of constructing dwellings and placing furniture in a way that is optimal for its inhabitants. Over time, the directions for building a house according to feng shui also became referred to as the turtle, phoenix, dragon, or tiger, rather than north, south, east, or west.

Eventually, these colors and animals were extended to urban planning. Cities began to be constructed with four gates, each named for the animal protector of that direction. Even today, the gates in Chinese cities are commonly referred to not as north, south, east, or west, but by reference to the animal—tortoise, phoenix, dragon, or tiger—linked to that direction.

The celestial directions associated with symbols and colors were brought to Japan and Korea in the sixth and seventh centuries CE, where they also began to appear as protector spirits on tombs. Since the transmission of these symbols occurred at approximately the same time as the introduction of Buddhism in Japan, the four colors and associated animals assumed additional meanings. The four representatives of the directions became known as *Shitenno*, or Buddhist protectors of the four directions. They dwelled on the sacred Mount Meru (see Map 32) and acted as guardians who protected the four continents upon which humans resided.

In addition to their roles as protectors, these four original compass directions have become part of popular culture. In a gambling game called "Placing the Treasure," players make bets on the animal associated with each of the directions. And in martial arts films, the heroes often represent the four cardinal directions.

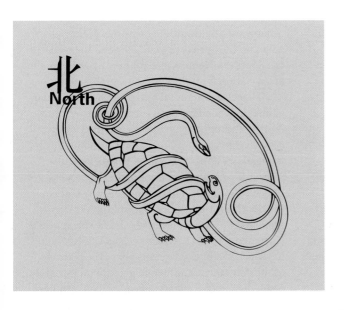

北
North

南
South

東
East

西
West

◄ **TOP LEFT AND RIGHT**
The Serpent-Tortoise (north) and the Red Phoenix (south).

◄ **BOTTOM LEFT AND RIGHT**
The Blue-Green Dragon (east) and the White Tiger (west) as depicted at the Beijing Ancient Observatory.

12

Albrecht Dürer, Map of Constellations,

1515 CE

• • •

Albrecht Dürer, Map of
Constellations, 1515
Pair of woodcuts depicting the
northern and southern skies
Bernard J. Shapero
Rare Books, London
Nuremberg, Germany

With this woodcut print of the northern and southern skies in 1515, the great German artist Albrecht Dürer (1471–1528), became the first to depict the constellations in the new style of the Renaissance.

During the Renaissance, artists sought to return to classical models styled after those of ancient Greece and Rome. Dürer traveled to Italy to study the techniques of the leading Italian Renaissance artists, such as Giovanni Bellini and Bellini's brother-in-law, Andrea Mantegna.

Incorporating the techniques he had learned in Italy, Albrecht Dürer became the greatest Renaissance artist in northern Europe. In addition to painting and engraving, Dürer's fame also resides in his extraordinary transformation of the art of printing on wood, elevating the crudely carved pictures common to the fourteenth and fifteenth centuries into works of art. His most famous woodcut was the *Four Horsemen of the Apocalypse*, created in 1497–1498. His depiction of the northern and southern skies, shown at right, also attests to his skill in woodblock printing.

Dürer's northern hemispheric sky (on the left) is densely populated with constellations, while the southern skies seem almost empty by comparison. The reasons for this difference have to do with both history and geography.

The classic catalog of stars that originated in ancient Mesopotamia largely included stars from the northern skies. Mesopotamia, Alexandria, and Egypt (another important center of astronomy in antiquity and home to Ptolemy), as well as the entire Mediterranean lie considerably north of the equator. Astronomers from Asian civilizations with strong sky-watching traditions, such as India and China, also made most of their observations north of the equator. Hence, observers from Europe, North Africa, and Asia knew far more about the stars in the Northern Hemisphere than they did about stars in the Southern Hemisphere. Not until the nineteenth and twentieth centuries did people from Asia and Europe come to understand the cultures of the Southern Hemisphere sufficiently well to gain appreciation for how they depicted their skies.

However, one small group of Europeans had gained independent knowledge of southern skies. By 1515 Portuguese navigators had frequently crossed the equator to reach Brazil and had navigated around the Cape of Good Hope in southern Africa to reach India. In the process, they discovered and began to use many stars in the Southern Hemisphere for sailing. While knowledge of those discoveries had likely reached Nuremberg by 1515, artists such as Dürer would have lacked sufficient details about the placement of the new stars to be able to map them. Hence, his depiction of the stars reflects the old groupings handed down from Mesopotamia and Ptolemy.

To depict the southern skies, Dürer relied upon ancient information about these constellations. Because the Earth's axis rotates at close to 1° every 71.5 years, several southern constellations that were no longer visible north of the equator, such as Pictus notis, the "Southern Triangle," and the entire constellation Argos Arx (a torch-bearing arm, only a portion of which was still visible from northern skies) are included in Dürer's woodcut.

Perhaps most importantly, Dürer's prints marked the beginning of drawing constellations in the Renaissance style, following Greco-Roman models. Dürer retained some of al-Sufi's prototypes (see Map 7), but most of his Renaissance drawings supplanted the models first drawn by Al-Sufi in the ninth century. The use of classically inspired drawings for star groupings would continue in the West for the next two hundred years. As seen on the right, Albrecht Dürer's Sagittarius is bare-chested in the style of classical nudes, with a toga streaming over one shoulder. In contrast, al-Sufi's Sagittarius wears a turban and his upper body remains modestly cloaked in the garb of an elite Persian hunter.

◄ **TOP LEFT**
Albrecht Dürer's drawings of the stars around the North Pole.

◄ **TOP RIGHT**
Albrecht Dürer's drawings of the stars near the South Pole. Note how few there are compared to the North Pole.

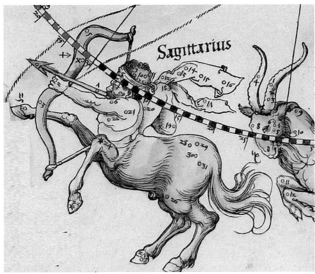

◄ **BOTTOM LEFT AND RIGHT**
Dürer's depiction of Sagittarius compared to al-Sufi's from five hundred years earlier.

Part **2**

Roads, Rivers, and Routes: 3000 BCE – 1360 CE

The earliest land maps developed after humans began to settle down and plant crops, domesticate animals, and develop crafts. Such settlements began around 10,000–8,000 BCE, largely near the great river valleys of Asia Minor and Mesopotamia, Egypt, India, and China. The link between settlements and the first land maps stems from the requirements for mapping.

Since creating images of places required time, humans had to remain in one place long enough to accumulate detailed information about their surroundings. Maps were thus only possible with the growth of fixed settlements. People also needed sufficient leisure time to draw images of their surroundings. In order to do so, the society in which they lived had to produce a food surplus capable of supporting specialized craftsmen who had the time to create visual representations of geographical knowledge.

Moreover, in order to create maps, people also needed to be able to learn the positions of places relative to one another. Only when they lived permanently near a set of established locations and places could humans begin to record the positions of such places on a map.

Maps of the terrestrial world could have first emerged in any one of four early civilizations: western India (in the Indus River Valley), China (along the Yellow River), Egypt, and the ancient Near East. Of these four, the earliest known maps first appeared in the ancient Near East and Egypt. No evidence survives of maps from the other early civilizations.

In the Indus Valley, between 2600 BC and 1900 BCE, craftsmen carved small pieces of a soft stone called *steatite* measuring from a half inch to just over two and a half inches. Because no one has managed to decipher the symbols on these stone seals, it has remained impossible to determine whether any of these constituted maps.

Somewhat different circumstances surround the decipherment of artifacts from the early settlements along the Yellow River Valley in China (1600–1046 BCE). Animal bones or shells were cleaned of meat and then scraped and smoothed to create suitably flat surfaces. Pits or hollows were then drilled or chiseled partway through the bone or shell. While some of the designs may have illustrated the sky, none appear to depict places on the ground.

Controversy continues to surround one claim to the first map. Nearly 10,000 years ago the earliest known village, called Çatal Höyük (*c.* 7500–5700 BCE), flourished in a small, well-watered area of what is now central Turkey. When archeologists initially uncovered a wall painting with squares and dark centers, some claimed it constituted the first map. Since then many other scholars have disagreed, contending that the spots depict a leopard rather than an urban settlement. Until further information becomes available and a definitive answer is reached, there is no way of settling the disagreement between the two sides. Hence it remains excluded from this volume.

However, southeast of modern Turkey, in present day Iraq and Syria, lies a broad, well-watered plain which the Greeks called "Mesopotamia,"

Timeline of world history

c. 3000
Earliest writing (Sumer)

c. 2300 BCE
Earliest known road map (Mesopotamia)

2050–1070 BCE
Middle and New Kingdom Egypt

c. 1800 BCE
Spread of iron technology

since 800 BCE
Trans-Mediterranean trade

c. 550–323 BCE
Persian Empire, Alexander's Empire

since 300 BCE
Silk Roads; Indian Ocean trade

c. 321–185 BCE
Mauryan Empire, India

240 BCE – 476 CE
Roman Empire

c. 239 BCE
Earliest surviving Chinese map

221 BCE – 220s CE
Han Empire

c. 350 CE
Earliest surviving Roman road map

630 CE onwards
Rise and spread of Islam; growing trans-Saharan trade

c. 1360 CE
Earliest surviving road map of Britain

meaning "land between rivers." This region covered several thousand square miles, all generously supplied with water by the 1,180-mile (1,850-kilometer)-long Tigris and the nearly 2,000-mile (3,000-kilometer)-long Euphrates rivers. Around 8000 BCE, agricultural communities appeared in the northern reaches of this region. Sometime between 5500 and 4000 BCE, irrigation canals and waterways cropped up toward the southern reaches of the Tigris and Euphrates. The first towns in this region emerged around 3000 BCE. Not long after, around 2300 BCE, the first undisputed terrestrial maps were drawn. The history of land maps—plans of cities, and trade and travel routes—is thus far briefer than the history of humankind. Long before people settled down, pastoralists and herders created maps of the skies, not the land. But despite their relative late appearance as a form of human expression, maps of the Earth have played crucial roles in both mundane and sacred undertakings.

Since mapping began with settled societies, two fundamental characteristics of sedentary life became the principal subjects of the earliest maps: agricultural fields and towns or cities. Not long after, a third category emerged—the route map.

The earliest maps measured fields and towns. By 4000 BCE, Mesopotamians developed a system of measurement for land parcels. Three thousand six hundred square meters equaled one *field*. Ancient Egyptians also developed a measure called the *royal cubit*, roughly a 20-inch square, that they used for building. While techniques to reduce these measures to exact scale did not yet exist, early mapmakers estimated shapes, proportions, and relative location. A canal would be drawn in approximately its correct

position within a city, relative to other major landmarks. By the time of the Romans, mapmakers were transferring very meticulous measurements onto marble.

To map a road or a route required a longer period of time, since it involved assembling information from a variety of sources. First, mapmakers needed to compile a list of places from travelers who had traversed the route. Before the advent of road maps, long-distance travelers often created lists of place names that would anticipate the series of locations they would encounter if they were traveling in the right direction. Today, a traveler might check the sequence of names of stops or towns along a railway line to make sure he or she was heading in the right direction. The sequence of place names supplies a rudimentary understanding of direction along a route.

While most route maps from antiquity concerned land journeys, there are a group of famous exceptions, also composed with great detail, showing a different set of places that a traveler would encounter along the way. These maps originated in Egypt during the Middle Kingdom (2055–1650 BCE) and depict the path through the afterlife. Believing that negotiating the passage from death to eternal life was complicated and difficult, Egyptians began drawing maps inside wooden coffins that illustrated the correct route as well as the blind alleys along the way. The maps were accompanied by extensive writings that described the various traps and difficulties that the dead would encounter during the journey.

For thousands of years, route maps were made without any additional specific information about direction. Before the advent of the magnetic compass, directions were likely to be supplied by referring to the rising or setting sun, or to the feel of the wind, or to prominent mountains or coasts. None of these measures were very precise, but a mapmaker incorporated whatever information he had in order to provide approximate directions. Some maps provided the shapes of mountains or other noticeable landscape features to steer the traveler in the correct direction.

Some mapmakers also added to their drawings stopping or resting points along the way. Since individual travelers may have stopped at different locations along the same route, or simply compiled different lists, a mapmaker would need time to gather enough information to create a comprehensive list of the most frequently encountered stops. Today's highway mapmakers also collect lists of places, only their lists include gas stations, roadside attractions, and rest stops. In the case of conflicting or missing information, our historical mapmaker would have needed to evaluate the reliability of information about similar places with slightly different spellings.

Yet another feature that mapmakers of the past noted were the distances between locations. Travelers found such information valuable for several reasons. First, it allowed them to estimate how long they could travel on a route before having to stop overnight. Advance knowledge of the approximate distances allowed the travelers to calculate the amount of supplies that they would need to carry or acquire at different places.

In ancient times, there were no uniform measures of distance. Without standardization, the separation between places would often be expressed in a variety of different measures on the same map. Space could be measured in time or by distance. For time, travelers usually referred to days or parts of days (not hours). Measures of distance were more complicated and included furlongs, stadia, leagues, paces (steps), rods, or parasangs. Often a single traveler would employ multiple measures of distance, each based upon the standard measure of the people from whom he requested information. So a route maker might be told, or read in a report, that one city might be a day's or half day's journey from the next one, the succeeding city might be described as 10 leagues away, while further on a place might be 50 parasangs away (a Persian measure).

After gathering the information, mapmakers still had to decide where to place the locations and routes they had uncovered. Three features of route maps mattered to travelers: the sequence of place names, distances, and a rudimentary indication of direction.

To create a map required an additional step, drawing a picture. Lines needed to be drawn, symbols had to be chosen to represent city gates or town walls, and colors chosen for the roads as well as for the surrounding terrain. Because of the amount of information that had to be gathered, and the time and energy expended on creating visual representations, only the most widely used routes were mapped before the nineteenth century. The most common route maps from before the modern era showed imperial communication hubs, merchants' trade routes (whether by river or land), and sea journeys for trade.

13

Ancient Mesopotamia: The Town of Nippur, *c.* 2300 BCE

• ◆ •

Terracotta fragment with map of city
of Nippur, from Tell Telloh, Iraq
c. 2300 BCE
De Agostini Picture Library
The Bridgeman Art Library
Hilprecht-Sammlung Friedrich-
Schiller-Universitat, Jena

The first undisputed land maps are from Mesopotamia, from sometime around 2300 BCE. The creation of the first maps in Mesopotamia is linked to the development of an early form of writing, first proto-cuneiform and then **cuneiform**. Both writing systems consisted of sharp, angular shapes, which were likely the easiest to draw with precision in the clay material in which they were made. These earliest known writers pressed sharp sticks into a flattened piece of clay, drawing lines that would become fixed once the clay dried. They used these same tools and techniques to create maps; as a result, the maps consisted of straight lines and sharp angles, with simple circular shapes. The Tigris and Euphrates are long, curving rivers, but on these earliest maps they appear as straight lines.

One reason why these Mesopotamian drawings are considered the first maps is that they contain labels for places. They also exhibit a uniform style. Dozens of geographical tablets have survived from ancient Mesopotamia; each portrays features in a similar manner.

Since their maps were created after humans began to farm and settle into villages, not surprisingly the earliest examples show fields and towns. And since agrarian communities depend upon water to grow their food, many of the earliest maps also depicted important irrigation canals and rivers.

The clay map on the right shows a fortified town, Nippur, located on the Euphrates River 112 miles (180 kilometers) south of present-day Baghdad. The Euphrates is on the left side of the map; an irrigation canal appears as a set of parallel lines across the top of the map. A second canal, paralleling the Euphrates, appears on the right.

Just to the right of the banks of the Euphrates are a series of lines indicating the city walls, which extend from left to right across the map to form an irregular rectangle bounded by the second canal. The walls enclose a large temple and a park, marking this place as a religious site as well as one susceptible to military attacks (hence the need for walls). A number of gates appear along the walls to allow people and animals in and out of the town.

Nippur was an important religious site throughout several different Mesopotamian dynasties. During the third millennium BCE, the kings of Sumer and Akkadia sought to control the town since it was the seat of the god Enlil, who controlled human fate. In subsequent centuries Nippur was conquered by the Elamites and the Kassites.

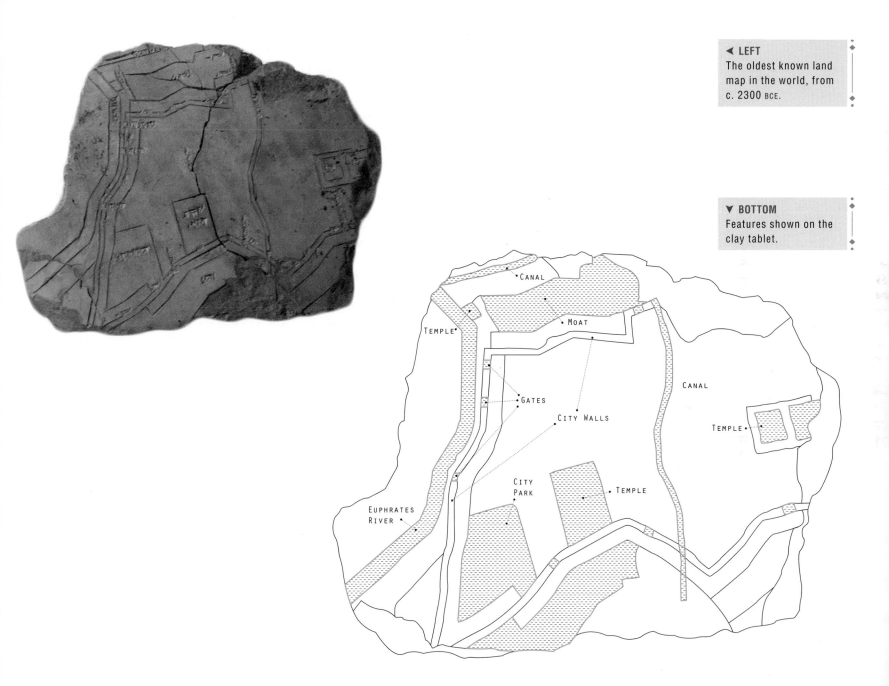

◀ **LEFT**
The oldest known land map in the world, from c. 2300 BCE.

▼ **BOTTOM**
Features shown on the clay tablet.

CANAL

TEMPLE

MOAT

CANAL

GATES

CITY WALLS

TEMPLE

CITY PARK

TEMPLE

EUPHRATES RIVER

14

Map of the Route to Paradise, Egypt, 1985–1795 BCE

• ◆ •

Outer coffin from the tomb of Gua,
Deir el-Bersha
Egypt. 12th Dynasty, 1985–1795 BCE
260.5 × 92 cm.
British Museum, London,
Great Britain

Outer coffin
1985–1795 BCE
Sameh Abdel Mohsen, Photographer
The Egyptian Museum, Cairo

This unusual image, from the second millennium BCE, is a good example of the ancient Egyptian tradition in which the main features of the heavens and the Earth are described and mapped. The Greeks later named such representations **cosmographies**, or cosmographical maps, because they described the entire cosmos.

Ancient Egyptian society was preoccupied with the afterlife. From the very beginning of agriculture in the Nile Valley in the sixth millennium BCE (not long after the birth of ancient civilization between the Tigris and Euphrates rivers), Egyptians placed great importance upon burial rites, initially placing the deceased in shrouds and interring them facing the sunset (west). During the Old Kingdom (c. 2686–2181 BCE) Egyptians began to build giant pyramids as final resting places for their rulers. They engaged in elaborate mummification of the bodies and carefully buried the dead with food and transportation that would help them make the journey through the afterlife, an intermediate state on the way to joining the sun and enjoying eternal life.

During the Middle Kingdom (c. 2055–1650 BCE), members of the elite began to be buried inside decorated wooden boxes. Mummies were placed in the boxes, and a pair of large eyes (known as *Wedjat*, or the "Eye of Horus") were painted on the outside, aligned with the eyes of the deceased, so that the dead person could see out of the coffin.

Inscribed and painted along the sides of the coffin were a series of instructions and spells (unimaginatively called "coffin texts") as guides for the dead to read as they journeyed toward eternal life. These "coffin texts" reflected a belief that the trip through the netherworld would be full of hazards and obstacles. Fearful that the dead might not remember all of the many instructions for overcoming the many obstacles they would encounter, Egyptians began writing down the instructions (and even magical spells) for the dead inside the coffins, so that the deceased could consult them as they journeyed through the underworld. The texts were written so that the mummy could read them from head to toe. As before, the ultimate goal was to join the sun and hence eternal life—but several spells in the coffin books now allowed the deceased to transform themselves into fire, air, grain, a child, or even an animal.

Other spells allowed family members to find each other in the afterlife. The world's first cosmographical maps were set underneath the mummies. These maps illustrated the journey that the deceased would take with the sun god, first by water (as shown with wavy lines), and then by land, (indicated by sharp angular lines). The first journey involved traveling from east to west along a waterway through the inner sky and then back again from west to east by land through the outer sky. These journeys were described in the coffin texts as the "Book of the Two Ways," one waterborne, the other by land. In some coffins they appeared in separate colors, with the water route shown in white and the land path in black. In still other maps a dangerous world of flames separates the two paths. As with early Mesopotamian maps, agreement that these images constitute true maps is based on the writing accompanying the representations. Egyptians invented a system of writing called **hieroglyphics** around 3400 BCE. By the time of the Middle Kingdom, they had begun to use a form of cursive for faster writing. But the instructions for the dead remained in carefully carved hieroglyphics. Imagine the danger that the deceased would experience if he or she could not decipher the handwriting inside the coffin!

15

Road Map to the Egyptian Quarries, 1150 BCE

• ◆ •

Turin Papyrus reconstruction
Courtesy James A. Harrell

This map shows a 9-mile (15-km) stretch of a valley and seasonal waterway (or *wadi*) in the central part of Egypt between the Nile River and the Red Sea. The waterway, called Wadi Hammamat ("Valley of Many Baths"), appears as the clear, road-like area filled with green, white, and brown specks. It shows the path to the quarries for two precious materials—gold and a grayish-green stone called bekhen-stone that ancient Egyptians prized for plates, statues, and jewelry. Like other maps that show long winding roads (or rivers—see Map 13) on a narrow writing surface, the pathway actually has far more twists and turns than the mapmaker could possibly fit in. The many tears and gaps of this map are the result of both its age and the fragile, paper-like material called **papyrus** on which it was drawn.

This map dates to the era of ancient Egyptian history called the New Kingdom, when the rulers were named Ramses, meaning "Born of the sun god Ra." The pharaoh at the time of this map was Ramses IV (1155–1149 BCE). The map depicts the route taken by numerous mining expeditions he sponsored to this region.

This map is unusual for its accurate depiction of the types of rocks in the region, and it is often called the first geological map. For example, the green, white, and brown specks that appear along the valley bottom represent the kind of gravel that lay along the route. The dark greenish areas are hills that rise up on either side of the gravel pathway. The hills are composed of a gray sandstone and fine, grainy stone called siltstone. The grey-green bekhen-stone is a rare combination of the grey sandstone and siltstone, and is only found in this particular location in Egypt. Ancient Egyptians prized this grey-green stone for jewelry and orna-mentation both because of its color and its scarcity. The quarry where the stone was mined appears on the map as a lighter grey-green oval close to the gravel pathway near the bend in the road.

The papyrus also refers to an expedition sent to the quarry to collect a chunk of this stone to use for a carved portrait of the most famous of the sun god pharaohs, Ramses II, also known as Ramses the Great (1279–1213 BCE) and husband to the famous Queen Nefertiti. Ramses II had commanded an army of over 100,000 men, conquering areas to the east, west, and south. According to the papyrus, those who transported the stone "deposited it in the Place of Truth beside the Temple of Usermaatre Setepenre, the great God [i.e., near the Valley of Kings in Thebes], left it at the enclosure of the Tomb and there it lay being half worked in one year."

The second place described in great detail on the map is the site of the nearby gold mines, indi-cated by a symbol that can be easily located because of the large white polygon which is the temple to the god Amun. Just to the left is a hill with what looks like three pinkish-brown rivers, distinguished by their color from the surrounding rock, which actually are gold-bearing quartz veins. Just below the gold-bearing rocks are four small rectangles indicating the gold mining town. The settlement itself was much larger, so the rectangles only indi-cate the site of the town. The papyrus also gives the distance from the gold quarry to the bekhen-stone quarry, but the exact length appears on a part of the papyrus that has been destroyed.

On the edge of the map, two labels indicate the "path to the sea." Although the bekhen-stone was destined for a pharaoh's tomb, the Wadi Hammamat was also the principal route from the Nile to the Red Sea and from there, east to Arabia. It is believed that the route that Moses took out of Egypt in the Book of Exodus followed a similar wadi to the north of the one shown on this map.

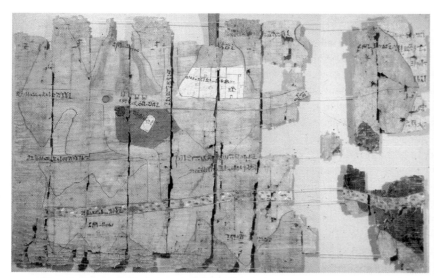

◄ **LEFT**
The papyrus map
showing mines, the
nearby mining town,
and the route to the
Red Sea, 1150 BCE.

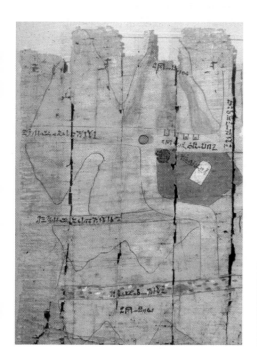

◄ **LEFT**
Close-up of the gold
deposits (pink streaks)
and the nearby mining
town.

Mediterranean Sea

Jerusalem

Gaza

Dead Sea

Nile Delta

Giza

Sinai
Peninsula

Akhetaten

Red Sea

River Nile

Wadi Hammamat

Qena   *Quseir*

Thebes   Luxor   *Bend in wadi
shown above*

New Kingdom Egypt.

37

16

Rivers and Roads:
The Oldest Map in
China, *c.* 239 BCE

• • •

Oldest Chinese map, showing the Wei
River in northwestern China
Ink on wood, 269 BCE
Gansu Provincial Research Institute
of Antiquities and Archeology
Tianshui, Gansu, China

Found only a few decades ago buried in a tomb in China are a series of seven painted wooden panels, faded and brown with age, each containing a set of serpentine black lines. At first, no one was entirely sure what these lines represented. But after they were restored, a careful reading revealed ancient Chinese characters indicating that these panels were, in fact, ancient maps.

The wooden boards date to the Warring States Period when what we now know as China was a group of feuding fiefdoms. Between 475 BCE and 221 BCE, seven major kingdoms (Qi, Chu, Yan, Han, Zhao, Wei, and Qin) fought each other in the central and eastern portions of the region. The briefly victorious Qin built tombs in a giant fan shape around the present day city of Fangmatan. Near the end of the wars, around 239 BCE, the wooden boards were placed inside one of these tombs.

The sinuous lines that dominate the image on the left are predominantly rivers, but some also signify roads or drainage divides. The only way a road can be distinguished from a waterway is by the Chinese character placed next to it.

Other features on the map are more clearly differentiated. Settlements are labeled with a character enclosed within a square. Mountain passes are identified by a pair of black circles with the color filled in.

One of the more unusual features of the surviving maps is the manner in which forests are identified. The predominant species of tree—cedar, fir, pine—is given. But the maps fail to disclose why its viewers would want this information, whether for fuel, lumber for constructing fortifications, or for hunting animals.

While some of the lines signify roads, the majority show the tributaries of the Wei River in west-central China. The centrality of rivers tells us something about the importance of waterways in ancient China. For thousands of years the two major rivers, the Yangzi and the Yellow, dominated the landscape and provided water for agriculture along with serving as major transportation routes.

Both rivers begin high in the Tibetan plateau and traverse thousands of miles before finally emptying into the Pacific. The Yangzi, 3,915 miles (6,300 km) in length, is the largest river in China and the third largest in the world. Only the Nile in Africa and the Amazon in Brazil are longer. The Yellow River is China's second largest at 3,395 miles (5,464 km). Along its banks, much of ancient Chinese civilization was born.

The Wei River, depicted in these panels, is the largest tributary of the Yellow River and the birthplace of many of China's most important ruling dynasties for over two millennia, beginning around 1000 BCE and ending around 900 CE. In addition to the Qin (221–207 BCE), the region had been dominated previously by the Zhou (1046–256 BCE). Later the Han (206–220 CE) and Tang (618–907 CE) dynasties would arise from its fertile watershed.

While 66 place names have been deciphered on the map, only three correspond to any modern settlement, suggesting that perhaps the towns have either disappeared or moved with the changing course of the Wei River. The map is oriented to the north, with the word "north" appearing at the top.

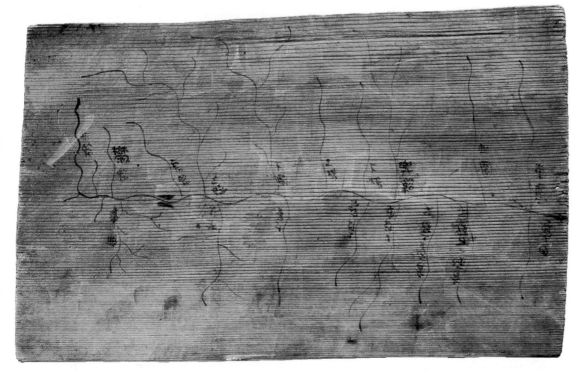

◄ **LEFT**
The oldest Chinese map
(ink on wood) showing
the Wei River in north-
western China *c.* 239 BCE.

▼ **BOTTOM**
Map showing the Wei
and Yellow rivers.

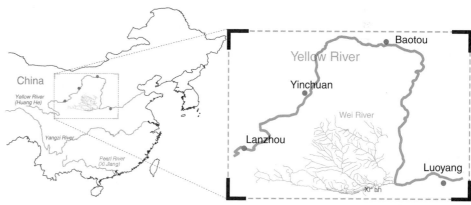

China

Yellow River
(Huang He)

Yangzi River

Pearl River
(Xi Jiang)

Yellow River

Baotou

Yinchuan

Wei River

Lanzhou

Xi'an

Luoyang

17

Rome Mapped in Marble: The Severan Marbles, 203–211 CE

• • •

Frammento di mappa da via Anicia
Soprintendenza Speciale per i Beni
Archeologici di Roma

The largest known urban map from ancient times shows the city of Rome. Composed entirely of massive chunks of marble, 150 pieces in total, the map was attached with pegs to the outside wall of a building. Together, these massive marble chunks measured nearly 2,520 square feet (240 square meters), covering the entire outside wall of the Temple of Peace. Today, all that remains of this once giant map are over a thousand small marble fragments similar to the fragment from an earlier map, pictured on the right, showing the temple of Castor and Pollux.

Visible from a great distance, the Severan map was made under the rule of the first Roman to seize power by a military coup, Septimius Severus. Completed between 203 and 211 CE, the map was chiseled out of marble at a time when the Roman Empire held sway from Britain to Armenia. Both its size and location suggest that the map was created to glorify the city of Rome and its people.

The framework for the map are the streets of Rome, carefully laid out on a giant grid. But the map's orientation is distinctive. South, or more precisely southeast, lies at the top of the map and northwest at the bottom. This angle parallels the angle of the Italian peninsula itself, which extends from southeast to northwest. Furthermore, the map is aligned along the major route to the Sanctuary of Jupiter, patron god of ancient Rome and its people.

None of the streets are named, only the giant temples and public buildings. Seeing the names of these towering buildings on a map may have allowed Romans to use the marble wall as a sort of guide that showed how to get around the vast and teeming metropolis. About 1 million people lived in Rome when the marble map was created: an extraordinary figure for the ancient world.

Yet another function may have come from another distinctive feature of the map. The streets that crisscross the city merely represent a massive urban outline. All of the care and detail of the map has been reserved for showing the structure and design of each and every one of the buildings. Thus, this giant map is really a carefully rendered series of architectural drawings. The walls, doorways, and staircases (both indoor and outdoor) of private homes and public meeting places, covered walkways (arcades), columns on large buildings, and columns joined together across the top (colonnades) are all shown. Doorways appear as breaks in a wall; arcades emerge as dashed lines; indoor staircases are registered with a V or a triangle; outdoor stairways consist of short perpendicular lines in between two parallel lines. Two-story buildings appear with top and bottom floors drawn separately; ground floor stores appear open for business.

Public buildings show the greatest architectural detail and are frequently named, unlike private residences. These named places, however, may well have served as reference points along streets without names and buildings without numbers. Such a public display of architecture exposed the interiors of the city's famous temples to the gaze of its citizens. But even more important, this massive map made the interior world of private buildings visible. The size of shops, apartments, and homes: all were exposed to every passerby. Romans did not need to guess at what lay behind the facades of buildings they walked by each day: like an x-ray, the map revealed the city's architectural bones.

NORTH

ROAD TO SANCTUARY

TIBER RIVER

N ⟵⊙

◀ TOP LEFT
Fragments of the earliest surviving marble map of Rome, created 50 to 100 years before the giant Severan map. Architectural symbols are identical to those used in the Severan map.

◀ TOP RIGHT
How Italy would appear if oriented in the same direction as the Severan marble map.

◀ LEFT
Diagram showing the pieces of the entire map with the Tiber River curving through the city. The map is aligned in the direction of the Temple of Jupiter, an important sanctuary.

18

All Roads Lead to Rome: The Peutinger Table, *c.* 350–400 CE

• ◆ •

Tabula Peutingeriana
Österreichische Nationalbibliothek

At its height at the end of the first century CE, the Roman Empire stretched south from Great Britain to the Straits of Gibraltar and eastward across the Mediterranean to the eastern shores of the Black Sea. Rome controlled a total of 6.5 million square kilometers (approximately 2.5 million square miles) of territory. The vast size of the Roman Empire still impresses today.

Between 27 BCE – 14 CE, the Roman emperor Augustus ordered the construction of a vast network of stone roads. With all roads leading to Rome, messages flowed quickly inward, as did orders sent out to the provinces. In later centuries the roads were widened to allow the swift deployment of troops. In all, an astonishing 43,350 miles (70,000 kilometers) of roads were constructed.

The city of Rome had been founded at the end of the sixth century BCE, and it soon set out to defeat its neighbors on the Italian peninsula. In the third century BCE, Romans launched naval attacks across Mediterranean that defeated the North African–based Carthaginians in the Punic Wars. By the mid-second century BCE, Romans controlled sea traffic in the central Mediterranean and increased their territorial control by more than 800-fold. In the sixth century BCE, the Romans controlled a territory of 10,000 square kilometers (3,861 square miles)—an area slightly smaller than Connecticut. By the end of the Punic Wars, the Romans controlled an area slightly larger than the state of Texas (308,882 square miles or 800,000 square kilometers).

Shortly after achieving its maximum extent, groups on the borders of the empire began chipping away at its size. Around 350 CE, not long after the capital of the declining empire was moved east to Constantinople (Istanbul), the original of this extensive map of Roman roads shown on the right was created. (The surviving copy was created by

an unknown monk around 1200 CE). Measuring 7 meters or 23 feet long, the map was just under a foot (11 inches or 30 centimeters) high.

The shape of the map suggests that it may have been meant to be rolled up and carried along on journeys, or, as some suggest, perhaps it simply was a display piece intended to celebrate Roman imperial power. As a result of its limited height, north–south distances are compressed, giving the map exaggerated east–west directions. Thus, triangular-shaped Sicily is stretched and flattened into a thin parallelogram. An already long and narrow Italian peninsula is absurdly elongated.

The map provides only the most general indication of direction, and only from east to west. The focus of the map, however, seems to have been distance. Roads appear in red, with a zigzag indicating a stopping point or perhaps a relay station where messages were originally handed over to a new carrier. Between the zigzags the distances appear in red Roman numerals. Sometimes the distances refer to Roman miles, but in Gaul (France) they refer to French miles, which were 50 percent longer. In Persia the distances are given in parasangs, an ancient measurement whose exact distance remains disputed.

Only a few other colors appear on the map. Mountains appear as overlapping brown semicircles. Water is green, and several large square structures (which may have been castles) show blue interiors. Five hundred different places were marked with icons and place names. Cities and towns most frequently appear as a pair of houses, each with a front door and flat, circular, or angled roof depending upon their location. Temples are shown as single angle-roofed houses viewed from the side. A handful of walled cities are drawn, as are the famous lighthouses opposite Alexandria and Constantinople.

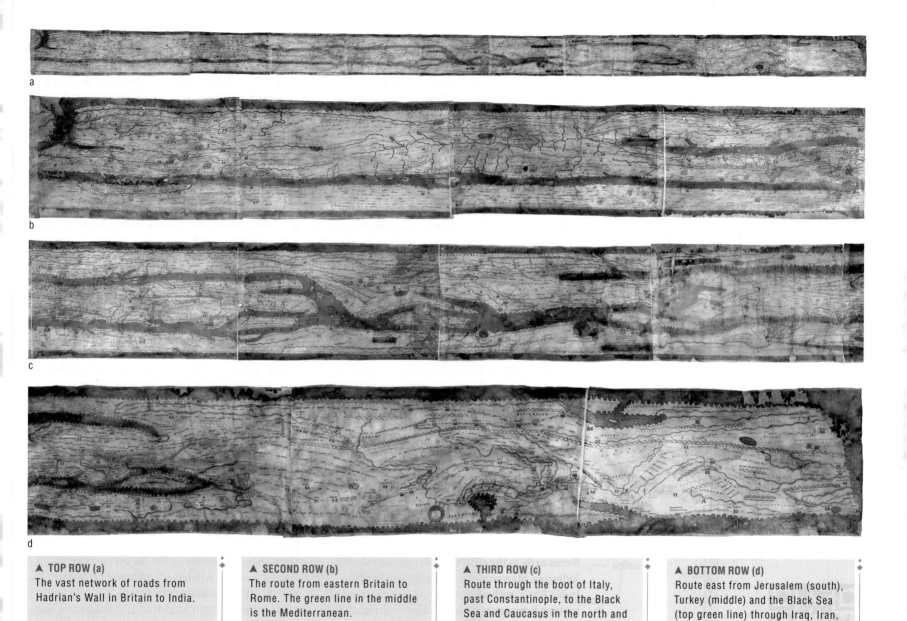

a

b

c

d

▲ TOP ROW (a)
The vast network of roads from Hadrian's Wall in Britain to India.

▲ SECOND ROW (b)
The route from eastern Britain to Rome. The green line in the middle is the Mediterranean.

▲ THIRD ROW (c)
Route through the boot of Italy, past Constantinople, to the Black Sea and Caucasus in the north and Mount Sinai (Arabian peninsula) in the south.

▲ BOTTOM ROW (d)
Route east from Jerusalem (south), Turkey (middle) and the Black Sea (top green line) through Iraq, Iran, and Afghanistan, ending in India.

21

Crusader Jerusalem,
c. 1200 CE

• ◆ •

Jerusalem as the center of the world,
c. 1200
Collective manuscript
North-West France
Shelf-mark: 76 F 5, fol. 1r
Koninklijke Bibliotheek, National
Library of the Netherlands

This Crusader map of Jerusalem, drawn about 100 years after the First Crusade (1096–1099 CE), tells the story of the newly captured city. At the bottom of the image, mounted Crusaders drive Fatamids out of the city. Above the Crusaders rests the city of Jerusalem, set inside a circle filled with the names of Christian buildings and with crosses atop the churches. The Muslim buildings have been removed from the map just as surely as the Christian forces drove the actual Muslims from the city.

The city of Jerusalem was actually a many-sided polygon, entirely enclosed by fortified walls. However, the mapmaker substituted the simpler geometric form of a circle for the actual boundaries (see Map 24). He similarly transformed the streets of Jerusalem that curved and weaved their way through the city into simple straight lines. And, as with many such medieval Christian images, the map is oriented to the east, which appears at the top of the map.

The city's fortifications stand out in white against a dark blue background, while its gates appear as green tubes with red shutters on either side signifying the doors. The gate of St. Stephen appears on the left-hand side, with a kneeling saint enveloped by a Byzantine style golden halo. Above St. Stephen and on the other side of the gate, four humble Christian pilgrims appear to march toward the gate. At the beginning of St. Stephen's street, inside the city walls (in the lower left-hand quadrant) appears the most important destination for crusaders, the former Church of the Holy Sepulchre.

At the top of the image representing the church , near a gold cross surrounded by gold circles, the words "Golgotha" and "Calvary" appear, indicating the place of the crucifixion. Next to the gold cross is a green square that encloses a red circle. Inside the circle, a green tomb appears with thin bands of gold and green beneath. Written in Latin in black letters within the red circle are the words, "Sepulchre of Our Lord." Razed in 1009 by a Fatamid caliph irritated by Easter pilgrims, the Church of the Holy Sepulchre once stood upon that spot. Although later partially rebuilt, the church's destruction by a Muslim leader fueled the public outrage that motivated the crusaders. No crusader could consider his journey complete unless he had prayed at the Holy Sepulchre. Prince Godfrey of Bouillon (1060–1110), the first crusader ruler of Jerusalem, took the title of "Defender of the Holy Sepulchre," making it clear that the destruction of the church provoked the First Crusade. The destroyed church was no bigger than other churches depicted but it dominates the map, with its large size being proportional to its importance to the Crusades.

In depicting a victorious Christianity, the Crusader map renames formerly Muslim places. The most conspicuous rechristening occurs in the upper right-hand quadrant containing the famous al-Aqsa Mosque (also known as the Dome of the Rock), where the Prophet Muhammed ascended to heaven. The mosque has disappeared. In its place rises a building shorn of Muslim insignia and labeled "Solomon's Temple."

Similarly effaced from the map are the Jewish quarters, which should have been depicted in the bottom right quadrant of the map next to the tower of biblical King David. Jews fought alongside Muslims to defend their city from invasion, and the crusaders were violently anti-Semitic. Filling in the place where the Jewish quarter had been, the mapmaker placed a "Latin Church." However, the actual Latin Church was in the northern part of Jerusalem—so the mapmaker repositioned it to erase any signs of a Jewish presence in the city.

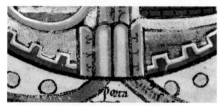

Temple of Solomon (al-Aqsa Mosque).

Gates of Jerusalem (Jaffa Gate).

The Church of the Holy Sepulchre.

David's Citadel (blue bricks on left) with former Jewish quarter (right).

Crusaders driving out Muslims.

22

Gough Map of Britain: Rivers and Routes, c. 1360 CE

••••

The Gough Map of Great Britain
(also known as The Bodleian Map)
c. 1360 CE
Drawn in pen, ink, and colored
washes on two skins of vellum
115 × 56cm
The Bodleian Library,
University of Oxford

Britain's first transport map was initially created around 1360 CE, about 145 years after the Magna Carta. The Gough map is a transportation map that links population centers by both rivers and routes. Distances sometimes appear in red Roman numerals alongside red lines traversing the land, but they are absent along the river passages.

Of the two modes of transport, rivers claim a far larger role in the map. Thick green lines twirl vividly across the landscape, heading mostly toward the sea, while the light red overland lines are only visible on careful scrutiny. Both the river and land routes link towns, hamlets, villages, and cities, some of which also include churches, castles, and fortifications. All these settlements are marked by simple, repetitive icons. Red roofs decorate single houses, indicating smaller towns; white groups of houses denote larger towns. Houses are drawn with a rectangular side, square front entrance, are topped by a triangle indicating the top of the roof, and closed off with a straight line at the end. The rectangles for churches also include a triangular spire with a cross at the top. Fortified cities and castles have long rectangles with arches for doorways and standard crenellation across the top. Only the city of London (detail at bottom right) shows any artistic distinction, with a giant gate and several imposing towers within its walls.

The significance of the Gough map, however, owes to the fact that it provides the first geographically recognizable shape of Britain. The overall appearance of the island resembles a man's shoe, with Scotland as the long flat front of the shoe and the ankle resembling the southern third of Britain.

Since the map is oriented to the east facing the continent, rotating it clockwise displays the first glimpse of a recognizable England with Scotland directly to the north. This correct placement of Scotland relative to England, together with the many towns properly situated relative to one another, indicates the skill with which the map was made.

This map dates from the final quarter of the fourteenth century and was then copied and partially updated early in the next century. The greatest accuracy appears on the east and southern coasts of England, from which Edward III (king of England at the time the map was made) launched several military expeditions against France. But other areas appear to reflect geographic information from an earlier time. For example, next to the Isle of Man (which was under Norwegian control until 1270) the first four letters of Norway appear, suggesting that the mapmaker started to write "Norway" and then learned of the loss, so he stopped writing in the middle of the word.

Other areas reflected a shortage of geographic information. Edward I (r. 1272–1307) had invaded Wales but knew little about Scotland, whereas Edward III knew a great deal after having invaded it several times. Yet, little additional information on Scotland appears to have made its way onto the map. Thus, it contains geographic information acquired at different points in time. Like many maps produced in the Middle Ages, the Gough map incorporates the state of geographic knowledge both from the historical past as well from the era of its construction.

England, Scotland, and Wales.

A detail from the Gough map showing London and environs.

▲ TOP
The Gough Map from c. 1360 CE (and partly updated later) shows England lying on its west side facing the unlabeled coastline of France. The large green waterway at the bottom right side of the map shows the Bristol Channel. The Thames appears as a much smaller waterway almost directly opposite, at the top of the map.

Part **3**

Mapping the World
600 BCE – 1450 CE

Long before satellites sent back images of the Earth from space, people in many parts of the globe tried to understand or to imagine what the entire world or even the universe looked like. Before the modern period, in both Asia and Europe, religious elites produced a type of world map that sought to define humans' place in the universe. Known as **cosmological maps**, the earliest are from ancient Egypt (see Map 14). Religious men often were the only members of a society that had the leisure and contemplative time to pursue questions concerning humans' relationship to the universe.

Three religions founded in India—Hinduism, Buddhism, and Jainism—shared similar sacred texts about a whole world centered on a high mountain named *Meru*, thought to be in the Himalayas but whose exact location is much debated. From Meru the world spread out in a series of seas and continents, which both Buddhists and Jains (but not Hindus) drew on maps (see Maps 32 and 33).

In medieval Christianity, another religious elite also possessed both the learning and the leisure to imagine the shape of the universe. Many Western clerics envisioned a circular world oriented toward the east because that was where Jerusalem lay. Instead of a mountain in the Himalayas, they oriented world maps toward this sacred city in the eastern Mediterranean (see Map 24).

Religious leaders were not the only ones who depicted the larger world or even the universe. In some societies and cultures, maps became a way of seeking to represent all the spaces that were known to be inhabited. In trying to portray this entire realm of human habitation, mapmakers had to picture faraway locations. Possessing only minimal, partial, and sometimes erroneous information, they primarily engaged in acts of the imagination. The visual form of maps allowed them to use symbols and icons to represent what the world might look like (see Map 28).

Another group of world maps were assembled more scientifically. Medieval Arabic and Turkish maps of the world focused upon secular geography, producing an overview of the societies with which there was contact and trade, and indicating their approximate location. These maps often showed major geographic features—the Indian Ocean, the mountains of Central Asia—and spelled out the names of the people residing near these places. In this way, the known world was catalogued and mapped (see Maps 26 and 27).

Many medieval people observed the differences in temperature and climate when they traded and traveled in different parts of the world; their travel-ogues often incorporated information on these topics. Mapmakers drew upon this information to note, alongside the outline of landmasses, suggestions of what the climate might be like (see Map 25).

Finally, political or imperial ambitions sometimes provided the underlying reason for the creation of world maps. In these maps, religious considerations were eliminated or became subordinated to secular goals. The maps created by the legendary mapmaker to the ambitious King Roger II of Sicily (see Map 29), and another map for an equally ambitious king, Afonso VI of Portugal (see Map 31), are good specimens in this genre.

Timeline of world history

c. 650–550 BCE
Zoroaster

c. 600 BCE
Earliest surviving world map (Babylon)

c. 599–527 BCE
BCE Mahavira

c. 623–543 BCE
Buddha

551–479 BCE
Confucius

since 100 BCE
Mediterranean-Atlantic trade

c. 3–33 CE
Jesus Christ

200s and on
Spread of Buddhism to East Asia

300s and on
Spread of Christianity in Roman World

c. 1072 CE
Earliest surviving Turkish world map

1098 CE
First Crusade

1040s–1090 CE
Turkish migrations into Middle East

1000–1200 CE
Spread of Islam to West Africa

c. 1200 CE
First Buddhist world maps, Japan

c. 1300 CE
Earliest surviving Ptolemaic world map

23

Babylonian World Map, *c.* 600 BCE

• • •

Map of the world
700–500 BCE
Rock carving
Sippar, southern Iraq, Babylonian

This tiny tablet measures only 4.8 inches by 3.2 inches (122 × 82 mm), but it contains one of history's most famous maps—the first geographic attempt to represent the entire known world. Made from clay, the classic mapmaking material of ancient Mesopotamia (see Map 13), the tablet sketches the world centered upon the ancient town of Babylon.

The map's point of view is fundamentally geographical. The clay tablet shows a flat circle with what appear to be stars attached to the outer edge of the circle. The giant round shape represents an immense river surrounding most of the world, and labeled as "the Bitter River." Attached to the Bitter River are four triangles that appear as stars. According to the writing above the map, eight such triangles were originally represented; four of the star-like appendages have been lost. According to the famous Babylonian myth, *The Epic of Gilgamesh*, a great flood once covered the land. When the waters receded, these eight identically labeled "regions" appeared, each separated from each other by an identical distance. According to some sources the triangles symbolize mountains, but nothing further about them appears on the tablet.

The ancient city of Babylon lies at the center of the map, marked by the large rectangle inside and toward the top of the circle. The horizontally labeled city crosses the Euphrates, just as the city itself once sat on both sides of the river.

One of the most fabled cities of antiquity, the city of Babylon rose to prominence when it became the capital of Hammurabi's empire (1728–1686 BCE). Hammurabi most likely first posted his 281 laws—the world's first legal code—on a giant clay tablet 2.25 meters (7.4 feet) tall in this city. However, Hammurabi had been dead for over a millennium when this map was created.

This map dates from the time of the legendary Hanging Gardens of Babylon, a terraced landscape a hundred feet square, gradually rising high above the Euphrates and densely covered with fragrant greenery. Reputedly created by king Nebuchadnezzar II around 600 BCE, the gardens attracted visitors from as far away as ancient Greece. The Greeks compiled guides to the most impressive sites of the ancient world and designated these gardens as one of the Seven Wonders of the World. However, the gardens were destroyed by earthquakes during the second century BCE and were never rebuilt.

On the Babylonian world map, the Euphrates vertically dominates the frame, while its sister river, the equally important Tigris, is entirely absent. Instead of the Tigris, the map emphasizes the place where the two rivers join together near present-day Basra in southern Iraq. A second, smaller horizontal rectangle at the bottom of the Euphrates is labeled "marsh" on the eastern side and "outflow" on the west, corresponding to the 200-kilometer (120-mile) Shatt al-Arab (Coast/Beach of the Arab) or Arvand River (Persian) formed by the confluence of the Euphrates and the Tigris and emptying into the Persian Gulf.

The small circles indicate either cities or kingdoms, but do not appear in correct geographic relationship to Babylon. The circle labeled "Assyria" to the east of Babylon actually represents a kingdom several hundred kilometers to the northeast. The northern area called "Habban" is similarly incorrectly situated, since it lies around present-day Kermanshah in western Iran. While the name of the ancient kingdom of Urartu appears above that of Assyria, it actually lay far to the north, near where the boundaries of Iran, Turkey, and Armenia meet today. A semicircle in the top right is labeled "mountains." Both the Tigris and the Euphrates originated in mountains to the northeast—the Euphrates in the Zagros Mountains of Turkey and the Tigris further to the east in the Toros (Taurus) Mountains.

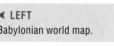

Ancient Mesopotamia, showing places indicated on the world map.

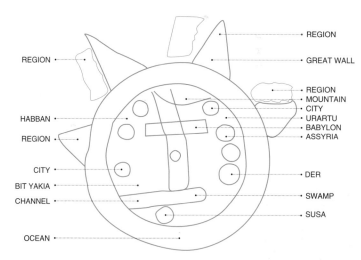

REGION
GREAT WALL
REGION
MOUNTAIN
CITY
URARTU
BABYLON
ASSYRIA
DER
SWAMP
SUSA

REGION
HABBAN
REGION
CITY
BIT YAKIA
CHANNEL
OCEAN

Diagram showing places described on the Babylonian world map.

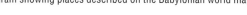

24

Medieval Christian T-O Map, *c.* 600 CE

•••

Isidore, Bishop of Seville.
(*c.* 560–636 CE)
Etymologiae (Etymologies), page 2
Augsburg: Guntherus Ziner, 1472
Vollbehr Collection
Rare Book and Special Collections
Division, Library of Congress

With its simple vertical and horizontal lines enclosed by a giant circle, this medieval European map resembles a simpler version of the ancient Babylonian world map on the previous page. Over a thousand years separate the two maps. While mirroring the Babylonian map's formal appearance, this map covers a far greater geographical area, since in the intervening time the size of the known world had expanded far beyond the valley of the Tigris and Euphrates known to the Babylonians.

The earliest known example of such a drawing appears in the *Etymologies* of Isidore of Seville (560–636 CE). In the section in his book that treats the Earth, the map appears as a small drawing at the top of a page. Like its Mesopotamian predecessor, Isidore's diagram has the world encircled by an ocean. That ocean flows continuously around the land, enclosing it completely. Inside that giant circle, bisected by the "T" is what Isidore calls the three parts of the world.

The top half of the circle—and the largest section of the map—is labeled "Asia." Much of the area labeled Asia would be familiar to readers today. Both the Ganges and Indus rivers in India are mentioned in Isidore's book, as are Sri Lanka, Persia, Mesopotamia, Syria, Palestine, and Judea.

The two much smaller portions of the world are Africa and Europe, each half the size of Asia. Europe appears on the left-hand side, while an equally sized Africa appears on the right. In the *Etymologies*, Africa extends from the Nile through the Straits of Gibraltar to the Atlantic. Europe appears in identical form, running along the Mediterranean from Greece to Spain, then north to Gaul (France) and Germany.

At the center of the map, where the horizontal and vertical lines intersect, lies the city of Jerusalem, which most medieval readers would recognize even

if, as shown on the example on the right, it was not named. The intersecting lines direct the viewer's eye toward the hub of the map—Christendom's sacred city. The centering on Jerusalem also explains the map's orientation. East lies at the top (*Oriens*), since from the perspective of people living in Africa and Europe Jerusalem lay to their east. The shape of the map became so popular and familiar that it even earned a nickname. The vertical bar crossed with a horizontal bar resembles the letter T, while the circle enclosing the "T" looks like the letter O. Hence these maps have become widely referred to as **T-O maps**.

Other medieval maps also employed simple lines. "Zonal" maps separated the world into broad climate zones: temperate, frigid, and torrid (see Map 25). But the T-O outline with its symmetry, simplicity, and implicit religious message remained the most popular of all world maps circulating during the Middle Ages. Sometimes they are grouped into a larger category of maps known as **mappamundi,** literally "maps of the world."

T-O and Babylonian maps both diagram the world; that is, they outline spatial relationships. Outlines are employed when a group of people have become aware of their spatial relationship to other places but lack necessary information to visualize that connection in greater detail. In Map 23, ancient Mesopotamians had become spatially aware of places a considerable distance away, but lacked either the information or a means of determining direction or distance between themselves and these faraway places. Similarly, the European T-O maps convey an appreciation of a vast world that they could conceptually imagine but could not fully represent. Creators of the T-O maps laid out basic directions—Asia to the east, Africa to the south—as well as relative areas—Africa and Europe were virtually identical in size, but Asia's area was double, equal to that of the two other parts combined. Since all that was known of Africa at the time was the northern section, the map depicted known areas of the world proportionally. While greater detail could not be illustrated, world diagrams conveyed an understanding of connections to larger, distant, and as yet unrepresentable spaces.

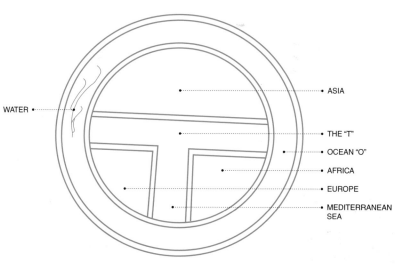

A diagram showing some of the labels on the T-O map.

WATER

ASIA

THE "T"

OCEAN "O"

AFRICA

EUROPE

MEDITERRANEAN SEA

25

World Climate Map, *c.* Fifth Century CE

• ◆ •

MS. D'Orville 77, folio 100r.
The Bodelian Library,
University of Oxford

The earliest known sketch of the world according to climate zones first appears in a book from Late Antiquity with a very odd title.

The map, from the *Commentary on Dream of Scipio*, divides the world into five zones, originally created by the Greek philosopher Aristotle (384–322 BCE). The map is divided according to Aristotle's description of two separate temperature bands in the north, a parallel number of identical bands in the south, and a single band in the middle. At the top and bottom of the map are the poles—labeled as the "north frigid zone" and the "south frigid zone." Just below the freezing zone on the north and just above the frigid zone on the south are two identically labeled "temperate zones," described as the most suitable for human habitation. In between lies a region of burning heat that was usually called *torride* in Latin ("torrid zone" in English) by such famous Classical writers as Cicero (106–43 BCE), Strabo (63/64 BCE – 24 CE), and Pliny (23–79 CE).

While no one seemed compelled to draw a map to accompany the descriptions provided by these Roman writers, climate zone maps appear in a commentary on Cicero's *Dream of Scipio,* composed toward the end of the Roman Empire by the writer Macrobius (395–423 CE). In the dream, the Roman general Scipio Aemilianus (185–129 BCE) finds himself transported into the heavens, looking down upon North Africa "from a high place full of stars." Scipio's grandfather tries to impress upon him the vast size of the universe and his insignificance in the world. To do so, Scipio's grandfather describes the enormous size of the world, using Aristotle's separation of the world into five different zones of climate.

While some of the maps that were included in the *Commentary on the Dream of Scipio* contain no geographical referents whatsoever, the version of the map shown here places specific geographical features in each zone. The entire north side of the

Mediterranean is included in the north temperate zone. The unlabeled Black Sea appears as a mushroom cloud in the middle of the Mediterranean with a clearly distinct Anatolia (Turkey) next to it. Also included in this north temperate zone is the Caspian Sea, which appears with a label on the far right. The southern shores of the Mediterranean belong to the very hot regions. North Africa from the Straits of Hercules to the coast of Egypt is labeled as being part of the Nile River and is included in the very hot region, as is the Indian Ocean. At the far right of the upper torrid zone is an apparent peninsula, which could be either India or Sri Lanka.

The excessively hot region is split in two by an ocean. It may be that caravan traders bearing gold up from West Central Africa talked about a body of water to the south, which could be the Gulf of Guinea. However, since no European had explored that seacoast, the map sketched a possibility— namely, that the water extended straight through the continent of Africa. Thus, an additional hot region of Africa extends below this (fictional) body of water extending across the middle of the continent. Just below this region, labeled *perusta*, is the southern temperate zone. But the text states that this southern hemispheric temperate zone would be too difficult to reach because it would be impossible to traverse the hot zone. Only the northern temperate zone remained truly habitable.

Several other features of this map are worth noting. While many of the self-consciously Christian maps of the world (Maps 24 and 28) are oriented toward the east, this map has north on top, much as in today's maps. The majority of these world climate maps were oriented north, which suggests that this orientation may have influenced later cartographic development of the northward direction.

The idea of a world divided by horizontal zones endured for a very long time. During the Middle

Ages, versions of world maps by al-Idrisi (see Map 29) and other Islamic cartographers further developed the idea of climate zones. As mapmakers began to incorporate latitude (a horizontal division based upon mathematics), they continued to associate climate with horizontal zones well into the seventeenth century (see Map 30).

Look, the inhabited portions of the earth are tiny and few, the rest is vast desert dividing one inhabited area from another. The inhabitants of earth are so removed from each other that they cannot even communicate with one another. The place where you live is so very far away from other populated areas; some people live in areas on the opposite side of the globe. Do you expect them to honor or glorify your name? Look at all the different zones enveloping the earth; the two most widely separated from one another, at opposite poles of the heavens, are fixed with an icy cold, while the midmost zone burns with the heat of the sun. Only the two zones between these extremes are habitable The zone which lies south of yours has no connection or means of connection with your zone, because they are prevented from crossing the midmost zone. If you look at your own northern zone, you can't help but notice just how small a section of this region can be regarded as yours. The territory you occupy, your vast Empire, is nothing more than a small island, narrow from north to south, a bit wider east to west, surrounded by the sea ...

—Cicero, *Dream of Scipio,* Book 6 of *On the Commonwealth*

Diagram showing the climate zones as first described by Aristotle, depicted on the map above.

26

Medieval Islamic Map of the World, *c.* 1300 CE

• ◆ •

Late 17th century copy of a
14th century map
'Umar bin Muzaffar Ibn al-Wardi.
*Kharidat al-'Aja'ib wa Faridat
al-Ghara'ib.* (*The Pearl of Wonders and
the Uniqueness of Things Strange*).
Near East Section, African
and Middle Eastern Division,
Library of Congress

Many world maps from medieval Islam stylistically resemble their contemporary Christian T-O maps. In both traditions, the known world appears as a flat circular disk bounded by an encircling sea. Europe and Africa are shown as wedges separated by the Mediterranean, which is drawn as a straight line.

However, several features distinguish the Islamic world maps from their Christian counterparts. The most significant change is the inclusion of the Indian Ocean, which generally occupies a larger space in the Muslim maps. In the map shown on the right, the Indian Ocean appears as an open wrench, pointing to the right and wrapping itself around the Arabian peninsula.

The size and centrality of the Indian Ocean is due to the important role it played in Muslim trade during the Middle Ages. Unlike their Christian counterparts, who largely confined themselves to the Mediterranean and other waters close to the European coast, Muslim merchants traded in both the Mediterranean and Indian Ocean from the ninth century CE onward. Taking advantage of the monsoon wind system (see Map 76), Muslims regularly sailed between East Africa, India, and Arabia. A seasonal reversal in the current along the east coast of Africa also allowed Muslim merchants to travel as far south as the gold-producing region of Sofala in what is today Mozambique.

Trade contributed to the another important distinguishing characteristic of Islamic world maps: namely, the exaggerated extension of east Africa. On the map at the right, pie-shaped Africa has been enlarged by the addition of a large curved semicircle attached to the bottom of the continent and extending to the east. The easiest way to follow this addition is to look for the path of the River Nile (colored red). Across the bottom of the Indian Ocean, the Nile makes a ninety degree turn and goes almost as far as India (see diagram). As a result of this eastward extension of Africa, the relative sizes of the two western continents shifted. In the Christian T-O maps, Europe and Africa each appear as pie-shaped wedges of equal size. However, in this Islamic map, Europe retains its pie-shaped dimension, but it is significantly smaller relative to Africa.

The map also shows the Nile extending in three directions. It flows southward, as in most maps, including Christian T-O maps. In addition to the newly introduced sharp eastward turn, the map also reflects a misconception about the Nile, widely held until the fifteenth century; namely, that the Nile also branched off to the west and flowed to the Atlantic. Although this feature sometimes appears in Christian maps, it is usually absent from ones that follow the T-O mapping tradition.

There are other differences between this Muslim world map and its Christian counterparts that reveal Muslims' greater geographic awareness of the world beyond the Mediterranean. These include the appearance of the Persian Gulf on the other side of the wrench that clutches Arabia. A little below what would be the handle of the wrench, two swirls resembling spectacles indicate the Black and Caspian Seas. Although both bodies of water occasionally appear in T-O maps, in this map they possess an unusual shape. Finally, toward the left section of the map, a rectangle denotes India.

As with most medieval Islamic maps, south lies at the top of the map, whereas Christian maps were oriented toward the east. Although the map illustrates greater detail, it retains the diagrammatic style of the Christian T-O map, suggesting the exchange of ideas about mapping, if not the maps themselves, between Christians and Muslims during the Middle Ages.

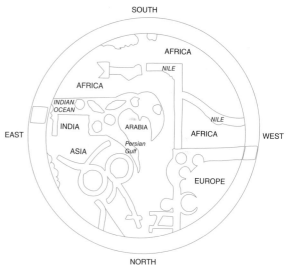

SOUTH

AFRICA

NILE

AFRICA

INDIAN
OCEAN

NILE

EAST

INDIA

ARABIA

AFRICA

WEST

ASIA

Persian
Gulf

EUROPE

NORTH

Diagram showing the places named on the world map.

27

First Map of Turkish Central Asia, 1072 CE

• ◆ •

Mahmud Kashgari bin Husayn
bin Muhammad
Kitab divan logat el Turk, 1072 CE
[n.p.] (1917–19)
Library of Congress, African and
Middle Eastern Division

A different perspective on the world emerges from this earliest known map drawn by a Turk. The cartographer highlighted his homelands—the vast Turkish-speaking swathe of Central Asia—in a book designed to inform Arabic-speaking Muslims about the steppes and its peoples.

Central Asia is an immense region of deserts, mountains, and steppes. At the time of this map, it lay at the heart of the Silk Road. The route began in China, depicted in Map 27 as the center of a large red box representing the Great Wall. Once beyond the Great Wall, Silk Road merchants would usually spend at least four months traveling through Turkish territories.

The map's creator, Muhammed al-Kashgari, belonged to the ruling family in the Turkish town of Barskon (Barsgan) in what today is the modern Central Asian Republic of Kyrgyzstan. His family claimed descent from the Karahan khan, Karahanli Kasgarli'nin, the first Turkish leader to convert to Islam in 932 CE. Thrust into political exile in 1047–1048 CE, al-Kashgari traveled through Central Asia for the next twenty years, visiting cities and villages and collecting stories, recording oral literature, dialects, and customs from different Turkish communities.

In 1072 CE al-Kasghari was invited to the capital of the eastern Islamic empire, ruled by Seljuk Turks. Having conquered Iran in the tenth century, the Seljuk Turks came to power in Baghdad in the eleventh century, ruling over an empire that stretched from Afghanistan to the Mediterranean. At the invitation of the leader of the Seljuk Turks, al-Kasghari moved to Baghdad where he composed both the map and the first Arabic–Turkish dictionary. The dictionary contained approximately 7500 words and phrases, including popular sayings and a section on Turkish customs and rituals. Al-Kasghari recounts how, when two Turks met each other they would identify themselves by the names of their nation, tribe, clan, and kin group, in that order.

The Central Asian steppes are a huge land-locked region. Hence, the core of this map shows land. The names of Turkish towns and cities are placed accurately along the northern and southern routes of the Silk Road. The seas that are so central to other Muslim world maps (such as Map 26) are named but not distinctively colored or noted. In fact, these bodies of water appear considerably smaller than the steppes. The only distinctively colored body of water is the apostrophe-shaped Caspian Sea on the eastern edge of Central Asia. On the rim of the map the encircling sea is colored dark green, while elsewhere rivers are lighter green, mountains appear in red, and cities are marked in yellow.

Even though water routes and bodies of water assume a secondary role, the map nonetheless spans an immense geographic region from Iberia at the western end of the Mediterranean to Japan, which is a semicircle and labeled "Cabarka." China is located to the east of in the little hook just to the left of this Japan semicircle. The thick red lines are the giant mountain ranges fringing China. Al-Kashgari identifies the Muslim kingdoms around the Mediterranean including the Maghreb and Andalucia, as well as Egypt and Alexandria. Important trading areas noted along the Red Sea include Yemen, Ethiopia, and Somalia, demonstrating the author's vast geographic knowledge. The province of Kashmir in northern India also appears, as does India itself.

Turkish Central Asia declined after 1110 CE, as high local tariffs hurt trade and religious orthodoxy stifled the region's most original thinkers. The Seljuk Turks' power declined after the First Crusade (1096–1099 CE), and a little over a century later invasions would alter the complexion of Central Asia immensely. Still, Turkic languages—similar to the Turkish in al-Kasghari's dictionary—remain widely spoken throughout Central Asia, particularly in Turkmenistan, Uzbekistan, Kyrgyzstan, Kazakhstan, and western China.

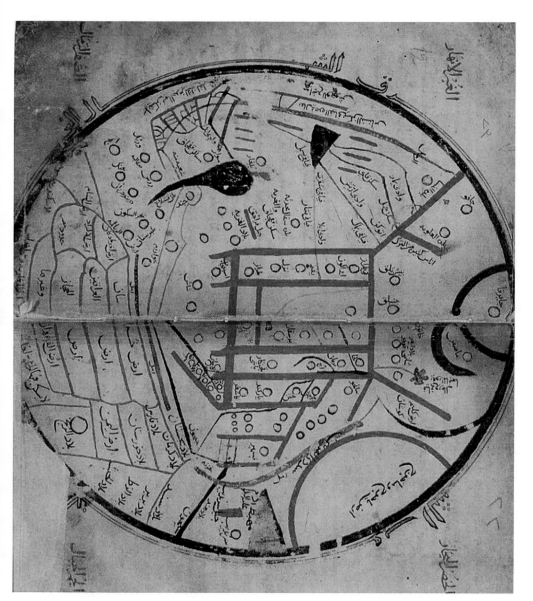

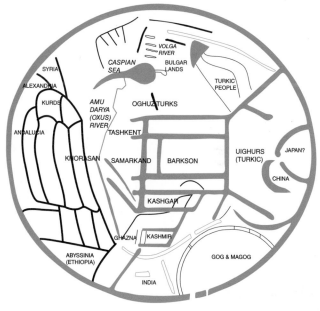

◀ LEFT
Earliest known map of the world drawn by a Turk.

Diagram showing some of the locations labeled on the map.

28

The Hereford Mappamundi,

c. 1300 CE

• ◆ •

Mappa Mundi, c. 1290 CE
Vellum
Richard of Haldingham
(Richard de Bello) (fl.c.1260–1305)
Hereford Cathedral,
Herefordshire, UK

This map of the world is in Hereford Cathedral in the county of Herefordshire in England, near the border with Wales. The largest surviving mappamundi (world map) from the Middle Ages, the map was created around 1300 CE by a clergyman named "Richard of Haldingham or Lafford" (Holdingham and Sleaford in Lincolnshire, England). Nothing further is known about Richard than his name, except that he apparently bequeathed his creation to Hereford Cathedral.

While Europe is considered to have been disconnected from the rest of the world during the Middle Ages, this map shows unmistakable knowledge of Africa and an awareness of the world beyond the Mediterranean.

The map's basic outline derives from the schematic principle of the T-O map (see Map 24), a "T" shaped inland sea and rivers surrounded by an encircling ocean in the form of the letter "O." Like the T-O maps, the Hereford mappamundi divides the world into three central parts: Europe, Africa, and Asia. The top of the map lies to the east and Jerusalem appears in the center.

The Hereford map, however, soon departs from the clarity of the outline, modifying, embellishing, and sometimes muddling it. Someone involved in making the map reversed the designations for Africa and Europe so that the English Channel appears under the label "Africa" while the Nile surfaces under the label "Europe." The idea of the tripartite world first enshrined by Isidore of Seville remains clear, but someone inexplicably reversed the labels.

Other modifications include a different understanding of the Nile, which instead of remaining on the right side of the "T" now appears as a small rectangle. The river's course follows that of the Islamic mappamundi from the same time period. It makes an eastward turn and travels almost to the base of the Red Sea near the top of the map. As with Islamic maps from the same period (see Map 26), Africa has increased considerably in size, appearing in the Hereford map with a shape like a slice of lemon.

This map differs significantly from other medieval world-view maps because it embellishes the basic outline with additional bodies of water, including the English Channel (a semicircle) on the bottom left, and the Red Sea diagonally opposite on the upper right (a slightly drunken "H"). The Hereford mappamundi also includes place names, pictures, commentary, and even Biblical events. The map's immense size—a 52-inch (132cm) circle drawn on a single, chopping-board-shaped calfskin measuring 64 by 52 inches (1.58 x 1.33 meters), making it the largest known T-O map—furnishes the space for all this additional information. Undoubtedly, the map took years to make by many different artisans with varying degrees of skill. Among the 420 places mentioned in the map are the Indus and Ganges rivers in India, Sri Lanka, the Tigris and Euphrates Rivers, and the city of Babylon in Mesopotamia. It also includes the Black Sea and the adjacent Sea of Azov, the Caspian Sea, the Persian Gulf, and the Red Sea. Egypt, the Nile, Greece, and the Straits of Gibraltar are also depicted. Naturally, both Britain and Ireland appear on the map, although both are sketched as long slivers.

The Garden of Eden, a place of dubious geographic value, is depicted at the top of the map, perhaps in India. Its presence is unsurprising. During the Middle Ages many people thought that the Biblical Garden of Eden could actually be found on Earth.

◄ LEFT
The Hereford
Mappamundi, *c.* 1300 CE.

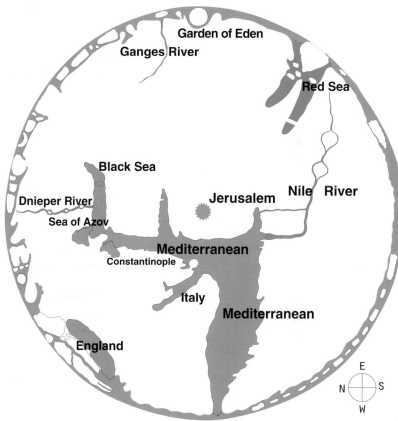

Garden of Eden

Ganges River

Red Sea

Black Sea

Dnieper River

Jerusalem

Nile   River

Sea of Azov

Mediterranean

Constantinople

Italy

Mediterranean

England

E
N ✛ S
W

Diagram showing a few of the 420 places depicted on the Hereford Mappamundi.

29

Idrisi's Circular Map of the World,

1165 CE

● ◆ ●

Idrisi's Circular Map of the World
c. 1165 CE
(copy from 1553)
MS_Pococke_375_3b_4a
The Bodleian Library,
University of Oxford

The Spanish-educated Muslim scholar Mohammed al-Idrisi (1099–1165 CE) completed this map just before his death. He created it not for a Muslim leader but for a Christian king, Roger II of Sicily. Roger's father conquered Sicily in 1078 as part of the same eleventh-century Norman overseas invasions that overtook England in 1066.

Of the two Norman conquests, Sicily was far richer and far more important at the time. For nearly a thousand years the island had functioned as a crucial transit point for shipping gold and other goods from Africa to Europe. Before the Normans, the island had been under the Fatamids; their ongoing military struggle with the Normans is highlighted by the warning regarding Sicily on Map 20, the Fatamid nautical route map of the Mediterranean. With the conquest of Sicily, Normans controlled trade across the central Mediterranean.

Roger II, son of the original Norman conqueror Roger I, engaged in successful military campaigns on the Italian peninsula. However, Roger II also wanted to assemble a compendium of geographic knowledge about the entire world. Fluent in Arabic and tolerant of the island's Muslim inhabitants, he invited Mohammed al-Idrisi, one of the leading Islamic scholars of the day, to create such an overview. King Roger provided al-Idrisi with access to historical geographical works, as well as accounts about the rest of the world from Christian and Muslim merchants and pilgrims, past and present. From these widely varied sources, al-Idrisi created a rich sourcebook on humanity, illustrated with a series of regional maps as well as one large overview of the entire world, presented here.

Al-Idrisi took his task seriously, devoting decades of his life and working with unknown numbers of assistants in compiling the detailed regional maps. While al-Idrisi held his work to a high standard (crosschecking and verifying sources), he followed his own injunctions most closely for that area of the world he knew best, namely the western Mediterranean (both the African and European coasts). But by the time he reached regions with little contact with Sicily (such as India) he took shortcuts by copying the work of earlier geographers without paying such careful attention to discrepancies between accounts, or even to more recent reports regarding population settlements that had been abandoned.

The world map included in his compendium echoed the basic shape of the classic Babylonian, medieval Christian, and Islamic world views. The Earth is circular, surrounded by a continually moving, uninterrupted ocean. Three separate areas are named—Africa, Europe, and Asia. However, al-Idrisi's world map (or the earlier model he may have used) also shows distinctive features. Like other Islamic maps of the world, al-Idrisi's map includes both the Mediterranean and Indian Oceans. Like the world map created over a hundred years later by al-Wardi (Map 26), al-Idrisi shows Africa as a crescent-shaped area, with a square on the western side but tilting sharply northward south of the Red Sea. The Arabian peninsula is also visible.

Al-Idrisi's skill as a cartographer really shines in his grasp of European and Mediterranean geography, which was superior to that of his predecessors. Spain appears as a peninsula extending toward the Atlantic, its rivers and mountains correctly displayed. Italy also appears as a long peninsula intruding into the Mediterranean with Sicily correctly drawn next to a sharp point, the emerging toe of boot-shaped Italy. On the other side of Greece, the rarely-seen Black Sea emerges and directly across the Mediterranean the Nile River delta appears in remarkable detail. For regions further east, al-Idrisi provides less accuracy. He illustrates the coast of India as flat (rather than triangular in shape) and he depicts the economically important island of Sri Lanka, which in the twelfth century was the world's only source of cinnamon, as disproportionately large relative to India. Al-Idrisi also shows the Nile traveling north (correct) as well as west (incorrect). He also depicts the Indus river in India, as well as the rivers of the East African coast.

SOUTH

EAST

WEST

NORTH

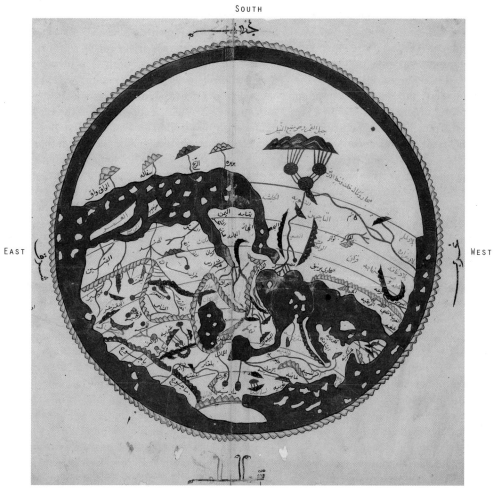

NORTH

WEST

EAST

SOUTH

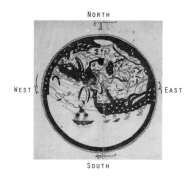

◄ FAR LEFT

Al-Idrisi's Circular Map of the World (1165). Created with south at the top in the Islamic style, the smaller version of the map on the right and the diagram below have been rotated to show north on top.

NORTH

INGILTIRRAH
(ANGLE-TERRE)

PECHENEGS
(TURKISH TRIBE)

MAGOG

BRITANNY   POLAND   BULGHARS   GOG
AL-ANDALUS   THE   (JATHULIYAH   "MOUNTAIN OF THE BARRIER"
           (BALKANS)   (BUILT BY ALEXANDER THE
                   MACEDONIA   ALANS   GREAT)
              VENETIAN   (SYTHIANS)   KHAZAR
FORTHEST   GULF   (TURKISH   KHIMSHIR
MAGHREB   SICILY   CASPIAN   TRIBE)   (TURKISH
                                  SEA   TRIBE)
              MEDITERRANEAN   CYPRUS
                                       KHORASAN   TILE
MAGHRAWAH   (ATLAS MTNS)   FARS   INDIA   CHINA
(BERBERS)   EGYPT   AL-SIND
LAND OF THE   YEMEN   JAVA
LAMLAM   CEYLON   WAQWAQ
         DESERT AND SAND   ETHIOPIA   INDIAN OCEAN
THE   BEYOND THE EQUATOR NUBIA   WAQWAQ   WAQWAQ
WESTERN   SOFALA
DARK   THE ZANJ (MOZAMBIQUE)
SEA

WEST   EAST

SOUTH

67

30

Earliest Known Ptolemaic Map of the World,

c. 1300 CE

•••

Claudius Ptolemy
Map of the world; from the British
Isles and Europe, the Mediterranean Sea
and North Africa,
to the Middle East, Arabia, and Asia
Originally produced in Greece,
Monastery of Vatopedi, Mount
Athos, early 14th century
The British Library

This map from about 1300 CE outlines Europe, Africa, and Asia, with many of the same characteristics as the world map by al-Idrisi (see Map 29). Spain sticks far out into the Atlantic, Italy appears as a peninsula entering the Mediterranean, and the Arabian peninsula extends into the northern Indian Ocean. Major rivers' origins are depicted with a semicircle, India is flat rather than triangular in shape, and Sri Lanka remains disproportionately large. The upper right-hand corner of the map is covered with mountains, indicated by the same curves used in Map 29. All these features are similar to those created by al-Idrisi in 1165.

However, there are some significant differences between the two maps. First, this newer map takes the overall shape of one third of a circle. No ocean surrounds the land masses; in fact, both Africa and Asia extend to the bottom and right-hand edges of the map, as if there were no or very little ocean separating them.

The map suggests that it is impossible to sail around Africa, and that Asia lies only a short distance from the western European coast. This map also has greater information on mainland Southeast Asia. By 1300 CE, Muslim traders were long familiar with the region's lucrative commodities, especially spices. The landmass appears to extend like a lizard's tail, hooking back into the Indian Ocean.

Finally, this is one of the first maps to show the world surrounded by air instead of by water. Lining the top, bottom, and sides of the map are putti, heavenly spirits blowing winds from nine different directions.

This and later similar maps were for centuries thought to have been based on models first created by the second-century CE Greco-Roman scholar Claudius Ptolemy. However, there is no evidence of any map by Ptolemy prior to the thirteenth century, a hundred years after al-Idrisi. While Muslim scholars often expressed admiration for Ptolemy's contributions to astronomy, there is no evidence of anyone praising him for his contributions to cartography. Instead, "Ptolemy" appeared as the author of maps very similar to al-Idrisi's during a propaganda offensive launched by Byzantium as its territory was steadily being eroded by Muslim forces. The suspicious political and military circumstances surrounding the sudden appearance of the Ptolemaic map, nearly identical to the widely imitated al-Idrisi model, suggests that al-Idrisi is the true author of the map and the so-called "Ptolemaic" versions are merely copies. Or, perhaps, there may have been earlier copies of Ptolemaic style maps that were improved upon by al-Idrisi and other medieval Islamic cartographers, which the Byzantines decided to conveniently forget. During the next two hundred years, a wide variety of maps were suddenly reintroduced, as if created by Ptolemy, who had been for over a thousand years. By attributing the maps to a long-deceased Greek, Renaissance propagandists eliminated the need to acknowledge that these "Ptolemaic" maps had were based upon knowledge of the world acquired by Muslim merchants and travelers over the course of several centuries.

One of the areas most frequently traveled by Muslim traders during the Middle Ages was the Indian Ocean basin (see Maps 26 and 29). The Peutinger Table (see Map 18) shows the easternmost borders of the Roman Empire a few hundred years after Ptolemy. But there is no information to suggest that Romans around 150 CE could map the southeast Asian peninsula or other Indian Ocean areas with any certainty. Arab merchants, in contrast, knew this region intimately—the Indian Ocean was a Muslim "lake." Hence, information on India, Sri Lanka, Southeast Asia, and Central Asia, all of which appear on this map, were likely not mapped on "Ptolemaic" maps such as this one until 1300 CE—and they were mapped by Muslims, not by ancient Greeks.

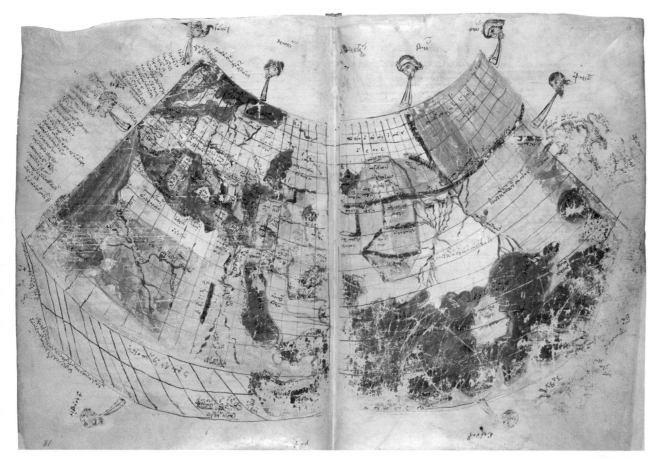

Outline of the Ptolemaic world map.

31

Fra Mauro's Map of the World, 1448–1459 {}

• ◆ •

Fra Mauro, Map of the World, 1459
Circular planisphere drawn on
parchment and set in a wooden frame
About two meters in diameter
Biblioteca Marciana, Venice, Italy

Commissioned by King Afonso V in 1448 {}, at the beginning of the great Age of Discovery, construction of this map was entrusted to a reportedly excellent Venetian mapmaker who belonged to an obscure sect of Catholic hermits, the Camaldolese, who occupied a large monastery on the island of Murano just off the coast of Venice. The map's central architect is known only as Fra (Brother) Mauro. In addition to outlining the map and choosing its content, Mauro hired a team of painters (at the king's expense) who worked for three years to embellish and color it. The result is a map with brilliant reds, blues, and even gold.

Before undertaking his assignment, Fra Mauro received from Afonso new Portuguese maps of the Mediterranean and West African coast. The king asked Fra Mauro to incorporate this new knowledge into a complete world map. However, the Portuguese maps were true sea charts created from measurements of actual coastlines, yielding a jagged, modern-looking style. Traces of these maps can be seen in Fra Mauro's outlines of the Mediterranean and part of the Atlantic shoreline. (For a good example of this nautical style of mapping see Map 36.) In providing coastal maps with irregular shapes, however, the king expected that Fra Mauro would be able to fill in missing details from the rest of the world with coastlines similar in style.

King Afonso was doomed to be disappointed. Contrary to what the king had heard of Fra Mauro's reputation, the monk was in no position to provide the kind of details that King Afonso desired, for the simple reason that no one had collected that kind of data on the shorelines of the world. Where shores on the king's maps appeared as irregular, ragged shapes, Fra Mauro's coastlines are smoothly scalloped and evenly serrated. Fra Mauro merely improvised coastlines because he was unable to draw them based upon actual measurement.

In one respect, the reports King Afonso had heard about Fra Mauro were correct. The monk did indeed possess knowledge of many parts of the world, but his knowledge was verbal and textual rather than nautical and mathematical. Fra Mauro expressed his knowledge by smothering the map with words.

Of all the maps in this book, this one is one of the most verbose, containing line after line of text. Shorter commentaries appear in red text on stylized banners scattered throughout the ocean, while longer expositions in red and blue are crammed into the landscape. Around the edge of the map, eight multi-line texts discourse on subjects like astronomy and mapmaking. The map contains no less than 2,921 such separate labels, mostly place names. But one third of the identifications consist of garrulous commentaries on everything from human societies to the environment, from history to economics. Many of the commentaries resemble disjointed medieval travelogues that lump together any and all information about a place regardless of its source or the interests of the readers. These haphazard interventions make reading the map feel like listening to a tiresome, elderly uncle endlessly reminisce about his travels.

Mauro's basic design reflects the classic T-O map in the Islamic tradition (see Map 26) with its tripartite division of the world, a separate Indian Ocean, a clearly delineated Arabian peninsula, and an East African coast tipping at an oblique angle into the Indian Ocean south of Asia. Finally, Mauro adopts the traditional orientation of medieval Islamic maps with south at the top. If the clean shapes of the marble map of Rome (see Map 17) or the Fatamid chart of the eastern Mediterranean (see Map 20) epitomize high points in classical minimalist design, this expansive, extravagantly ornate and florid map embodies an early and unforgettable baroque.

◄ **LEFT**
World map created by the
Italian monk Fra Mauro for
King Afonso V of Portugal.

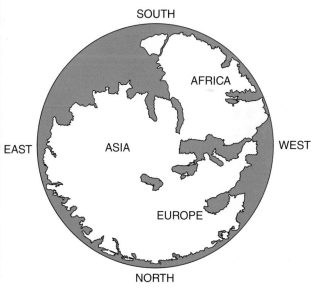

Diagram of Fra Mauro's world map.

32

Buddhist World Map from Japan, 1710 CE

• ◆ •

Buddhist Map of the World
by Rokashi Hotan, 1710 CE
Woodblock
Height: 45 in (114.3 cm).
Width: 56.5 in (143.5 cm)
Namba Collection, Kobe City Museum

With this map, we move to a cartographic and cosmological tradition that is wholly different than that of the preceding maps we have just explored. Map 32 belongs to the tradition of Buddhist cosmological maps from Japan. Buddhism was first introduced into Japan in the first half of the sixth century CE. It soon became, and has remained, the country's most widely professed religion.

According to Buddhist tradition, its founder was born as the royal prince Siddhartha Gautama in 624 BCE in Lumbini (Sanskrit meaning "the lovely") in the foothills of the Himalayas. After he renounced his worldly pursuits to devote his life to religion, Siddhartha pursued various ideas and approaches. At some point in his travels, he arrived near the town of Bodh Gaya in northeast India, approximately 400 kilometers (250 miles) south of his birthplace. There he reportedly remained motionless as he meditated for six years. Then, on the verge of attaining ultimate contemplative wisdom, he traveled to the nearby town and sat beneath a fig tree, continuing to meditate, without moving, until several weeks passed and he achieved full enlightenment. In Sanskrit, the name *Buddha* signifies "the awakened one." From that moment on, the Buddha traveled continually until the end of his life, teaching what he had learned.

Japanese Buddhists began producing simple maps in the century after the religion's introduction to the islands. Starting in the mid-thirteenth century, Japanese mapmakers began to develop their own mapping traditions. However, the basic structure of Japanese maps share a lot in common not only with other Buddhist maps, but with other religious maps drawn on the Indian subcontinent.

Three of the major religions originating in India—Jainism, Hinduism, Buddhism—describe Mount Meru (*Sumishen* in Japanese) as the center of the world, resting upon a landmass called *Jambudvip*, which means "rose apple tree island." Jambudvip is encircled by continents and oceans, all of which are surrounded by an outer ocean. All Japanese Buddhist maps follow this fundamental and distinctive cosmography whose origins lie in South Asia. However, on the earliest Japanese Buddhist map from the thirteenth century, as well as on many subsequent ones, including Map 32, the seven concentric bands of water and of land are missing. Only the final body of brackish water surrounds the island of Jambudvip.

From the thirteenth century on, Japanese maps began to diverge from the traditional Buddhist/South Asian model by incorporating physical geography. Mythical Jambudvip is shaped like an upside down egg, with five separate parts of India identified below Meru: North, Central, East, West and South India. Even Sri Lanka appears to the southwest of India in the waters off the coast of Jambudvip. While the map accurately portrays directions southward, it is somewhat less accurate to the north. Nepal and China appear as small parallel blocks, east of Meru, while Japan is more correctly situated northeast of China and outside the island of Jambudvip. Farther north appear Central Asian stopping points on the Silk Road, including Turkestan, Tashkent and Bukhara (Uzbekistan).

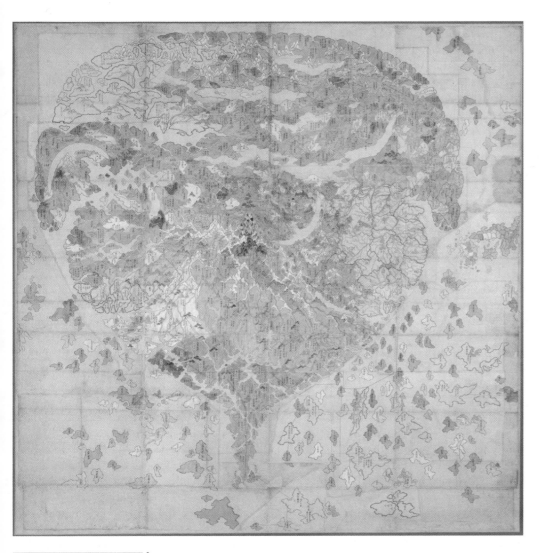

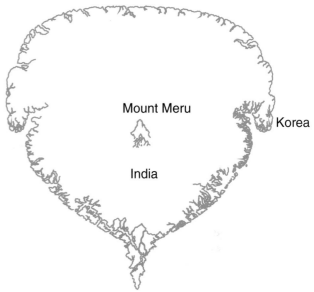

Diagram showing Mount Meru on the Buddhist world map.

Map of India and surrounding countries showing location of Buddha's birthplace.

▲ ABOVE
Japanese Buddhist world map. Though the map shown here was created in 1710, it follows the style of the earliest such map from the thirteenth century.

33

Jain World Map

• ◆ •

Manusyaloka (The Human World)
19th century
Western Rajasthan
Fabric
Southern Asian Section,
Asian Division, Library of Congress

Although their religion is older than Christianity, until the nineteenth century Jains did not permit the majority of their believers to see or study any of their sacred texts. Likewise, until the nineteenth century, maps were kept apart from believers and nonbelievers alike.

The foundational Jain religious texts, called *Agamas*, were richly illustrated manuscripts composed between the sixth and third century BCE, in a language called *Prakrit*. When Prakrit ceased being used around the tenth century CE, the scriptures became unintelligible even to many Jain leaders. Lacking the permission to do research, or the language skills necessary to comprehend these scriptures, many Jains simply venerated the sacred books (including the maps) as ritual objects rather than as texts to study or interpret. This situation changed in the nineteenth century when a new generation of Western-educated Jains insisted upon viewing these texts. Their efforts to translate the *Agamas* were assisted by the worldwide revival of interest in deciphering ancient languages such as cuneiform and hieroglyphics.

The *Agamas* were composed sometime after the death of the great Jain holy man Mahavira, who is thought to have died sometime between 525 and 510 BCE. As a child Mahavira was anointed atop the mythical mount Meru, located somewhere in northern India (see Map 32). Hence, in the Jain world map Mount Meru rests at the world's center, on the island of the rose apple tree (Jambudvip).

The entire middle world is where humans and animals dwell. Spreading out in concentric circles from the land containing Mount Meru are a series of ring-shaped oceans. Like a real ocean, the first is a giant salty body of water. However, that salty sea is ringed by a giant circular continent that in turn is encompassed by yet another ocean, called the "black ocean." According to Jain texts, this pattern of ring-shaped land surrounded by ocean repeats itself six more times, but on Map 33, only two are shown.

The final ocean, known as Swayambhu Raman, appears red and encloses the entire middle world where humans and animals dwell. Not depicted on this map are the heavens above and the seven-layered hell below the circular human and animal world.

Although additional continents and oceans intervene between the first landmass and the ocean, the pattern found on the Jain map is a familiar one. In ancient Babylonian, medieval Christian, and Muslim world-view maps an ocean circles the world's lands, most likely reflecting the belief that this world's size was finite.

Jain maps, however, take a different approach to another geographical feature—mountains. The northern boundary of the subcontinent is rimmed by the Himalayas, the highest and most spectacular mountain range in the world. For both Jains and Hindus, mountains enjoyed special religious significance and were considered to be the places where holy men achieved enlightenment. Giant temples were built in the Himalayan foothills, as well as in other regions with significant elevation, and the faithful were encouraged to undertake pilgrimages to these mountaintop temples. On this Jain map the mountains are denoted by the sixteen upright rectangles on either side of Mount Meru.

Both Hinduism and Jainism envision Mount Meru as a central island ringed by circular land masses and oceans. However, no matter how explicitly the ancient Hindu texts, the Vedas, described this similarly conceived cosmos, Hindus, unlike Jains, never visualized these spatial relationships on maps.

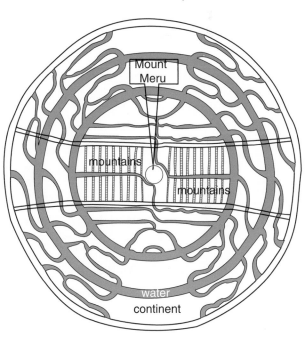

◄ **LEFT**
Jain world map, entitled
Manusyaloka, Map of the
World of Man.

Diagram of the Jain world map.

4

An Expanding World, 1300–1570

Maps in Part Four

Previously uncharted areas of the planet began appearing on maps as knowledge of the world expanded dramatically between 1300 and 1570. Improved sailing ships, which could maneuver with greater speed and stability, and were increasingly able to handle adverse weather conditions, powered this growth. Since European ships were the first to reach the shores of Africa, the Americas, and other previously unmapped areas of the world, maps created for navigation led the way in charting large tracts of the Earth for the first time.

Techniques that were first developed in the Mediterranean around 1275, and which steadily improved over the course of the following centuries, produced an explosion of cartographic knowledge. Coastlines were mapped using notations provided by European and North African seamen. Accurate directions were established by marrying an Arabic mapmaking technique with a Chinese compass. Although these new maps emerged in the Mediterranean, they were the product of many cultural strands.

The first map in this Part is a classic Mediterranean sailing map. It shows the immense amount of accumulated knowledge of the Mediterranean and Atlantic coastlines by 1375. The brilliant colors and figures were added to the basic sailing chart in order to make this map as beautiful as possible for presentation to the King of France (see Map 34).

Mediterranean techniques of mapping coastlines were also applied to the previously uncharted coastlines of West Africa. As Portuguese ships gathered increasing amounts of information about the coastline and the hazards to navigation along the route, they made ever larger maps of Africa with ever greater precision, so that by the end of the fifteenth century that continent was the first to be mapped in its entirety. Iberian ships were the first to cross the Atlantic, and the techniques of mapmaking developed by Portugal were used to sketch out the new coastlines found across the ocean. By 1502, the first clear map of Africa and the eastern Americas had been produced by Portuguese cartographers in Lisbon (see Map 39).

Not long after, the same techniques of Mediterranean coastal mapping were applied to other regions the Portuguese penetrated—the Indian Ocean, and eventually the Spice Islands in what is now Indonesia. Mapping followed closely on the heels of imperial expansion.

From Portugal these skills were transferred to Spain as several prominent Portuguese cartographers followed Magellan when he circumnavigated the globe in the second decade of the sixteenth century. The maps created in the wake of his voyage showed the outlines of the coasts of most of the world for the first time (see Map 44).

Maps designed for navigation reached their peak with the development of a map by Gerhard Mercator in 1569 that allowed pilots to keep track of their progress across the ocean with a straight line drawn on a sheepskin or paper (see Map 47).

The final major development in cartography during this period was the creation of the atlas, a collection of maps organized by dividing nautical charts of the world into discrete sections that could be bound together and sold as books (see maps 45 and 46). While none of these atlas maps were used for navigation, they provided the reading public with facsimiles of the nautical charts that illustrated new patterns of trade, economics, and power.

Timeline of world history

1000–1300
North Atlantic warm spell

1100s
Compass introduced to the Mediterranean from China

c. 1200
First portolan charts

1206–1360s
Mongol hegemony

1300–1800
Little Ice Age

1300s–mid-1400s
Plague in Eurasia

1300
First known Mediterranean sea chart in Arabic

from 1350s
Rise of the Ottomans

1368–1644
Ming dynasty, China

from mid-1400s
Rise of Incas, Aztecs. Beginnings of oceanic imperialism

1497
Vasco da Gama reaches India; nautical astrolabe invented

1502
First European map to include the Americas
First map to include lines of latitude

1569
Mercator's world map

1570
First atlas, published by Abraham Ortelius

34

Catalan World Map, 1375

• • •

Chart of the Mediterranean
and Black Sea, 1375 CE
Abraham Cresques
Catalan map, illuminated
manuscript on vellum
Bibliothèque national de France

In 1375, a Jewish mapmaker completed this map at the request of King John I of Aragon (Spain), who then sent the map to France's King Charles V. Because it was a royal gift the map was painted with the finest pigments, which is why the colors remain so bright more than six centuries later.

Abraham Cresques, the mapmaker, belonged to a prolific and talented group of Jewish cartographers based on the island of Majorca, largest of the Balearic Islands off the eastern coast of Spain. Part of a long-established Jewish-Catalan community that suffered periodic violence at the hands of the Christian majority, Cresques ranks among the best cartographers of the fourteenth century.

Cresques' map resembles a small book. It consists of six pages, with a leather binding and brightly colored parchment pages glued to a lightweight wooden backing. If all the pages were added together they would form a rectangle 64 × 300 cm (25 by 318 in). The first two pages contain cosmological information: the spherical earth, calculations for feast days on a calendar, and astronomical information, including a lunar cycle inserted in order to help navigators determine the time of the tides.

The next four pages contain a map of the world in consecutive sections, starting from the Canary Islands off the west coast of Africa to China in the east. The first two map pages cover the Mediterranean, with North Africa and Western Europe visible on the left. The island of Majorca appears in gold leaf near the edge of the first page. The second map page covers the area from Italy to the Black Sea in the north and from roughly modern Libya to the Red Sea (in red) and the Holy Lands. The coastlines of these first pages were drawn according to the emerging technology of nautical charts with direction and shapes similar to those of modern maps. The third map page shows Turkey with a green Ottoman Sultan, and to his right lies the Arabian peninsula, with a seated blue historical figure, the

Queen of Sheba from the book of Prophets in the Old Testament/Tanakh. Right next to her is the holy city of Mecca, portrayed with minarets and the Kaaba in the center. According to Muslim tradition the Kaaba ("the cube") contains the first building created by Adam, and its black and gold covering clearly appears in Cresques' depiction. The fourth and easternmost segment of the map (far right) contains only the most general outlines of China and Central Asia, with hundreds of colored dots perhaps indicating Indonesia's many islands. Cresques' drawings of both Turkey and China differ from the sharply angled Ptolemaic maps (see Map 30). Cresques' shapes of the East are gently rounded curves filled with brightly colored figures reminiscent more of al-Idrisi's 1165 CE map (see Map 29).

A final distinctive characteristic of this map is the extent of the detailed locations and accurately rendered figures in North Africa. The Jewish community of Majorca had emigrated from North Africa at the start of the thirteenth century, and is thought to have retained information on the places and peoples from their home region. For example, on Cresques' map, the Atlas Mountains are accurately depicted forming a long chain along the northern rim of Africa. But Cresques' most detailed graphics center on the Sahara. A Berber tribesman, his face swathed in cloth against the blowing desert sand, travels on a camel to meet the King of Mali, who is seated on a golden throne and holding a golden ball in his right hand. The camels is depicted accurately, both its overall shape and its gait, suggesting firsthand experience or precise historical accounts of the animal. This face-to-face meeting of the two men illustrates the gold trade, in which Berbers purchased gold in Mali and then transported it via caravan north to Africa's Mediterranean ports. The map portrays Saharan Africa as a densely settled area with many towns including Melli (Mali) and Tenbuch (Timbuktu).

◄ **TOP**
The world map of Abraham Cresques.

◄ **BOTTOM**
Detail from the bottom left panels showing a Berber on camelback approaching Mansa Musa, the king of Mali.

35

Arabic Portolan,

c. 1300

• • •

Maghreb/Mogrebina Chart, c. 1300 CE
Veneranda Biblioteca Ambrosiana

This is the first known Mediterranean sea chart in Arabic, created with the new **portolan** technique used to design charts for sailing with a compass. The center of the map is a sixteen-point compass with lines extending out in all directions. Unsigned and undated, the map provides few clues about the identity of its author. Only the handwriting, spelling, and the territory displayed on the chart provide hints as to its origin and possible uses.

The style of this map is that of a working portolan chart. The name *portolan* comes from the word port and refers to its purpose and function. The map lists the names of nearly 300 ports in the western Mediterranean and Europe. Charts that were designed for presentation to monarchs were embellished with beautiful colors. Images of people, rulers, or animals were often included, as in the Catalan map of the world (see Map 34). On Map 35, as was common on charts designed to be used by navigators, only the three most essential features appear: a compass rose (for directions), the names of the ports (for location), and a scale indicating approximate distance (top right and bottom right corners). Such measures of distance were imprecise but provided a navigator with basic information.

The person or persons for whom this map was made remains a mystery. Most likely, however, the chart was created for the sailors and merchants residing in the Zayyanid kingdom that today constitutes the western part of Algeria. During the thirteenth and fourteenth centuries, the Zayyanid capital city of Tlemcen dominated the trade between Africa and Europe. Tlemcen's most famous resident was Ibn Khaldun (1332–1406 CE)—politician, teacher, and author of one of the first and greatest books of world history, the *Muqaddimah*.

Handwriting styles differed from one area of the Arabic-speaking world to another and changed over time. The type of Arabic writing used on this map was customarily employed in Spain and North Africa between the thirteenth and the fourteenth centuries, the period during which Mediterranean portolan charts developed. Since the map portrays the western Mediterranean, especially the Iberian peninsula, it seems safe to assume that the map's designer was from the Spanish Arabic world, an area that was frequently referred to in Arabic as the *Maghreb*, or "the West." The concept of the "West" in the Muslim world encompassed Iberia and North Africa, the western fringe of Arabic-speaking lands. Even though subsequent discoveries have expanded the boundaries of the western world across the Atlantic, the term "Maghreb" remains tied to its original locale.

The second clue to the possible creator of this map lies in the way in which the names were spelled in Arabic. Since portolan charts depended on the accumulation of information provided by many different ships' captains, the spellings of port names provides a clue as to the source. Alternatively, spellings could also indicate the language most familiar to the mapmaker. Only two of the areas shown in this map had significant numbers of chart makers when this map was most likely produced: northwestern Italy (Genoa and Pisa) and Catalonia (the eastern Mediterranean coast of Spain, including Mallorca). The largest numbers of distinctive spellings come from Catalonia and only four are Italian in origin, suggesting that either the navigators or the chart makers came from Catalonia. Since Catalonia (part of the kingdom of Aragon) had significant numbers of Muslim inhabitants, this region seems the most likely source of information and perhaps even the residence of the creator of this map. In the century after this map was made, Tlemcen's trade evaporated and the former Zayyanid kingdom became a protectorate of the king of Aragon.

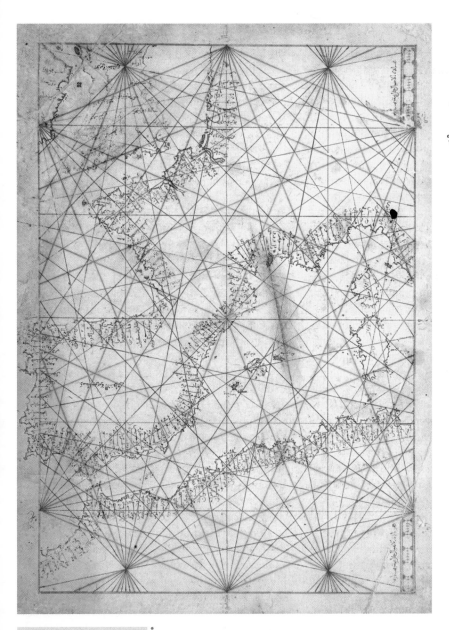

▲ ABOVE
Arabic portolan, *c.* 1300 CE.

Map showing the entire region
included on the portolan. The
blue dots indicate named ports.

36

Nautical Chart of the Mediterranean and the Atlantic Coasts of Europe and Africa, 1511

●◆●

Carte de l'Océan Atlantique Nord-Est, de la Mer Méditerranée et de la Mer Noire, 1511 CE
Salvat. de Pilestrina (Mallorca)
Facsimilé manuscrit / par Otto Progel*. Munich : [s.n.], [avant 1843]
Bibliothèque national de France

One glance at Map 36 and the shapes are immediately recognizable. The familiar outline of Europe, the Mediterranean, and North Africa make this map appear modern in comparison to the Arabic portolan from 200 years earlier (see Map 35).

The Mediterranean appears at the center, and the bright Red Sea to the southeast juts out along the map's right edge. Straight up from the Red Sea, the outlines of the Black Sea are clearly identifiable. Smaller shapes also materialize in familiar form. The boot-shaped Italian peninsula stands out near the center. To the west, Spain is discernible and to the north the British Isles appear somewhat less well sketched.

Although embellished with brilliant colors and supplementary drawings, this map belongs to the same genre of nautical charts as Map 35. In fact, it represents one of the most beautifully colored examples of a portolan.

The portolan tradition originated in the Mediterranean with maps such as the 1065 Islamic Fatamid map (Map 20). Like the 1065 map, this portolan chart has the names of all the ports written in sequence along the coast. Just as before, the first letter of the name appears parallel to the coast, while the rest of the letters spell out the name toward the interior. Additionally, the names of the ports are written so that they can be easily read by a pilot traveling toward the coast.

A pilot sailing from eastern or central Mediterranean—or even Mallorca—would turn the map clockwise so that he could read the names of the ports as he traveled westward. Writing the names of the ports in the direction that a pilot could easily follow by swiveling the chart is an Islamic Mediterranean invention.

Several major differences separate the older Islamic charts from this early modern one. The most conspicuous difference is the dramatic increase in the number of named ports. From a distance the coastline appears shaded in, although this is merely the result of the closely packed names lining the coast. Furthermore, unlike Map 20, the map covers the entire Mediterranean coast and includes the Atlantic coasts of both Africa and Europe.

In addition to the increase in the number of ports, the portolan charts, such as the one shown here, display a marked improvement of the representation of the direction of sailing between one port and another. Much of this improvement stems from increased use of the **compass**, introduced from China at the end of the twelfth century. Whereas earlier maps could only indicate four general directions (north, south, east, and west), these new maps have 32 different directions. With this refinement it became easier to draw more precise directions of the coastline from one port to the next, resulting in the creation of more precise outlines that more closely resemble modern maps.

Other features of the map may not be so immediately apparent. The overall contours of the map are determined by its material, sheepskin, with the handle-like left-hand side owing its shape to the neck of the sheep from which it came. In this area an image of the Virgin Mary carrying the infant Jesus in her arms appears, drawn near the Azores Islands one-third of the way across the Atlantic. This decorative image of Mary offers protection for those sailing into the dangerous Atlantic Ocean.

Surrounding the map are seven circles outlined in deep blue, with profiles of wavy- and curly-haired young men. On the outside of the circles, as if being blown through their lips, are the names of different winds. These figures are decorative directional indicators added for their artistic appeal. Pilots who might use a section of this map for navigation would use the compass rose rather than the ornamental faces as a guide.

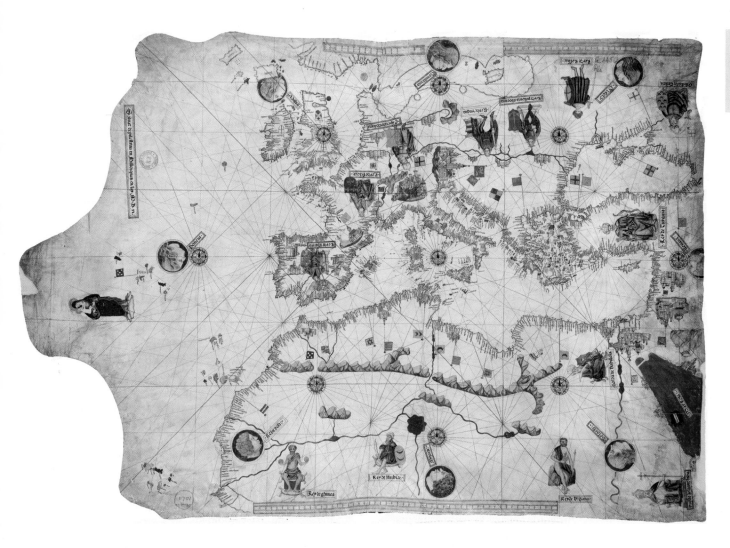

37

Which Way is North:
An Introduction to the
History of Directions
in the West

• • •

Drawings by author and Tsvetelina
Zdraveva from compass roses on maps
in chapters 31, 40, and the author's website
"Latitude: The Art and Science of
Fifteenth Century Navigation"

One of the most intriguing aspects of mapping has been how different cultures have represented direction. We have become so accustomed to the convention of placing north on top, east to the right, west to the left, and south on the bottom that it rarely occurs to us to think of maps in other ways. However, this convention only became customary in the Atlantic during the fifteenth century, made necessary by the need for mariners to work with maps created by people they had never met or spoken to before. In other words, direction needed to be transparent when maps were shared among strangers or passed down from one generation to the next. Those looking at a map and those traveling for the first time through the world's oceans to new lands had to know where directions could be found.

Historically, societies have oriented maps in a variety of different directions employing a variety of different symbols. The oldest indicator of direction appears on an ancient Mesopotamian clay tablet describing the heavens (see Map 23). Sunrise and sunset were "east" and "west" respectively, while unrelated factors defined others. Mountain ranges northeast of present-day Iraq provided the name for another direction ("mountain wind") while the west was described as "mardu," a word for the Amorite immigrants who arrived from that direction around 2000 BCE.

Other maps in this book display different orientations. The plan of Rome (see Map 16) was oriented toward the city's principal shrine, located to its southeast . Christian maps often faced east toward Jerusalem; Islamic maps often placed south on top, perhaps situating Mecca at the center of the map. Britain's first road map (see Map 22) faced east toward France. Printed Chinese maps placed north at the top but wrote *east*, *west*, and *south* so that the map could be read from any direction. In short, maps have historically been oriented in many ways.

Today we assume that north lies at the top and that a compass, triangle, or arrow will be drawn on the map indicating that direction. These conventions are followed throughout most of the world today.

The use of the **compass rose** as the symbol for north originates in the nautical tradition. The compass itself is an instrument that always points toward Earth's magnetic north pole. Introduced into the Mediterranean from China in the twelfth century, the compass began to be used for navigation. Although Mediterranean sea charts accurately depicted direction, neither letters nor signs showed which way was north, south, east, or west. Hence, any collection of charts relied upon the navigator's knowledge of the coastline to correctly determine direction.

Once navigators pushed the boundaries of the well-traveled Mediterranean and began to sail down the west coast of Africa in the fifteenth century they began drawing maps of coastlines, rocks, sand bars, and islands that no European had ever seen before. No longer could navigators rely upon a pool of shared knowledge of direction. To someone unacquainted with or insufficiently knowledgeable about an area, simply being presented with the drawing of a coastline could lead to all kinds of misunderstandings, many with potentially fatal consequences. Since all the information contained on these new maps was novel, conventions had to be established so that the next mariner traveling down the coast would know exactly in which direction to travel and in which direction he needed to sail to avoid hazards and find safe harbors.

Fifteenth-century Portuguese cartographers of Africa initiated the process, keeping north on top perhaps because they were traveling in a north–south direction down the coast of Africa and they wished to keep home port on top (the north). Mapmakers began to experiment by placing compass roses with triangles pointing to north on some, but not all, of these maps.

After the first trans-Atlantic voyages, the need to include directional indicators only intensified. In 1504, Portuguese cartographer Pedro Reinel created a design on a map of the Atlantic that has remained popular ever since. Reinel embellished the traditional compass rose with a fleur-de-lis pointing north. Radiating out from the compass are lines for the standard sailing courses.

38

Map of the Known World by Martellus,

c. 1489

• • •

Henricus Martellus
Map of the world of Christopher
Columbus, 1489 CE
The British Library

This remarkable map shows the rapid development of knowledge of the west and south coasts of Africa during the fifteenth century. While many of its Asian and European features are borrowed from older, more traditional maps, the most original part of this map lies in its depiction of Africa.

In earlier maps of Africa, such as the T-O maps from the Christian tradition (see Map 24), and the Ptolemaic maps from the late Middle Ages and Renaissance (see Map 30), the map of Africa appeared as either a quarter-circle or a block. In either case, knowledge of West Africa terminated abruptly at the Sahara. Europeans did not travel south of the Sahara. Instead, North African traders from a variety of different communities led camel trains across the Sahara south to the interior of Africa, where they traded for the gold, salt, and slaves that they would transport north to the Mediterranean coast. At the major port cities along the North African coast, colonies of traders from Muslim Spain as well as Christian Italy awaited the arrival of the caravans to purchase goods that they would then transport by boat across the sea to Europe.

In an effort to outflank these caravan traders, and to travel directly to the source of the gold, salt, and slaves, Prince Henry of Portugal began to sponsor nautical expeditions along the coast in 1427. By the time of his death in 1460, his ships had only traveled as far south as northern Sierra Leone, the bottom of the semicircular western coast of Africa. Over the next twenty years, however, the number of Portuguese voyages that mapped the west coast of Africa increased dramatically. Between 1460 and 1487 the entire Gulf of Guinea was mapped, as well as the entire western coast of Africa, the Cape of Good Hope, and along the southeastern coast of Africa north to the Great Fish River, located in what is now South Africa, and which probably appears on the Portuguese map of 1488 shown on the right, and whose discovery was made by the experienced Portuguese fleet commander, Bartolomeu Dias (*c.* 1451–1500 CE).

During the course of this voyage, Dias was blown out to sea as he attempted to travel southward down the southwestern coast of Africa near modern day Namibia. After being blown out to sea for nearly a week, Dias continued to sail to the east, thinking that he would arrive at another portion of the west coast of Africa. However, after two days traveling to the east without catching sight of land, he decided to turn north and in less than a day reached land some distance east of the southern tip of Africa.

Thinking that he would eventually encounter land, much as Portuguese sailors had found when they encountered the coast of Guinea in the late 1460s, Dias continued to follow the coast of South Africa toward the east. Several hundred nautical miles later, he noted that the coast of Africa was no longer continuing in a straight line but had begun to turn in a northeast direction, and that there was no land in front of him. Facing a rebellion among his tired and hungry sailors, Dias made a final stop at the Great South River in eastern South Africa and returned to Lisbon in 1488.

Over the next nine years, Dias captained other expeditions to southern Africa, continuing northeast along the southeastern coast. Two of his expeditions mapped the entire Mozambique Channel north to the edge of the Arabian Sea, long traversed by sailors from Persia, Arabia, Africa, and China. Having reached the edge of the centuries-old and easily crossed Arabian Sea route, Portugal was ready to send a relatively small expedition, including one cargo ship, on a voyage to India. Vasco da Gama (*c.* 1460–1524) would head this expedition in 1497 and successfully return to Portugal in 1499.

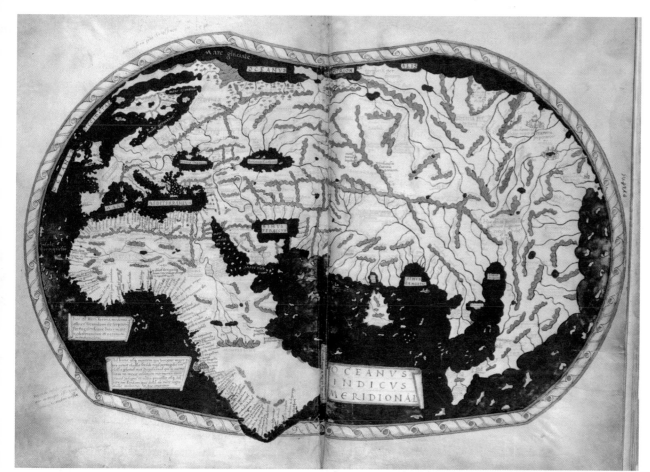

Diagram of the Martellus map.

39

First Map of America: The Cantino Map, 1502

• ◆ •

Carta del Cantino, 1502 CE
1050 mm by 200 mm, vellum
Biblioteca Estense, Modena, Italy

In 1502, Ercole I d'Este, Duke of Ferrara (in central Italy) sent a large sum of money to Alberto Cantino, his representative in the Portuguese capital of Lisbon, along with instructions to locate a Portuguese cartographer who could be bribed with a sufficiently large sum to make a copy of recent Portuguese discoveries. This map is the result.

Like many in Italy, Ercole I (1431–1505) recognized that the Portuguese discovery of a direct sea route to India would imperil the prosperity of many on the Italian peninsula. Italy earned a large part of its income by monopolizing trade from Asia, though the cost was high and required dangerous overland and sea journeys. For the overland portions of the journey, Italian merchants traveling with goods from Asia faced rulers who could decide to cut off trade or to deny them access for political, economic, or religious reasons, or even out of pure capriciousness. In short, the mixed overland and sea route was commercially unstable.

Once Vasco de Gama reached India in 1497, and the Portuguese began to trade directly with Asians, they only had to deal with local vendors and their intermediaries; the rest of the business depended solely upon the carrying capacity of their own vessels. While the Italians managed to cling to their revenues for a while longer, the death knell had been rung.

Many leaders of Italian city states, like the Duke of Ferrara, saw their economic decline approaching. They sought to gain access to the knowledge that would allow them to compete with the Portuguese. Specifically, they sought world nautical charts. The nautical chart on the right demonstrates how much of the world had been discovered by the Portuguese voyages of exploration.

All of the African coast had been mapped, much of it in a shape recognizable to modern viewers.

The chart shows the coast of India in its familiar triangle shape, revealing the discoveries made by the Portuguese. Compare Map 39 with Map 38, drawn just a little over a decade earlier: in the 1489 map, India is shown incorrectly as a stubby promontory.

On the left-hand side of Cantino's map appears something equally remarkable. In early April 1500, Portuguese ships came into contact with the coast of Brazil. We know that this map, showing the extensive coast of Brazil as well as portions of eastern Canada, was completed in November 1502, for that was the date that the copy was sent back to the duke. In just over two and a half years, Portuguese sailors had crossed the Atlantic and surveyed the territory that belonged to them by virtue of their 1494 treaty with Spain (the Treaty of Tordesillas), indicated by the dark vertical line cutting through the map about a third of the way from its left edge.

Portuguese mapmakers also had intelligence sources for Spanish maps of the Caribbean and a small portion of the coast of Florida and South America. But because the Spanish lacked technical skills in mapmaking, their possessions appeared distorted. Cuba and the Florida coast should be much smaller, and the area explored along the coast of Canada and Greenland should be vastly larger.

The Cantino map is the first to show the Americas as a continent. However, Africa, the Mediterranean, and India—all areas mapped directly from Portuguese intelligence—more closely resemble their actual shapes and sizes. It would not be until the Spanish conquest of the Aztec Empire in Mexico 1521 that the true significance of the discovery of the Americas would be felt.

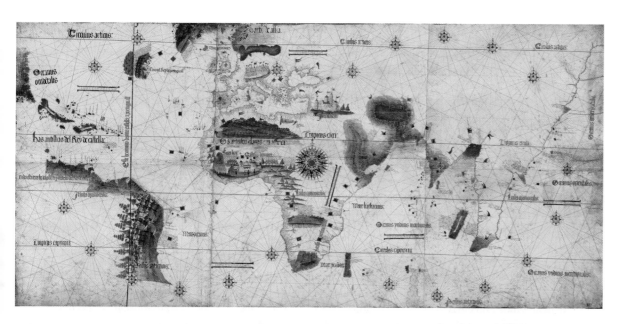

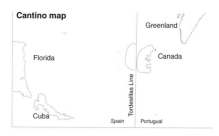

Cantino map

Actual shapes of Florida, Cuba, and Greenland

40

Latitude and Longitude: The Keys to Expanding the World

•◆•

Pedro Reinel
Nautical portolan chart of
Western Europe and Africa, 1504 CE
Bayerische Staatsbibliothek, Munchen

In 1440 no accurate map of the entire world existed anywhere on the planet. Regional and provincial maps existed in many different cultures, as did cosmological maps that described the universe from a religious or civilizational perspective. For the actual dimensions of the entire world, however, there were only guesses and conjectures, all incorrect. No one outside of the Americas was aware of the continent's existence; those residing in the Americas did not realize that people inhabited remote lands across the ocean.

Navigation was the key to unlocking this hidden knowledge. Since seventy percent of the world is covered by water, which was unknown to anyone in 1440, the separate landmasses of the world are all connected by sea, not by land. When Portuguese pilots in the 1420s and 1430s first began sailing against winds and currents into the Atlantic Ocean and then down the western coast of Africa, they were unknowingly embarking upon a quest that would equip them with knowledge of the methods needed to sail everywhere in the world. Prior to 1440, mariners all over the world relied upon local knowledge of winds, waves, and stars to sail. Acquiring that knowledge took time—decades, perhaps even centuries, of trial and error with many ships setting forth never to return until at first one, and then another, and finally a series of boats returned showing the path for crossing the seas.

But all such learning, acquired at great cost, was limited by the patterns of currents and winds in a particular part of the world. For centuries, travelers in the Arabian Sea relied upon seasonal reversals of winds and currents to travel from Africa to India. Once they sailed beyond those currents—in the vicinity of the Maldive or Chagas island groups in the middle of the Indian Ocean—they were lost. Similarly, ships in the South China Sea relied upon similar atmospheric conditions, coupled with a circular current, to sail back and forth to trading destinations as far away as Indonesia. However, if ships tried to sail outside this zone, even a little further east to Micronesia on the western edge of the Pacific, they would get lost. Polynesians who sailed tens of thousands of miles learned the currents, waves, swells and stars of the Pacific. However, even with the most extensive star knowledge of any navigators they could not venture beyond their sailing zone, either to the coast of the Americas to the east or Australia to the west (see Map 2). In the Atlantic, Scandinavian sailors had taken advantage of several relatively warm centuries to employ the midnight sun to travel at the height of summer across the northern rim of the Atlantic to Greenland and Canada. Since the midnight sun became less visible the farther south one traveled below the Arctic Circle, they could not sail into the middle of the Atlantic, let alone the Caribbean. In short, all of these regional navigation traditions, built slowly on trial and error, depended upon currents, winds, stars, and skies. But in the middle of the Atlantic no technique of traditional learning, no amount of trial and error, could provide a means with which to cross the ocean.

In the first decades of the fifteenth century, near the Canary Islands off the northwestern coast of Africa, neither winds nor currents would carry Portuguese ships in the southward direction they sought to travel. But the Portuguese came up with a novel solution: they used science to sail where nature only threw up impassable obstacles. In 1440, the Christian West was not well versed in the sciences used to solve navigational problems, such as trigonometry, astronomy, and accurate solar timekeeping. However, Jews and Muslims in Iberia had developed highly sophisticated scholarship in all three areas. In response to increasing anti-Semitic sentiment in other parts of Iberia, the rulers of Portugal welcomed refugee Jewish scientists and mapmakers, employing their talents to solve previously intractable navigational challenges.

Crucial to this novel approach to sailing was latitude. Mathematically challenging, fixing exact latitude required precise calculations of the daily changes in the path of the sun relative to the earth (taking into account the slight yearly changes in that path) and determination of the maximum height of the sun. It further required invention of a brand-new instrument to find the sun's daily elevation, the **nautical astrolabe** invented by the Jewish astronomer Abraham Zacuto in 1497. Thus, finding latitude was a scientific and technical achievement rather than a mechanical one. With accurate latitude, ships could successfully navigate anywhere in the world. Not surprisingly, less than a hundred years after the first use of this science, a Portuguese, Ferdinand Magellan, became the first to sail the previously uncharted waters of the South Atlantic and the North and South Pacific Oceans, showing the path to voyaging around the world (see Map 44).

Determining longitude was important, although precision was less crucial for navigation than it was to determine latitude. To establish a nearly exact measure of longitude, Jewish scientists in Portugal adapted a method based upon the pioneering work of the Islamic astronomer al-Biruni (973–1048). Though it involved no instruments, the lunar distance method first developed by al-Biruni was accurate enough so that as late as 1771, the British explorer James Cook used it to fix the longitude of his ship in the Pacific to within plus or minus three feet. It was only when European nations sought to establish colonial outposts on tiny Pacific islands at the same latitude but far apart in longitude—such as the ones in Polynesia explored by Cook (see Map 53)—that precise instruments become necessary. The **marine chronometer**, invented in 1774 by John Harrison, created a scientifically accurate longitudinal measuring device.

Although primarily resting upon achievements in astronomical observation and measurement in the Hebrew and Arabic scientific traditions, the new maps of the fifteenth and sixteenth centuries also drew upon an innovation from another part of the world—the compass. Originating in China, the compass was first widely used as a navigational instrument by Arab sailors during the twelfth century. One hundred years later Mediterranean mapmakers began to include compasses on the background of navigational charts, enabling sailors to follow their direction on a map (see Map 37).

With an accurate science for fixing latitude, and nearly precise knowledge for longitude, the science of mapmaking was transformed in the fifteenth and sixteenth centuries. Any place on Earth could be mapped mathematically in relation to any other place, and the direction in which one place lay in relation to another could be plotted using compass lines. By 1500 mapmakers could locate any newly discovered place in the world on a map, no matter how remote.

But the Jewish scientists who had invented these momentous technologies did not receive the appreciation of a grateful country. Threatened with expulsion by the Portuguese government in 1497 unless they converted to Christianity, the Jewish scientific community was scattered and their accumulated knowledge shattered. All that remains are their legacies: celestial navigation, the science of latitude, and new, accurate maps of the world.

1504 map by Pedro Reinel showing both lines of latitude and compass roses.

Navigator using nautical astrolabe, invented by Abraham Zacuto in 1497 CE.

41

Waldseemüller Map of the World, 1507

• • •

World Map, 1507 CE
One map on 12 sheets,
original woodcut
Martin Waldseemüller
Geography and Map Division,
Library of Congress

92

This flawed map, best known for a famous mistake, imitates a Portuguese world nautical map. Unlike Map 39, this map displays ignorance of many features that had been well known and correctly drawn by nautical map makers for a decade, and in some cases centuries. Since 1300, even an average chart maker had been able to correctly sketch the Mediterranean coast of Africa. But when creating this map, its maker, Martin Waldseemüller (c. 1470–1520), drew a straight line since he lacked even this fundamental, longstanding information. Another straight line substitutes for a different, more recently drawn area, namely the jagged west coast of Africa to Sierra Leone, which had been mapped by 1460. Portuguese voyages had also clearly demonstrated by 1499 that India was a peninsula. Yet Waldseemüller substituted a straight line for the information he lacked.

Only two areas of the Portuguese nautical chart appear correctly on this map. Africa south of the Equator resembles the cone-shape shown on Portuguese charts (see Map 39). But the top half of the continent follows the square shape found on the imaginary Ptolemaic maps. It also copies the Portuguese map of the east coast of South America, together with the Spanish Caribbean islands and Florida that are also found on Map 40.

The rest of the map mimics the geographically ill-informed Ptolemaic maps. A supersized Sri Lanka lies south of an unwisely straightened-out coast of India, while the Southeast Asian peninsula appears at three times its actual size and curves in the wrong direction toward the Indian Ocean. Even Europe is incorrectly depicted in a manner similar to both al-Idrisi's map of 1165 CE (see Map 29) and the Renaissance Ptolemaic versions, with a hyperextended Iberia and a backward-bending Italian peninsula (see Map 30).

Although most of its features would have appeared on any Ptolemaic map of the era, Map 41 is notable for one giant mistake in the Western Hemisphere. Waldseemüller had traveled to France from his native Germany at the invitation of the secretary to the Duke of Lorraine. As a result, he lacked any firsthand knowledge of the places he would depict on the map and had to rely upon the secondhand sources available to him. At the time of this map, he had access to few of the newly developed nautical charts of the world. Instead, he had access to the misleading accounts of Amerigo Vespucci (1454–1512), the Italian who claimed that he, and not the Portuguese, had discovered the Atlantic seaboard of Brazil. The Portuguese were deliberately silent about their discovery, which allowed Vespucci, who likely took part in the second Portuguese expedition to Brazil, to take the credit. As a result, instead of putting the original Portuguese name on the coast, *Terra de Vera Cruz* ("Land of the True Cross"), Waldseemüller placed the name, *America*. Thus, the first use of the name "America" was incorrect, and was used to designate not the entire hemisphere but just the southern half, especially the lengthy coast explored by the Portuguese.

A gifted mapmaker, Waldseemüller soon realized his mistake and the misleading nature of his information, and the name "America" never reappeared on any of his subsequent publications. Instead, he placed "True Cross" or "Brazil" along the South American coast. The quality of Waldseemuller's information would improve dramatically as the years went on and he continued to draw ever more accurate maps of the world, improving the sketches of Africa and South Asia as well as the Americas.

The unusual overall shape of the map also is characteristic of the time period, as European cartographers struggled with the new challenge of representing huge land masses never before encountered. The first decade of the sixteenth century marked the beginning of experimentation *trying to figure out shape of world also*

with different shapes for representing the world. The old three-way division of the world (Europe–Asia–Africa) had vanished, and something different needed to take its place. Waldseemüller's slightly curious choice features a top part resembling two curtain swags, while the lower part swings freely across the bottom. Another popular design tried out at this time was the heart-shaped map (see Map 43).

42

The Indian Ocean Remapped by Pedro Reinel, 1507

• ◆ •

Pedro Reinel
South Africa, East Africa, and the
Indian Ocean, c. 1507 CE
Codex Guelf. 98 Aug. 2°
Herzog August Bibliothek
Wolfenbuettel

Although Arabs began creating maps of the East African coast and the Indian Ocean in the eleventh century, they limited themselves to schematic diagrams (see maps 26 and 29), which nonetheless still provided more information than Christian mapmakers, who tended to reduce or minimize the size of the Indian Ocean since they traveled there infrequently and had less data at their disposal. However, both Arab and Christian maps of the Indian Ocean through the end of the fifteenth century shared two unique characteristics.

First, India's shoreline consistently appeared as a straight or occasionally jagged line with little or no hint of its status as a giant peninsula jutting into the Indian Ocean (see maps 28 and 29). The medieval Ptolemaic maps followed this same tradition, as did the slightly later Martellus and Fra Mauro maps (see maps 38 and 31). Even the giant Waldseemüller map (Map 41), created the same year as the map on the right, partly followed this distinct style.

Second, Christian and Arab maps showed the shores of eastern Africa bending in the wrong direction—into the Indian Ocean rather than gliding away from it. This trend, originally in Arab T-O maps, also appeared in Christian maps of the fifteenth century, including those by Fra Mauro and Martellus.

In 1507 Pedro Reinel produced this first detailed and directionally accurate map of the east coast of Africa. He also depicted the Indian subcontinent as a sizeable peninsula. This map resulted from the accumulation of knowledge gained after 1488 CE.

Following Bartolomeu Dias' voyage around the Cape of Good Hope in 1488, the Portuguese king sent three more expeditions to venture further along the coast. At this time, no one knew how far eastward the southern African shoreline extended (see Map 38), nor did anyone know in which direction the seaboard would lead. By the final voyage in 1496, Portuguese pilots realized that they had

finally reached the southern boundary of the well-traveled Arabian Sea.

During these initial exploratory voyages, Portuguese pilots outlined the rest of the remaining southern African coast. They then detailed the shoreline heading northeast against the Agulhas current along the Mozambique channel. On the other side of the passageway lay the island of Madagascar, which they initially only noted schematically on their charts because it merely presented an obstacle on the path eastward to India.

With this knowledge in hand, and having reached the southern boundary of the Arabian Sea, Vasco da Gama set off in 1497 on the first successful sea voyage around Africa to India. To ensure safe passage on the last leg of the voyage, da Gama enlisted a local pilot, Ahmad ibn Majid, to guide the ship along the centuries-old route across the Arabian Sea (the northwest quadrant of the Indian Ocean). But ibn Majid possessed only traditional oral and textual information about the region; he lacked any maps.

To complete the mapping of India and the East African coast northward from the land opposite Madagascar, the Portuguese crown sent several large fleets in quick succession: Pedro Alvares Cabral (1500), João da Nova (1501), Vasco da Gama (1502), Afonso de Albuquerque (1503 CE), and Francisco de Almeida (1505). Information from all these voyages was compiled in Lisbon by the talented Portuguese cartographer Pedro Reinel (1462 – c. 1542) into navigationally accurate outlines of the Indian Ocean. The map covers an expanded area, beginning at the mouth of the Congo River in Africa on the left and continuing along the western and part of the eastern coast of India. Sri Lanka appears correctly placed and sized relative to India. The map continues to the eastern and southern edge of the Malay peninsula on the right. The dark green island just off the peninsula's coast may be one of the

Andaman Islands, or even Sumatra, given the incorrect orientation of the peninsula that includes modern Myanmar (Burma), Thailand, and Malaysia.

This beautifully decorated chart surrounds the land with a brightly colored circle showing nearly all the 32 points of the compass, each with exquisitely colored compass roses. Portuguese flags (a small blue square with five white dots on a square blue background) appear next to decorative blue and red banners. The Nile appears on the left-hand side of the map as a thin upright blue line with a circle in the middle. Ships appear along the trade route to India, and four wind-blowing cherubs grace the four corners.

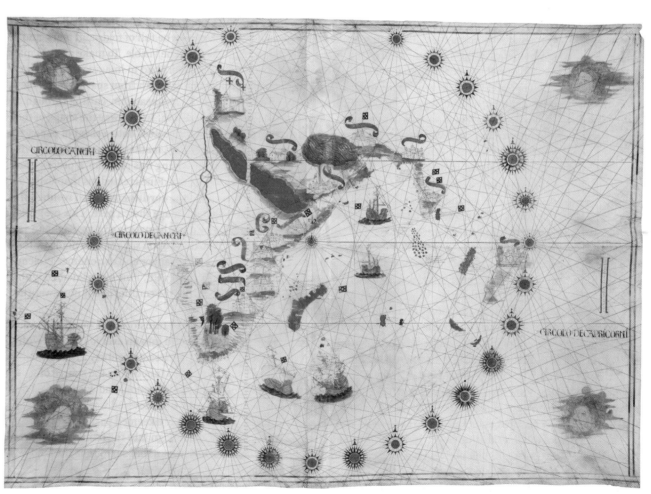

◄ **LEFT**
Pedro Reinel's map of East Africa and the Indian Ocean.

43

A Heart-Shaped Map

• ◆ •

Heart-shaped map of the world, 1536 CE
Oronce Finé
One map on two assembled pages
51 × 57 cm
Bibliothèque national de France

High in the sparsely settled French Alps, in a small town called Villard-Saint-Pancrace, a boy named Oronce Finé was born in 1494. Educated in medicine at Paris like his father and grandfather, Finé soon abandoned medicine for mathematics and astronomy, relatively unstudied subjects in Catholic France. In 1530, King Francis I founded the College Royal of Paris (forerunner of today's College de France) for lectureships in subjects not taught in the older University of Paris. Oronce Finé became the College's first professor of mathematics at the age of thirty-six.

Historians of science have not been kind to Finé. He failed to make any significant original contributions to geometry or astronomy. However, he possessed a gift for popularizing scientific ideas and his writings were widely translated and read in Western Europe during his lifetime.

The appeal of Finé's popular accounts of science stemmed partly from his use of expertly drawn visuals, a technique he continued to use during his ventures into geography. Finé's eye for good design also appears in the map on the right, whose prototype he first created in 1519. However, Map 43 reflects more than good illustration; it also reflects an emerging new development in sixteenth-century mapmaking.

The sixteenth century marked the beginning of a trend toward experimentation with different ways of representing the spherical shape of the earth on a flat surface. With the increasing number of expeditions to Asia, Africa, and the Americas, ordinary men and women became more cognizant of the circular shape of the Earth. Such recognition meant that mapmakers trying to show large sections of the Earth, or the world in its entirety, had to come to grips with the problem of representation: how to show a 3D object on a 2D surface. Although

scientific elites since [...] realized this problem [...] as well as ordinary p[...] century had never ne[...]

Today, cartogra[...] representing a 3D ob[...] Simply put, projectio[...] 3D object on paper. [...] lems associated with [...] would happen if you [...] sulting object would [...] only one side would [...] therefore, mapmake[...] looking down on the [...] were looking at a slic[...] the inside of the Ear[...] Earth would be "pro[...] the sixteenth centur[...] ing new ways of solv[...] continues to this day[...] projection called the[...] the heart-shaped im[...] was devised by a ma[...] Schoener, who drew[...] Greco-Roman geogr[...] in the second centur[...] other ways of using t[...] successful.

The heart shape [...] and unfamiliar worl[...] special powers. In si[...] heart was thought to[...] cognition, memory, [...] Rendering the newly[...] accessible and highl[...] transformed the fore[...] by the calm, blue oce[...] crimson backgroun[...]

46

Abraham Ortelius,

The Atlas, 1570,

Part B

• ◆ •

Ortelius, *Theatrum Orbis Terrarum*, 1570 CE
Library of Congress Geography and Map Division

From the vantage point of mapmaking, atlases also marked a shift in the style of representation. Mapmakers had to invent an entire new design vocabulary that would be consistent for all the maps contained in the book. They had to create conventions for indicating countries, provinces, cities, towns, villages, mountains, hills, forests, and a host of other features that had been simply irrelevant to the more functionalist designs of earlier maps.

Each map designer devised an entire range of icons to indicate features like forests or churches, sometimes borrowing from competitors and sometimes creating his own. In one atlas cities might be indicated by a simple building, while in another the same city might be drawn as a walled enclosure with multiple houses.

At first, no governing body dictated which icons could be employed in an atlas. The only requirement was that the representations remain consistent throughout the entire volume. Although the printing press had been invented a hundred years earlier, it was not until the middle of the sixteenth century that printers began to create a variety of distinctive fonts that would increase the legibility of words on a page as well as that of names on a map.

Whether printers first realized that a more legible type would increase their readership, or whether the growing demand for print led typographers to create new fonts, the result was the creation of different font styles for mapmaking. For example, Ortelius borrowed his friend Mercator's solution to the problem of how to clearly identify political divisions between countries and towns by creating a hierarchy of font sizes and types.

For the largest administrative group—the kingdom or country—he often employed a LARGE FONT with all capitalized letters. For towns and villages he usually employed a slightly smaller *italic font*.

The Ortelius atlases remained bestsellers, with forty different editions published between 1570 and 1612, and Ortelius added more and more maps to successive editions of his work. To this day, atlases have remained a popular literary genre, satisfying our continued curiosities about unknown lands.

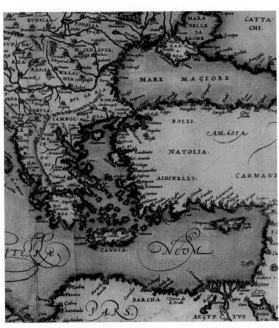

Detail from Ortelius' Atlas from 1570 showing the hierarchy of labels to designate countries, regions, seas, and settlements.

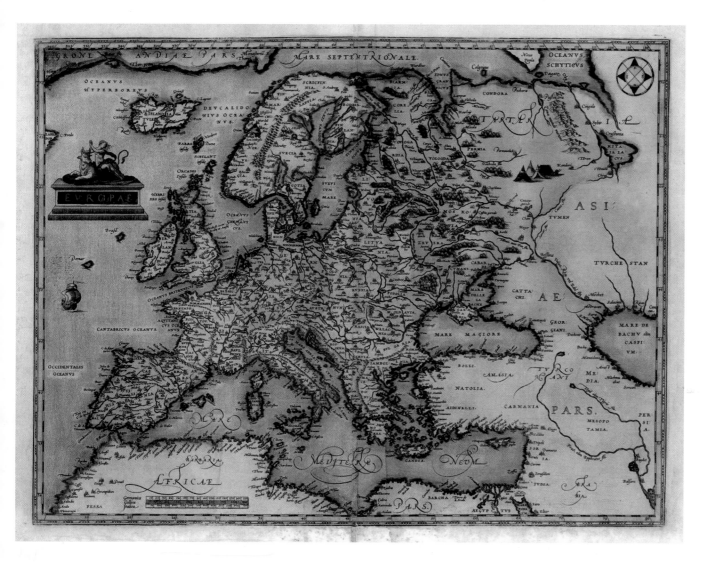

◄ **LEFT**
The map of Europe from
the first edition of Ortelius'
atlas.

103

47

Mercator's World Map,

1569

large enough map for sailors to plot in one whole map

. . .

Mercator, Nova et aucta orbis terrae descriptio, ad usum navigantium emendate accomodata 1569 CE
Maritime Museum, Rotterdam

In 1569, in what is now the northern German city of Duisberg, a Flemish mapmaker published a map that would revolutionize cartography. On twenty-one separate sheets of paper, cartographer Gerhard Mercator (1512–1594) printed an entire map of the world. Although apparently designed to be used in a series, when placed side by side these sheets created a giant map whose outlines would secure his place among the greatest mapmakers of all time.

With his publication, Mercator had solved a longstanding problem. For decades ocean pilots had complained that they were unable to plot their course at sea directly across a flat chart. Mercator's map permitted navigators to draw their route as a straight line through all the seven seas. A variation of his map continues to be used by the world's navies to this day.

The success of Mercator's system stems from the way in which it recreates, on a flat map, the angles on a circular globe. Thus, any line that a pilot draws on Mercator map would cross every latitude and longitude line just as if he were drawing his course on a rounded globe. In other words, thanks to Mercator, the reality of the curved surface of the earth can be represented as flat for purposes of navigation.

– Able to show earth curvature in a flat e surface

The question that has bedeviled scholars for centuries ever since is how Mercator managed to create his projection. Inclined to keep the secret of a potentially lucrative map—with potential sales to scores of navigators the world over—Mercator kept silent about the principles of his maps' construction until the day he died. Six months before he completed his map, he sought and obtained exclusive rights to print his map for a period of 14 years in the north German principality in which he resided, and a similar copyright for 10 years in the Netherlands. No historian—no matter how thorough—has ever found any written trace of the method that Mercator used to construct his chart. Mercator keenly understood the importance of intellectual property, and he shrewdly protected that intellectual property by not revealing to anyone (including his family and closest associates) how he had managed to create his map. Generations of historians and mathematicians have taken Mercator's reticence as a challenge, determined to ferret out the answer. In this sense, Mercator's secrecy has proven more enticing than any explanation he might have provided.

safeguarded his secrets, no one knows how he did

While celebrated as a northern European creation, the map's primary focus was on the sailing routes of the two major seagoing powers of the sixteenth century. Mercator's map includes the compass roses that pilots used for planning courses, but he plotted them around the areas regularly traversed by Spanish and Portuguese ships. The map may have been created in a city on the Rhine, but the navigational knowledge it displayed was that of Spanish and Portuguese pilots.

In the wake of the decolonization of Africa and Asia in the twentieth century, political critics challenged Mercator's map on grounds that it distorted the sizes of landmasses. Africa, for example, appears relatively small on a map that uses the Mercator projection. However, any projection that creates the landmass of countries in their proper proportion cannot be used for correct distances under any circumstances. Hence, navies and commercial fleets use the Mercator projection because it shows correct sailing distance and direction.(For more on the controversies on mapping and decolonization, see Map 85.)

May have Afri

but is for Spi

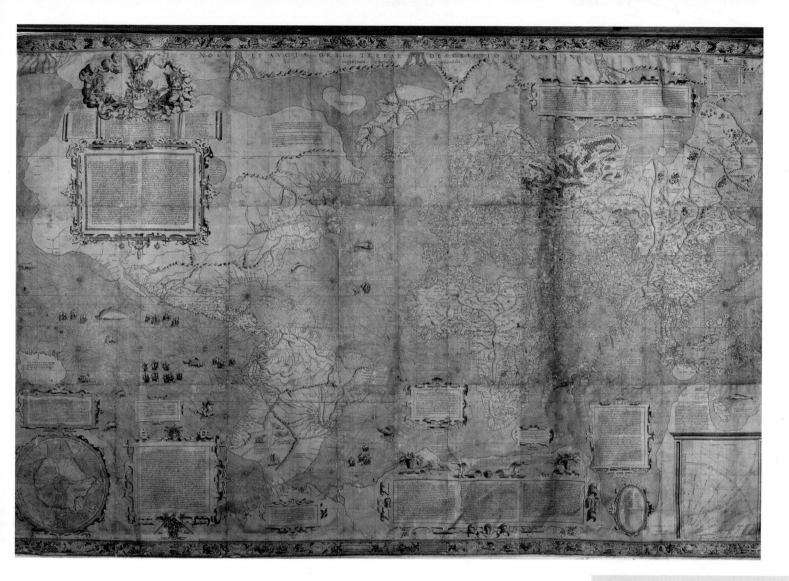

Toutepa   Oweha

Opopotea

Orivavie

Oroluma

Tinuna   Opoópooa

Ohetepoto   Tetupatupa cahow

Moenatavo

Ohetefoutou atu

Oheteoutoureva

Ohetetaiteare

Teoroorooatiwa -tea

Teamoorohete   Teatowhete

Part

5

Worlds Colliding,
c. 1550 – c. 1800

Maps in Part Five

For thousands of years, travelers in unfamiliar regions have asked locals where they can find shelter and food. Rarely, however, did they note such exchanges in writing or record the names of the individuals they met, or the nature of their conversations. Often the only indication we have today that someone had inquired about a location or direction is a notation upon the map that gives a measurement of distance in a local standard. These barest of notes are often the only surviving indications of otherwise unrecorded encounters and exchanges of information.

Historically these interactions were rarely preserved, except for occasional notations on maps, but the situation changed by the early sixteenth century. Like travelers before them, sixteenth-century visitors frequently sought out natives to locate rivers, ports, or the safest passageway through dangerous reefs or across high mountains, as well as safe places to set up camp or trade. The Europeans who created maps of areas in Africa and the New World sketched regions that might not be visited again by their peers for many years. Given the likelihood that a significant amount of time might elapse before the next person visited the same locale, European mapmakers began to include information about the natives who had provided them with valuable geographic knowledge. Identifying these indigenous providers of information was helpful to subsequent travelers, who might receive different or contradictory information from members of adjacent communities, or who might otherwise seek contact with peoples who had migrated, been defeated in war, or had ceased to exist. Finally, acknowledging these contributions allowed the European mappers to claim proof of greater authenticity and accuracy.

From about 1550 onward, native sources began to be acknowledged on European travel maps, and we sometimes have specific information about the contribution that natives made. This new willingness to acknowledge indigenous participation in mapmaking eventually led Europeans to discover that in many areas of the world geographic information was not recorded visually. In many places, local geographic knowledge was transmitted through verbal recitation or performance, so the act of creating a map (a fixed visual representation) introduced local peoples to a new way of rendering space. The maps drawn under these circumstances transported both colonizers and colonists into novel realms, since each side only imperfectly understood the premises of the other. While the dynamics of military power were unequal, the dynamics of knowledge exchange were more balanced as both Europeans and indigenous peoples sought to grasp the other culture's principles of representation. The resultant maps constitute unusual hybrids, in which European traditions of spatial representation combine with native knowledge to produce a third form of mapping that is neither wholly of one tradition nor the other. This cultural fusion is evident in the Tahiti map (see Map 53), the sketch of the Niger River (see Map 57), and the Chinese map of Southeast Asia (see Map 51).

Not all such exchanges entailed the exchange of relatively neutral information concerning trade routes or markets. Several European powers, including Portugal, Spain, England, France, and the Netherlands, established political and military

Timeline of world history

c. 1450–1650
Expansion of the Ottoman, Mughal, and Safavid Empires

since 1492
Columbian exchange

c. 1500–1600
Portuguese maritime empire at its height

since 1513
Atlantic navigation; discovery of Gulf Stream

1519–1522
Magellan's circumnavigation of the globe

1521
Cortés captures Tenochtitlán; Spanish conquest of the Aztec Empire (Mexico)

1532–1572
Spanish conquest of the Inca Empire (Peru)

mid-16th century
Atlantic slave trade accelerates

1549
First Jesuit missionaries arrive in China

since 1565
Pacific navigation; Japan current mastered

1550–1700
Scientific Revolution in the West

1639
Closing of Japan

since c. 1640
Decline of Central Asian steppelands

(continued)

control over large areas of the Americas. Spain, in particular, sought systematic geographic information about its empire in the 1570s, sending lengthy questionnaires to every part of the globe that they governed. Local officials often then turned to native informants, whose visual renderings show a wide variety of styles and graphic vocabularies (see Map 48).

Some of the maps in this section will appear odd to modern eyes. Lacking standardized technologies and scientific equipment to survey and measure, people in the past had imperfect ideas about locations, distances, the heights of mountains, the widths of rivers, or the lengths of coastlines. What matters, however, is how they chose to represent their world and what that representation tells us about how they saw it.

For the collision of different cultures could be as creative as it was destructive. Creole cultures, born out of the mixing of European and indigenous races, emerged soon after the first encounters. New languages, new cuisines, new ways of thought sprung up from Canada to the Spice Islands, from West Africa to the West Indies. The world converged, threaded together by an ever tighter web of cultural exchange. In Map 48, indigenous symbols for mountains and towns are the most conspicuous feature, but Christian churches and Spanish spellings can also be found next to the indigenous representations. Map 49 is another example of hybridization. A member of the Peruvian Inca elite, who had studied Spanish forms of mapping, chose to use his learning to mock subservience to an overlord he could not defeat by force of arms but whose geographic art he could master and manipulate.

Map 58 shows a Turkish map from the New (Cedid) Atlas that was created in 1803 based on a British model.

In other maps, native and European cartographic traditions are even more closely interwoven. In many parts of British controlled North America, deerskin was plentiful and was used for clothing, housing, and occasionally maps. Instead of colors that might fade on a partly tanned animal skin, indigenous communities used a more permanent method, poking a hole through the skin. A series of holes would indicate a variety of pathways or rivers (see Map 54).

In Arabic-speaking areas of Africa, elites wrote as well as read Arabic. But the geographic information that these leaders possessed appears to have been communicated orally rather than written down. When asked to draw the outlines of their territories or that of their trading partners, chiefs and kings did so, often writing the names in Arabic alongside the places they had drawn. In this, as in other instances, the native information was easily committed to paper using geometric shapes characteristic of European mapping. But such written depictions were only needed by outsiders, unfamiliar with the territory (see Map 57).

Other maps in Part 5 are the result of more violent types of collisions. Two military conflicts—the British campaign against the French in North America (1754–1763) and Napoleon's campaign against Russia (1812–1813)—led to the creation of very distinctive and innovative maps. British soldiers sketched their routes taken in battles against the French onto a durable material, hollowed-out animal horns, that would not fade despite exposure

Oryroa

Whaneanea·

to wind, rain, or snow, and yet were lightweight enough to be carried almost anywhere. The horns were also used to carry the powder needed to fire rifles (see Map 55).

In the case of the second unusual military map (see Map 59), which shows Napoleon's advance and retreat from Moscow, its creator did an immense amount of research on temperatures, geographic locations, and the dates of army movements in order to compile this information into a single dramatic visualization that has been held up as

one of the best examples of its kind. In other cases, such as the map of the Gold Coast of Africa (see Map 56), the mapmaker also had to compile information from a great many sources—indigenous Africans as well as the French, Portuguese, Dutch, and Danish traders—into a single map. Even though the resulting map demonstrates none of the originality of the Napoleonic-era map, it shows how mapmakers strove to incorporate information from many different sources into a single, seamless whole.

Oopati

Ohevatoutouai

Whaow

E Tatahieta
Oheroottea

Otaheite

Mytea.

Ohevanue

Oirotah

Oheteroa

Tometoaroaro

Oirotah

Itenue

Ohete maruiru

Oiropoe

48

Native Towns of Spanish Mexico, 1579

• ◆ •

Relación geográfica de Atengo, 1579 CE
Nettie Lee Benson Latin American
Collection, University of Texas Libraries,
University of Texas at Austin.

When Spaniards conquered the New World, they encountered thousands of native communities with unrelated languages, cultures, economies, and political structures. In order to survey this vast landed empire, which stretched from Colorado to Patagonia, King Philip II's official **cosmographer**, Juan Lopez Velasco, ordered a detailed geographic survey of the American communities. His 1577 questionnaire was very detailed, consisting of 50 separate questions covering population demographics, political jurisdictions, spoken languages, physical terrain, and native flora and fauna. While this time-consuming and expensive inquiry did not yield responses from many parts of the New World, the survey did receive answers from the Viceroyalty of New Spain, which today constitutes the modern states of Mexico and Guatemala.

Throughout New Spain, imperial officials often enlisted the aid of local leaders in drawing the layout of indigenous towns and regions. Some of these sketches appear to have been done by European officials with the help of native informants; others, such as the one at right, were done by both, and a majority were authored by indigenous creators. The comparatively large number of native geographic drawings stemmed from a remarkable system of writing in wide use prior to the Spanish conquest. Mayas, Aztecs, and others in this region had developed a sophisticated system of writing combining figures and hieroglyphics. During the sixteenth century, priests (notably Franciscans) encouraged natives to continue using their writing in order to convey religious concepts in a visual framework that their neighbors would understand.

When drawing urban, regional, or route maps for Lopez Velasco's *Geographic Reports*, these church-trained native writers primarily used indigenous icons to indicate both physical features such as hills, rivers, mountains, and caves, and to indicate the names of central places. In the map at right, displaying Misquiahuala (modern Mixquiahuala in the state of Hidalgo in Mexico), the icons running along the border all represent native symbols for different types of mountains surrounding the town. The long yellow curving shape coming up from the bottom of the map before veering off to the left represents the main river. The water detours around a very large red and yellow mountain symbol, bearing the name of the region, *Misquiahuala*, which means "place of the mesquite circles." Hence, on the mountain appear symbols for various kinds of mesquite, cacti, and agaves, with a red circle in the center. Finally, the center-right space is dominated by three seated native figures stacked vertically, with the largest figure facing Mount Misquiahuala. The progressively smaller figures below face the opposite direction. Although these figures are not identified, they most likely represented the regional chieftains from each of the three separate areas.

Alongside the colored and decorated drawings, by the Nahua-speaking natives there are several contrasting drawings and writings in pen and ink added by a Spanish scribe. Francisco Fernandez de Cordoba's strictly geometric lines and shapes provide a sharp contrast to the native symbols. Rather than focusing on the landscape he concentrated on the manmade environment, adding four meticulously drawn churches, three placed in front of the seated native leaders and a fourth to the side of the mesquite mountain. He also added carefully written Spanish names and descriptions. The contrast is sometimes striking. Next to the mountain covered with cacti, he describes the wide variety of wildlife present: deer, hare, rabbits, snakes, and mountain lions, which for him clearly were of greater importance than the native plants. The native artist represents the Spanish settlements with an extremely simple symbol, a rectangle partially open on one side, while Fernandez de Cordoba describes these places as sheep ranches and names their Spanish owners. The Spaniard's third major contribution to the map is a set of written directions indicating Misquiahuala's location relative to other Spanish settlements, especially those who do not require crossing mountains. At the bottom, for example, he indicates the town of Tula to the south, adding that "it lies on flat ground next to the river."

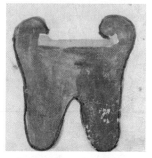

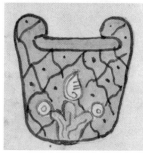

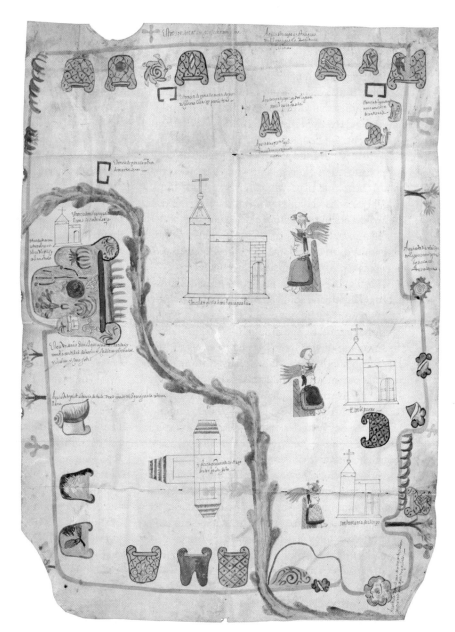

MEXICO

Misquiahuala

Hidalgo

Tula

Mexico City

Location of Misquiahuala (Mixquiahuala) in present-day Mexico.

49

Guaman Poma,
Mappamundi as
Satire, 1615

◆◆◆

Guman Poma de Ayala
Mappamundi del reino de las
In[dia]s, 1615 CE
El primer nueva coronica y
buen gobierno f. 948
Det Kongelige Bibliotek, Copenhagen

Imagine a 1,200-page handwritten "letter" addressed to King Philip III of Spain (*r.* 1598–1621) composed by a member of a minority native ethnic group from Peru. Imagine also that the work describes multiple abuses of political power by Spanish priests and bureaucrats. The likelihood that Philip III would read such a work was virtually nonexistent. Yet Felipe Guaman Poma de Ayala (1535–1616 CE) drafted exactly such a lengthy critical letter. Entitled "A New History and Good Government," the manuscript, which never reached the king, also contained nearly 400 drawings illustrating key events in the history of the conquest of Peru, as well as everyday occurrences and abuses of power by Spaniards in the colony. Ten percent of these drawings were maps.

Born in the year that Francisco Pizarro established the Spanish capital of Peru at Lima, Guaman Poma grew up during the civil wars between rival Spanish factions. By the time he was ten, the leader of the Incas had died and the Inca empire was securely in Spanish hands, except for a relatively minor rebellion that continued in a remote region until 1572. A native speaker of Quechua, the language of the Incas, Guaman Poma learned Spanish but did not quite achieve fluency in his second language. As a result, his writing is sometimes difficult to understand even though his handwriting is extraordinarily legible.

His drawings, however, powerfully depict the history of the conquest of Peru and the subsequent Spanish domination. Among his drawings are 38 city plans corresponding to each of the major cities in Peru, illustrating a wide variety of buildings and landscapes. At right is a unique drawing which Guaman Poma entitled a "world map" using the old Latin name *mappamundi*. In the map he demonstrates his familiarity with the basic requirements of the mappamundi style (see Map 28), but plays with both the form and iconography. The world is surrounded at top and bottom by oceans, into which Guaman Poma inserts drawings of a variety of sea animals—including a whale at the bottom and a mermaid at the top. In addition to the sea life characteristic of the medieval mappamundi, Guaman Poma adds the Spanish ships which brought troops and settlers to the former Inca realms. Where the classical medieval mappamundi placed Jerusalem at the center of the world, Guaman Poma places the ancient Inca capital, Cuzco, at the center.

Immediately above the city appear two coats of arms—the coat of arms of the Pope (in whose name the conquest took place) and the shield of the Spanish kingdoms of Castile and Leon, representing the political and military power of the conquerors. But far above those two conquering forces are the traditional Inca deities and supposed founders of the Inca dynasty: Mama Quilla, the Moon Goddess, on the upper left, and the sun god Inti on the upper right. The Catholic Church and the Spanish monarchy may control Cuzco, but the traditional celestial powers of the sun and the moon rise above all.

While traditional mappamundi shows the entire world, Guaman Poma's world encompasses just the Inca domains. Its east–west boundaries are the Pacific Ocean, delimited by semicircular lines at the bottom, and the giant peaks of the Andes at the top. Thus, east lies at the top just as in the traditional mappamundi. But the other division of the empire occurs along the two giant diagonals dividing the mappamundi into the four traditional sections of the Inca empire, with a giant "X" coming together at the center of Cuzco. To the left of the X lies the region of Peru north of Cuzco (Chinchaysuyo), and on the right lies the even larger area south of Cuzco (Collasuyo) extending into northern Chile. With skill and satire, Guaman Poma elevated traditional Inca beliefs within the apparent framework of a "European" map of the world.

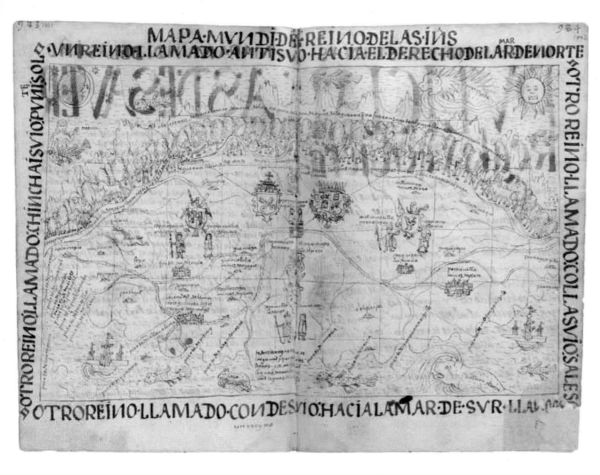

MAPA·MVNDI·DE·REINO·DELAS·INS

VN·REINO·LLAMADO·ANTISVO·HACIA·EL·DERECHO·DEL·AR·DE·NORTE

$OTRO·REINO·LLAMADO·CHINCHAISVIO·PVIISOLA

OTRO·REINO·LLAMADO·COLLASVIOSALES

$OTRO·REINO·LLAMADO·CONDESVIO·HACIA·LA·MAR·DE·SVR·LLA...

Moon Symbol

Northern Inca Rulers

Sun Symbol

Southern Inca Rulers

Pope's Blzaon

Inca Rulers, Cuzco

Castile's Blazon

Silver mines, Potosí

Whale

Ship to Panama

▲ TOP

▲ TOP
Felipe Guaman Poma de Ayala drew this satire of the European mapppa-mundi, or world map, in 1615. The map was not published until the twentieth century.

113

50

Northeast Coast of North America, 1607

• ◆ •

Champlain map of the northeast coast
of North America, 1607 CE
Facsimile of a manuscript, chart
on vellum
37 × 55 cm
Library of Congress Geography and
Map Division, Washington, D.C.

In May 1603, an expedition financed by the wealthy French fur merchant Aymar de Chaste reached the eastern shores of North America. On board one of de Chaste's three vessels was an ambitious young geographer named Samuel de Champlain (1567–1635). The voyagers mainly came to America to exchange their goods with the native Americans for furs. However, those on the third ship, including Champlain, were also charged with searching for a permanent trading base.

For nearly a century prior to this 1603 voyage, French boats had crossed the North Atlantic every March to fish in the bountiful waters off the coast of Nova Scotia, Newfoundland, and New England, setting up temporary base camps along the shore. With their boats loaded with catch, each August the fishermen would return across the Atlantic.

By the third decade of the sixteenth century, however, Spaniards had discovered not one but two enormous caches of previously unexpected gold and silver in the interior of Mexico and Peru. The French king, suspecting that similar wealth might exist in the northern regions of the Americas, charged Jacques Cartier (1491–1557) with exploring the interior in search of either riches or perhaps a passage to Asia. In 1534, Cartier sailed to Canada on the first expedition to explore beyond the Grand Banks, returning the following year and again in 1540–1541. When neither riches nor a passage to Asia appeared forthcoming, interest waned. Civil strife in France also postponed further travel. Nearly 40 years passed before French leaders again showed interest in the northeast coast of America. By that time, French merchants had realized that the only significant revenue to be gained in the New World would come from the fur trade.

Finding a place suitable for settlement in Canada required considerable geographic research. Frenchmen needed to reside near or within easy traveling distance to the Indians that traded the furs. They also required a sheltered harbor with easy access to the ocean so that the purchased pelts could be speedily transported overseas. Finally, and most importantly, they needed a place that could easily fend off an assault from European rivals. Making informed decisions regarding these considerations required native input.

Sailing up the St. Lawrence River, Champlain, like Cartier before him, found his path blocked by falls at present-day Montreal. Champlain, however, queried the natives about what lay upstream. Their geographic information (which included Niagara Falls and the Great Lakes) was so exceptionally accurate that it allowed Champlain to map these areas correctly without ever having seen them.

After returning to France for the winter, Champlain embarked the following year on a ship owned by de Chaste's successor, who wanted to find a warmer area to settle. Champlain therefore surveyed the "southerly" coasts of what today are the states of Massachusetts, New Hampshire, and Maine, rejecting them as potential settlement sites because they were not inhabited by fur traders, but by agriculturally inclined natives. He then returned north, leaving behind this map as a record of his journey.

Information provided by Indians directly influenced Champlain's map. On the way south to Nantucket, Champlain notes that the natives pointed out that he had missed the mouth of the Merrimack River (one of the largest rivers in the Northeast) because the entrance was partially hidden by an island. At present-day Rockport, Massachusetts, natives sketched for Champlain the entire span of the Massachusetts Bay from Cape Ann to Cape Cod, including Boston Harbor. While Champlain took his own measurements as he traveled south along the coast, the ghosts of Native American hands can be seen on his map.

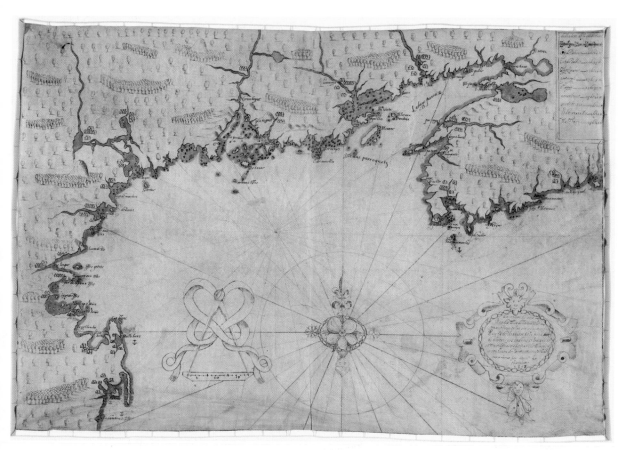

Map of northeastern coast of North America.

51

East and Southeast Asia, *c.* 1625

• ◆ •

Selden Map of China
MS.Selden supra 105
The Bodleian Library,
University of Oxford

On this recently discovered map, created in China in the 1620s, we can catch glimpses of two cartographic worlds coming together. The graceful rounded shapes of the coastlines of China, Indonesia, and Japan all belong to the Chinese tradition. In the upper right quadrant, west of Korea and alongside the traditional geomancer's compass, appear cartographic instruments recently introduced from the West—a ruler and a rectangle.

The encounter between Chinese and Western cartographic traditions began during the sixteenth century, when the Ming emperor allowed foreigners trained in astronomy and mapmaking to enter China. For centuries Chinese astronomers had played a crucial role in ascertaining exactly when the seasons changed, thereby legitimizing the authority of the emperor, who held a "mandate from heaven" (see Map 10). Impressed by the improved precision of astronomical measuring tools recently developed in the West, Chinese astronomers encouraged their use. Instruments that improved celestial timekeeping were welcome innovations.

In this way, Chinese officials were introduced to new cartographic techniques from the West. Among the most successful in introducing these methods to China was the Jesuit Matteo Ricci (1552–1610 CE), who organized the production of European style world maps.

While Ricci's world maps are important, of greater interest are the regional maps that emerged out of this encounter between East and West. The map at the right is a good example. Recently discovered in England by Robert Batchelor and David Helliwell, many features of this map, including both the language and symbolism, have been identified as highly distinctive and unusual. The geographic area covered by the map includes regions frequently overlooked in other Chinese maps: namely, the Philippines, Borneo, Vietnam, Laos, Cambodia, and Indonesia. Since much of this region is connected by sea, it is not surprising that this map was created in Fujian, a province of China that benefitted largely from maritime trade.

Regular overseas commerce between China and Southeast Asia began during the first millennium CE, with shipments of Chinese porcelain arriving in Borneo as early as the ninth century. Over the following centuries Chinese merchants sailed the South China Sea intermittently, trading for pearls and tortoise shells from the southern Philippines, camphor wood from Borneo, cloves from the Moluccas, and sandalwood from Timor. In the 1400s, during the first century of Ming rule, Chinese ship-building improved significantly and its maritime trade increased. Admiral Zheng He's (1371–1433) famous Treasure Fleet sailed in search of trade during this period. Chinese merchants began purchasing their cloves and sandalwood from the island of Java, which appears slightly oversized in this map. With expanding trade, however, came predators and smugglers. Faced with significant coastal piracy, Ming officials closed most of their ports and required merchants to use smaller ships. These measures had little effect.

During the century-long Ming restriction on overseas commerce, three ports remained open: Ningbo, which admitted ships from Japan, Fuzhou, which received ships from the Philippines, and Guangzhou, which accepted cargo from Indonesia. The ban eventually was lifted, as China's coastline with its many harbors would prove nearly impossible to patrol. Beginning in the sixteenth century, European cargo ships began carrying trade goods instead of Chinese ships, which would set an ominous precedent for the future.

KOREA   JAPAN

CHINA

○ Ningbo

FUJIAN ○ Fuzhou
Guangzhou ○

VIETNAM
LAOS

THAILAND   South China Sea   PHILIPPINES

CAMBODIA

PHIILIPPINES
(pearls, tortoise shells)

MALAYSIA

BORNEO (camphor)   Moluccas
(Malaku Islands)

Sumatra   Sulawesi

INDONESIA
Java

Map of East and Southeast Asia.

52

Nagasaki Harbor, Japan, 1764

• • •

Bunjiemon Ohata
Nagasaki, 1764 CE
University of British Columbia
Library

Of all the efforts at limiting foreign influence in the centuries after 1500, none was more successful than those adopted in Japan. For more than two hundred years, the majority of Japanese were forbidden to travel abroad, or even to have contact with foreigners. Carrying out such repressive measures required a military regime. This military dictatorship, closed all ports to foreign trade except that of Nagasaki in southern Japan. The dictatorship then monopolized trade with the outside world through this port from 1639 to 1859.

Initially, traders in Japanese port cities had welcomed the Portuguese ships that first appeared off the coast in 1543. Taking advantage of new sailing technologies, as well as abundant trade opportunities, Japanese merchants and pilots exploited the newcomers for their own benefit. The Portuguese presence provided the means by which legitimate trade ties with China could be renewed. Trade between the China and Japan had been curtailed by the Chinese emperor in retaliation for alleged Japanese pirate attacks. As representatives of a neutral country, Portuguese ships could openly carry goods between the two regions and, since they were designed to speedily transport heavy cargo, they could convey significant quantities of goods to the advantage of merchants in both China and Japan. Seeing potential profits of this trade, other Europeans soon appeared. The Portuguese were joined by English and then Dutch ships, all engaged in the same trade.

However, the Portuguese brought more than commercial products to Japan. They also introduced Jesuit priests, including the missionary St. Francis Xavier (1506–1552), who converted significant numbers of Japanese to Catholicism. The military dictators felt particularly threatened by the new religious faith, and they murdered many Catholics and drove the remnants of the community underground. From 1639 to 1867 Catholicism was outlawed in Japan.

The Dutch, however, had little or no interest in religious conversion. As a result, the Dutch were allowed to set up a permanent trading post on a small island in Nagasaki harbor and continued trading with Japan while other European powers were banned.

From 1603 to 1868 the country remained under the military control of the Tokugawa clan. Hence this era is known as the Tokugawa Shogunate. Under successive shoguns the clan centralized power, progressively weakening the authority of the traditional landlords, known as *daimyo*.

Although the Tokugawa military dictatorship prevented the Japanese from trading with the outside world for over two hundred years, by the middle of the nineteenth century internal conflict was tearing apart the once strong fabric of the shogunate. The demands to allow ships of other nations to trade, and to open other ports, became increasingly difficult to resist. The period of isolation eventually came to an end, brought about in part by visits to Japan by foreigner vessels such as those under the command of the American Commodore Matthew Perry in 1852 and 1854. The Tokugawa monopoly collapsed and Yokohama, Hakodate, and other ports were soon opened for trade.

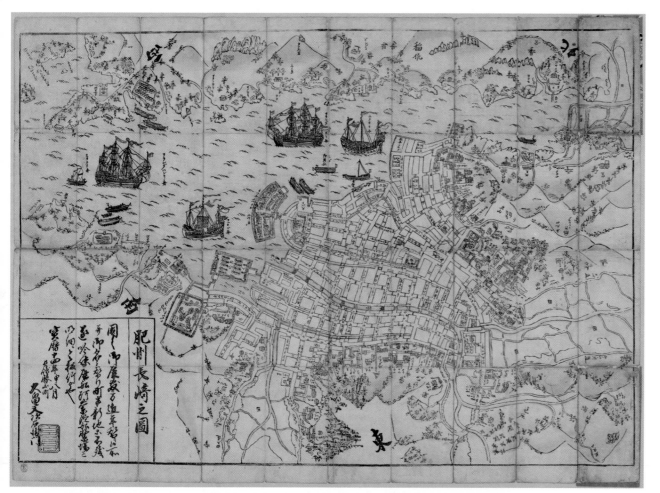

肥前長崎之圖

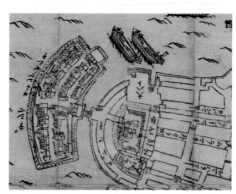

Japan and surrounding countries.

119

53

Tupaia's Map of Tahiti for Captain Cook, 1769

• ◆ •

James Cook
"A chart of the Society Islands, with
the native names, drawn by Lieut. James
Cook, in his first voyage," 1769 CE
The British Library

120

In 1768, Captain James Cook (1728–1779 CE) sailed from England to the South Pacific. Officially, his job was to determine the size of the solar system by timing the path of the planet Venus as it passed between the Earth and the sun.

But Cook was also given secret instructions from the British Admiralty to explore any southern land masses in the Pacific Ocean. Since French explorers Louis Antoine de Bougainville (1729–1811) and Jean-Francois-Marie de Surville (1717–1770) were also investigating the central Pacific at the same time as Cook, he was charged with gathering as much information as possible to forestall competitors.

On Tahiti, the principal island of what is now French Polynesia, Cook met one of the region's most skilled navigators, a native leader named Tupaia (or Tupia). When Cook inquired about the extent of the islands, Tupaia guided Cook across 300 nautical miles of open ocean to an island named Rurutu that was only six miles by three miles long. Tupaia accomplished the entire journey without the aid of either a compass or a chart, which astonished Cook. Throughout the journey, Cook repeatedly asked Tupaia for the direction between where they were on their journey, and where their starting point had been. Time and time again Tupaia pointed in the direction of Tahiti, and each time Cook saw that his compass indicated the identical direction. Naturally, Cook was extremely impressed by Tupaia.

Tupaia told Cook that he could similarly guide his ship, the *Endeavor*, toward 70 different islands in every direction around Tahiti. However, he added that he did not know the names of all of these islands. Thoroughly intrigued by a navigator who could sail with such precision, and interested in gathering information that would provide English explorers with an advantage in navigating this region, Cook asked Tupaia to help him create a map of the islands around Tahiti.

Like the other maps in this section that are the result of an exchange of information between European explorers and natives, the basic geographical knowledge in Map 53 originated with the indigenous informant, in this case, Tupaia. The result was a mixture of Tupaia's Tahitian geographic knowledge, Cook's knowledge of mapping, and the mistaken assumptions on the part of each man. For example, both men were concerned with winds, but Cook thought that when Tupaia referred to the *huatau*, "north wind," he meant what Europeans did when they used the term—namely that the wind came from the north—when in fact in Tahiti the term referred to the wind that went *toward* the north rather than away from it. Cook made the same mistake for *tapatoa* (south wind) and thus drew Tupaia's chart upside down. Fortunately the chart did not wind up backwards as well because Cook used sunrise and sunset to label east and west.

Tupaia was apparently as impressed with Cook as Cook was with Tupaia, because the Tahitian navigator later accompanied Cook south toward the islands of New Zealand, which had been settled from Tahiti approximately 500 years earlier. The extent to which Cook used Tupaia's knowledge in reaching New Zealand remains unclear.

Tupaia continued on with the *Endeavor* to Batavia (now Jakarta, in Indonesia), where Cook stopped for repairs in 1770. There Tupaia came into contact with malaria, a disease that would kill him. The legacy Tupaia bequeathed is the map on the right, which shows a small part of his vast navigational knowledge interpreted through the upside-down and backward prism of a Western cartographic and meteorological perspective.

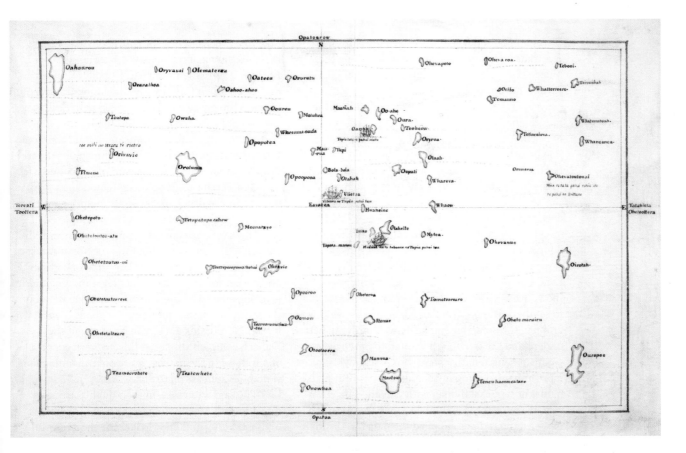

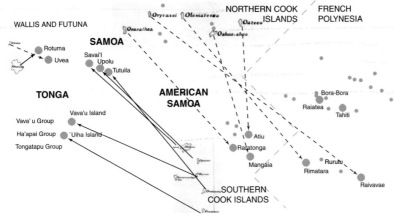

A map of the South Pacific overlaid on Tupaia's map, illustrating how Cook's mistaken understanding of the directions of winds reversed the position of islands. The blue circles represent the correct location of the islands.

54

North American Buckskin Map, 1774–1775

●●●

Map of buckskin from North America,
1774–1775 CE
Drawing on the hide of a deer.
3ft × 4ft
British Museum, London

Beginning in the seventeenth century, French traders (*coureur des bois*) traveled along the Mississippi and its many tributaries exchanging various European commodities for fur, especially beaver pelts. In the wake of France's defeat in the French and Indian War (1754–1763), a large part of North America was handed over to the British. The British settlers who came to the former territories of New France were not merely interested in the fur trade; they also wanted to grab control of the land. Despite the British government's formal declaration that private land purchases west of the Allegheny Mountains were illegal, private deals flourished.

In 1774–1775, a private group called the Wabash Land Company sought to purchase territory around the Wabash River, which flows from northern Ohio to southern Illinois, from an Algonquian speaking group in the area, the Piankashaw. In order to better understand the territory it wanted to purchase, the company sought native people for assistance. One or more unnamed company members wrote out place names on a buckskin map with pen and ink. However, in contrast to Champlain's map (see Map 50), in which the Indians supplied the data but the map was drawn by the explorer himself, the rivers appear to have been drawn by the Piankashaw. Pricking holes into the buckskin and employing indigenous symbols, they relied almost exclusively on their own knowledge.

The map shows the broad drainage basin between the Mississippi and Ohio rivers, but it indicates the positions of rivers schematically. The Wabash River runs down the middle of the map. Other rivers stick out diagonally. The Mississippi appears separately as an "L" shape running down the left side of the deerskin and across the bottom. Distances along the rivers reflect the time it would take to travel from one Indian village to another, much like ancient travel maps (See Map 18). Few European settlements appear. Notably absent is St. Louis, which was already a booming trade center in the eighteenth century. Fourteen native villages are marked with red circles and semicircles. Only two of these appear on European maps of the time. From the perspective of the Englishmen, the deerskin drawing created a written record of the boundaries of a land purchase. The phrase "Piankashaw sold," written in English, appears on the map, suggesting that the purchase had already been completed.

However, the concept of purchase was initially foreign to the native communities of North America. Customarily, lands would be lent from one group to another for a period of time. The fundamental principle of purchase—a permanent alienation of the land in exchange for money or goods—was foreign. It remains unclear to what extent the Wabash company disclosed this Western concept of purchase to the natives, since only an ambiguous statement appears on the map:

"The said witnesses, in their quality as interpreters . . . according to the best of their understanding and knowledge, and have faithfully and plainly explained to the said chiefs . . . to which they have set their ordinary marks, with their own hands." But exactly what the interpreters explained to the chiefs is unknown. They may have merely told them that they were certifying that the information on the map was correct—the message about a sale conveniently omitted, as was often the case in English and later American dealings with Algonquian people.

Ironically, British colonial governors struck down this particular land deal, most likely because they had their own ambitions for a chain of forts or fur trading posts along these rivers.

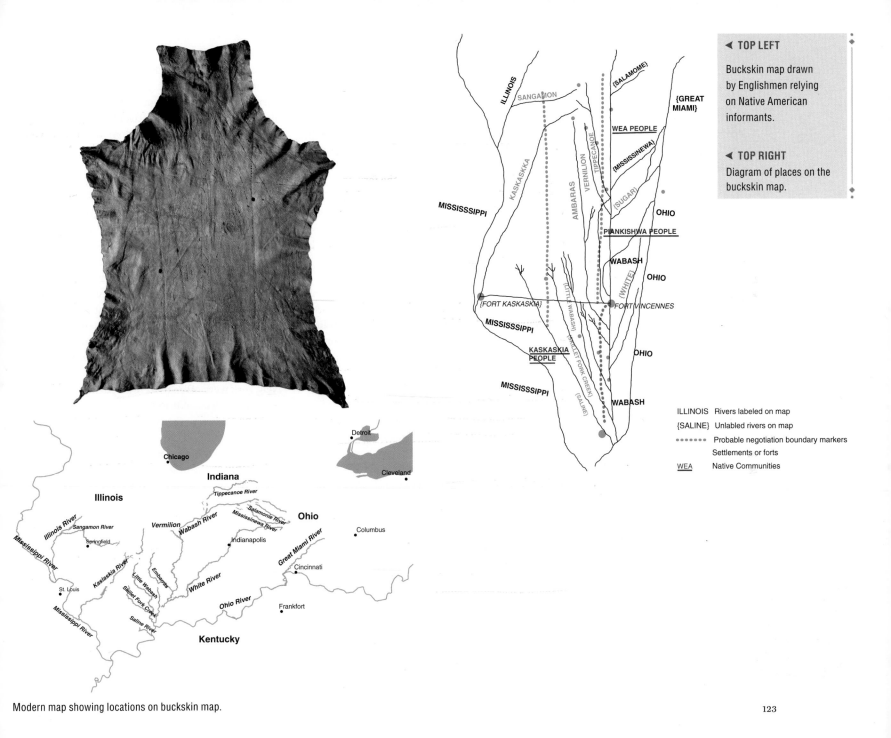

◄ TOP LEFT

Buckskin map drawn by Englishmen relying on Native American informants.

◄ TOP RIGHT

Diagram of places on the buckskin map.

ILLINOIS Rivers labeled on map

{SALINE} Unlabled rivers on map

• • • • • • • Probable negotiation boundary markers

       Settlements or forts

<u>WEA</u> Native Communities

Modern map showing locations on buckskin map.

55

Powder Horn Map,
1757–1760 CE

• ◆ •

Untitled pictorial depiction of rivers
and fortifications on conical powderhorn,
1757–1760 CE
Black/brown inks on bovine horn,
shellacked
32 cm. long, 9 cm. diameter
Library of Congress Geography and
Map Division Washington, D.C.

In the eighteenth century, muskets, long rifles, and flintlock rifles needed black gunpowder in order to fire. But gunpowder had to be kept separate from the rifle until the time came to use it.

Gunpowder fizzled when wet, so keeping it dry was crucial. Soldiers used many different objects for carrying their powder. Bull or ox horns were particularly favored, since they were lightweight. Soldiers would boil them in potash, and then scrape them clean and oil them for improved waterproofing. Wooden stoppers would then be placed on both ends of the horn to seal it shut. This rare example on the right is the only known powder horn map with pewter seals on both top and bottom.

Engraving these gunpowder horns with a knife had long been a popular pastime. Soot or plant dyes would be rubbed into the engravings to add color. Typical engravings showed animals, people, or cannon. However, during the French and Indian War (1754–1763) soldiers on the British side began carving maps onto their powder horns, creating a unique type of cartography.

Some maps on gunpowder horns may have been created simply to commemorate a fort, a town, or a battle. But others appear to have been used as durable, portable maps that remained intact and unchanged despite exposure to the elements. Such maps were elaborately and professionally engraved with intricate details, such as the river routes soldiers traversed.

Map 55 shows New York City at its base and illustrates two separate routes important during the French and Indian War. Both routes begin at Albany (150 miles north of New York City), with one route extending northward along the Hudson River to Lake Champlain and ending at Saint Jean sur Richelieu, southeast of Montreal. The second route heads westward along the Mohawk and Oswego Rivers to the shores of Lake Ontario. The tip of the horn shows the route from Lake Ontario, north along the Saint Lawrence River, past the Thousand Islands region to Montreal, where British soldiers defeated the French in the final battle of the French and Indian War.

This map belonged to a British soldier, as it has an elaborately carved English Royal coat of arms featuring a unicorn and lion supporting the crest on either side. Engraved below is the motto *Dieu et Mon Droit*, "God and My Right," referring to the divine right of the English monarchy.

An estimated 500 powder horn maps have survived, dating principally from either the French and Indian or the American Revolutionary wars. The majority portray key places in New York, while a handful of others show western Pennsylvania, especially Fort Pitt, Fort Necessity, and Fort Duquesne. However, maps of locations outside New York were often inaccurate, hence unlikely to have served as usable maps.

In addition to the North American powder horns that have survived, there are over two dozen known powder horns from Cuba that depict Havana, scene of an important battle between English and French troops during the Seven Years' War (1756–1763). Some soldiers carried their powder horn maps back to Europe with them as mementos of their experiences fighting in the American colonies.

The engraving of powder horns declined after the Revolutionary War when gunpowder began to be carried in premeasured amounts in containers or cartridges. A soldier ripped or bit off the base of the cartridge and poured the powder into the barrel, eliminating the need for guesswork regarding the correct amount of powder needed.

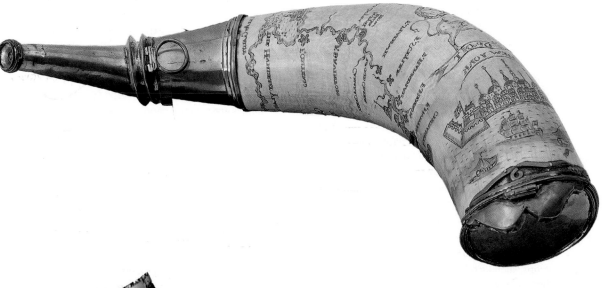

◀ **LEFT**
A map carved into the carrying case for gunpowder for use during the French and Indian War. British soldiers carried these horns back to England as a way to remember their combat experiences in North America.

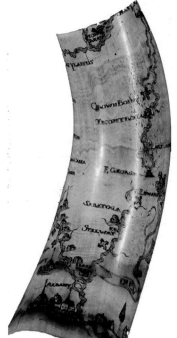

Detail showing the route from Albany to Canada.

Outline of the area depicted on the front and back of the powderhorn map.

Detail of New York.

125

56

Slaving on the Gold Coast of Africa, 1729

• ◆ •

Jean Baptiste Bourguignon D'Anville
A Map of the Gold Coast from
Isini to Alampi, 1729 CE
Author's Collection

Prospect of the coast from El Mina to
Mowri from Barbot & Smith, c. 1744 CE
Jean Barbot, *A Description of the
Coasts of North and South Guinea and
William Smith, A New Voyage to Guinea*
Author's Collection

Slavery has long been practiced throughout the world. It was widespread in the ancient Near East, Greece, and Rome, and in the great empires of Asia. Slave trading flourished in the Mediterranean and Black Seas, the Indian Ocean, and the South China Sea. In western Eurasia, a pattern developed in which Christian slaves would wind up in North Africa and the Middle East, and African slaves would be transported to Christian Europe.

However, a very unusual and particularly brutal kind of slavery appeared several decades after the discovery of the New World. When colonists came from Europe to settle the New World, they found territory that lent itself to agricultural production on an unprecedented scale. Underpinning this new large scale agriculture was the discovery of new cash crops, such as tobacco, as well as crops transplanted from other areas of the world, such as sugar and cotton. New factory-like farms, called plantations, emerged.

Decimation of the indigenous population, largely because of disease, created conditions for this unprecedented agricultural exploitation of the New World. Regardless of whether they were treated poorly or well, 90 percent of all native Americans died within a hundred years after the arrival of Europeans. These deaths left open wide areas of agriculturally productive lands with only a handful of individuals able to work the fields.

To fill that void a type of slavery developed which had previously only occurred on a limited scale, and within limited areas. As the Portuguese began to explore the coast of Africa in 1434, they engaged in slave trading on a relatively small scale, bringing Africans north to be sold throughout Europe. But as the native peoples of the New World began to die out over the course of the sixteenth century, their labor was gradually replaced by that of people captured in sub-Saharan Africa and enslaved.

From the west coast of Africa, shown in this map, a great many people were taken as slaves and transported across the Atlantic, primarily to work as farm labor on the plantations of the New World. Slave traders would bring slaves to be sold at these forts, where they would be held until the ships that would transport them across the Atlantic in the horrific "middle passage" arrived. The picture at right shows a European slave ship awaiting a fleet of canoes being rowed from the nearby fort. The landscape behind the boat shows how densely slave forts were concentrated along this coast, with no fewer than three separate forts—Elmina, Cape Coast ("Corse"), and Fort Royal—along with a military outpost (S. Jago).

The map reinforces the picture of European slaving operations amassed along the coast. The lines of text extending out from the coast into the Gulf of Guinea are not rivers and capes, but the names followed by a capital letter ("H" for Holland, "E" for English, "D" for Danish) that designate slave forts.

There were significant gold deposits in this region, and this map also displays the location of gold mines along with the different Akan-speaking communities in the region. The Ashante (Asiante) kingdom is described as "very powerful"; its defeated rival Denkyira, located in an Akan area called "Akim" is described as "very large and rich in gold" and borders a similar "Great Akkanni" labeled "formerly powerful and rich in gold."

A MAP of the GOLD COAST, from Issini to Alampi, by M. D'ANVILLE. April 1729.

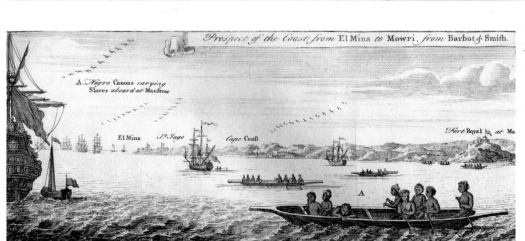

Prospect of the Coast from El Mina to Mowri, from Barbot & Smith.

A Negro Canoas carrying Slaves aboard at Manfrow

Greater Accra
Fort James
Fort Crèvecœur
Fort Good Hope
Fort Lijdzaamheid
Central Ghana
Ghana
Western Ghana
Fort Amsterdam
S. Jago
Fort Nassau
Elmina
Fort Komenda
Fort Vredenburgh
Fort San Sebastian
Fort San Antonio
Fort Orange
Fort Batenstein
Gross Friedrichsburg

Forts across W. Africa coast

Map of Africa with inset showing the Gold Coast.

57

The Niger River Described by a Fulani Ruler, 1824

• ◆ •

Dixon, Denham, Hugh Clapperton, Walter Oudney, and Abraham V. Salamé. *Narrative of Travels and Discoveries in Northern and Central Africa: In the Years 1822, 1823, and 1824.* London: John Murray, 1826.

Beginning in the early nineteenth century, Europeans repeatedly launched expensive overland expeditions into the interior of Africa. Sponsored by government, religious, or geographic societies, scores of British, French, and Germans set out on multiyear journeys to achieve geographic, economic, or religious objectives. David Livingstone (1813–1873), the famous British explorer who located the source of the Nile River, initially traveled to Africa to preach the Gospel, funded by the London Missionary Society. Hugh Clapperton (1788–1827), who sought to find the path of the third longest river in Africa, the Niger, secured government backing to set up trade missions. Like scores of other explorers, both Livingstone and Clapperton paid special attention to waterways. Since rivers formed a natural conduit for transporting bulky materials, they were key to establishing new trade routes to the interior.

All such travelers depended upon Africans. In addition to counting on African labor to carry the trade goods, food, and other supplies for the expedition, these explorers also often acquired both male and female slaves as servants and porters. When the opportunity presented itself, they also took advantage of African traditions of hospitality to obtain free food and housing. In order to find the places they were seeking, the explorers often had to ask Africans about the direction in which they should travel.

For an African expedition of 1822–1824, the British government sought to learn more about the course of the Niger River, which flowed through gold-producing areas of the Sudan. To that end they sent three members of the Royal Navy (!) on a mission to locate the river and to catalog the plants, animals, and minerals of potential commercial value. Dixon Denham, Hugh Clapperton, and Walter Oudney were to land at Tripoli (in current-day

Libya), cross the Sahara, and establish a permanent trade mission in the capital of the presumably still flourishing Bornu Empire, then centered southwest of Lake Chad. However, as the travelers discovered, Bornu had been surpassed by another empire known as the Sokoto Caliphate.

Created by a military invasion by the Muslim Fulani people in 1809, the Sokoto empire was ruled by Muhammad Bello ibn Uthman from 1815 to 1837. Clapperton, a co-director of a second British expedition (1825–1826), asked Sultan Bello to draw a path of the Niger River. Bello, who drew the map at the right, had some experience with spatial representation, having planned and directed construction of Sokoto, capital of the new caliphate.

Bello centered the map on his own palace, and mosque (a circle inside a square-ish figure in the center) near the intersection of the Rima and Sokoto Rivers. The two flow southwards a short distance before joining the Niger River (the thick black line).

On this map the Niger takes a sharp southeastern turn before heading to the Gulf of Guinea. On the bottom left a big circle indicates the river trading city of Idah, which in reality lies far to the right-hand side of the map along the Niger River. A line connects Idah to a small circle labeled Yoruba, the people who traded at Idah. At the very top left of the map, the Niger splits into three—with the largest circle indicating the legendary gold-trading center of Timbuktu. Just to the left of Timbuktu, a circle represents the ancient metropolis of Djenne. Both Djenne and Timbuktu are correctly placed along the Niger, but they are much further away from Sokoto than they appear on the map. Not surprisingly, Bello's most accurate geographic information concerns the native lands of the Fulani people, while his knowledge of the southward path of the Niger lacks precision.

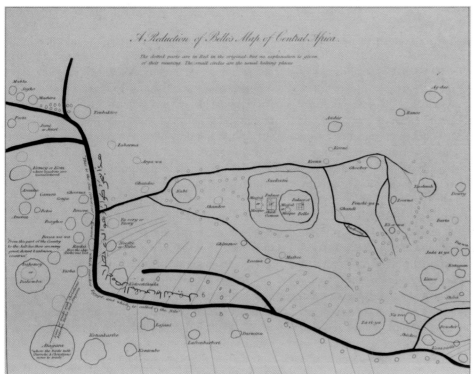

A Reduction of Bello's Map of Central Africa.

The dotted parts are in Red in the original: but no explanation is given
of their meaning. The small circles are the usual halting places

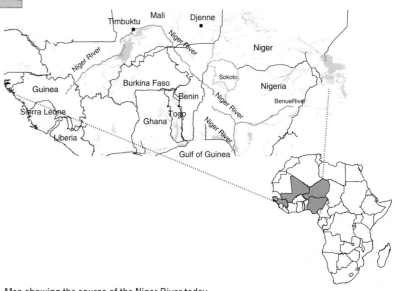

Map showing the course of the Niger River today.

58

The Cedid Atlas, 1803

• ◆ •

Maps based on William Faden's plates
for his General Atlas.
Cedid Atlas, Tab'hane-yi Hümayun
(Istanbul, Turkey), 1803
Library of Congress Geography and
Map Division Washington, D.C.

This rare example of Ottoman printing was the result of reform efforts of Sultan Selim III of Turkey, who ruled from 1789 to 1807. Selim III's reform efforts were propelled in part by a series of humiliating and economically destructive military losses to Russia at sea and on land.

For centuries, Ottoman rulers depended upon income from tariffs on goods transported over the lands and through the waters they controlled. From the sixteenth until the late eighteenth century, Ottomans had controlled one of the largest inland seas in Western Eurasia—the Black Sea (and its smaller sea, the Sea of Azov), as well two important chokepoints leading out to the eastern Mediterranean: the Dardanelles and the Bosporus Straits. Both the seas and the straits handled commerce from Central Asia and Russia. While there were alternative routes for goods from Asia, goods from Russia were forced to travel through Ottoman-dominated waters to reach the Mediterranean. After losing a series of wars with Russia during the eighteenth century, the Ottomans had to turn over control of the Sea of Azov and the western coast of the Black Sea, thereby forfeiting the transit fees they had relied upon.

Realizing that their military defeat stemmed partly from a failure to keep up with advances in military technology and training that were spreading throughout Europe, Selim embarked upon a program of modernization and invited once despised emissaries from Europe to help better equip and train the Ottoman navy and army.

This opening to the West included an embrace of science and engineering skills that had developed there over the last two centuries. The instructors invited from Europe included the very best. In 1795, one promising young French artillery officer was ordered to help upgrade the Ottoman armed forces. He was held back from his journey to take care of a more pressing matter. The officer was none other than Napoleon Bonaparte, who only four years later would seize control of France in a coup d'etat and lead France to a series of stunning, if temporary, military victories.

Among the skills the Ottomans desired were Western mapmaking techniques, which were to be taught to military engineers, while geographic knowledge was to be shared with officials of the foreign and war ministries.

To assist in the dissemination of this newly acquired knowledge, the production of paper and printing was encouraged. Hence the publication of the *Cedid* (New) *Atlas,* which was intended to train young military engineers and to provide geographic information to government officials. Although the plates for this atlas were created in Vienna, the atlas was printed and published by the Military Engineering School's printing press in Istanbul in 1803. The atlas consists of 24 separate, beautifully colored sheets, representing a translation of one of the great standards of Western mapmaking of the day, William Faden's *General Atlas.*

The map at right depicts Asia, including Russia in yellow and Turkey in a light red, but leaves the part of the Black Sea region conquered by Russia uncolored. Central Asia and Indochina both appear in a beautiful blue.

59

Napoleon's Advance and Retreat from Moscow, 1812–1813

• ◆ •

Carte figurative des pertes successives
en hommes de l'Armée Française dans la
campagne de Russie 1812–1813
Charles Joseph Minard, 1869
Collections de l'Ecole des Ponts,
Champs-sur-Marne, France

Sometimes maps convey more than spatial information. Occasionally they even manage to incorporate data about events that have occurred (or are occurring) on and across the terrain. In many older maps, drawings of camels might indicate a caravan route through the desert or a ferry might show a regular water crossing (see Maps 34 and 62).

The creator of the unusual map on the right manages to tell the story of a disastrous military attack and defeat. By superimposing a graph onto the map, he depicts the movements of Napoleon's army as it attacked and retreated from Moscow in the winter of 1812–1813.

This type of representation on a map is sometimes called a **cartogram**, because it presents statistical information in a diagrammatic form. In Map 59, the cartogram uses a kind of bar graph to show the size of Napoleon's army at various stages throughout its advance and retreat. But what makes this map special is that the mapmaker managed to build his cartogram around geographical distance.

A simple bar graph would simply have showed the number of men in Napoleon's army at any given point in time. The date would appear at the bottom of the graph, and the height of the bar would indicate the number of men in the army at that time. A second bar graph would be dated a few months later, and indicate the number of men in the army at that date. In this manner a progression of bar graphs would show the gradual decimation of Napoleon's army over the course of time, from month to month over the course of the year. The result would show when the numbers declined, but it would not show *where* they declined.

By contrast, the cartogram takes the information on the size of the army for each month, and places each bar graph on a map showing the location of Napoleon's soldiers. The constantly narrowing line represents the decline in French forces heading east (brown) and then returning west (black). The line below the main figure tracks the temperature of the brutal Russian winter. In this way, the numbers of soldiers in the army in any month also appear on a map that shows when and where these numbers declined. The result is a more complete image of the devastation that befell Napoleon's army. The cartogram's ability to convey the dynamics of Napoleon's troop movements through time and space, in a single static representation, make it particularly compelling. Its steadily decreasing graph manages to narrate an ill-advised military venture and its devastating cost in human lives. Edward Tufte (1942-), a pioneer in the field of data visualization, describes it as "the best statistical graph ever drawn."

However Minard sacrificed geographical accuracy in his pursuit of visual clarity. To dramatize Moscow's cold, for example, he repositioned the city nearly two hundred miles north of its actual location. To keep Napoelon's advance visually separate from his retreat, Minard both reversed the relative positions of Chjat and Wizma and additionally moved Wizma (Vayazma) nearly a hundred miles south so that it fell clearly in the line of Napoleon's retreat rather than its actual position above Napoleon's path of advance. While a brilliant cartogram, Minard's effort falls short as a map.

While cartograms are still employed today, to indicate the relative distribution of diseases, or levels of poverty, they are increasingly being displaced by dynamic computer displays that use a wide variety of animation programs.

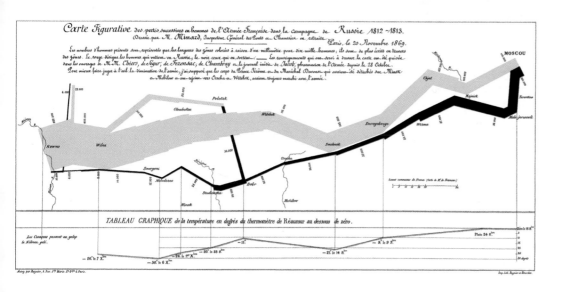

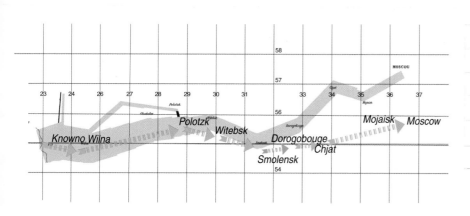

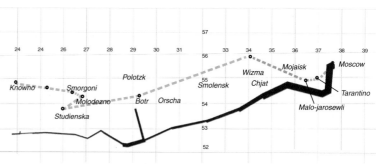

◄ TOP

Cartogram showing fatalities by month and location (with weather details) for Napoleon's advance and retreat on Moscow.

◄ MIDDLE

Napoleon's actual route. The brown line shows his advance, the black line his retreat.

▼ BOTTOM LEFT

The actual route of Napoleon's advance (in blue) juxtaposed with how it is shown on Minard's cartogram.

▼ BOTTOM RIGHT

The actual route of Napoleon's retreat (blue dashed lines) compared with how Minard depicted it on his cartogram.

Part **6**

Land Surveys
c. 800–1900

Maps in Part Six

Land surveys define surfaces, shapes, and boundaries. Historically, land surveys were commissioned to further political or economic interests. Government officials often wanted to know the size of properties in order to levy taxes or to divide up conquered territories among their armies. At other times, political leaders desired better information on the boundaries of their political and administrative units. Competition among opposing religious groups also led to surveys to fix the borders of their respective landholdings in order to control them better. Close observations of the dimensions of agricultural fields, the boundaries between farms, and the networks of irrigation systems all allowed governments or other organizations to allocate resources accordingly.

The land survey itself is a product of great antiquity. Both the Babylonians and the Egyptians undertook land surveys; to date, the oldest recovered land maps have come from Mesopotamia. Ancient Egyptians tabulated surveys of the Nile, but they either did not sketch their analyses or they committed them to extremely fragile material that have not survived the passing of time. Babylonians, however, did depict lands and irrigation ditches on maps. The image of the town of Nippur on a clay tablet (see Map 13) contains elements of a land survey with its depictions of a river and a canal and its placement of the city walls.

Romans also undertook agricultural surveys in order to allocate fields or decide where boundaries lay for large and small properties. The vast size of the Roman Empire, and the need for measurement of conquered lands to be subdivided, led to the emergence of surveying as a professional occupation that required skilled training.

As societies grew more complex, with many layers of competing authority over land, questions of boundaries, water rights, taxes, and political control all became increasingly contested. In response to these developments, land surveys grew more complex. In many societies even minute differences in the way land was used needed to be recorded, and many societies chose to map those differences.

The oldest land survey in Asia was conducted in Japan in the eighth century CE, as land was gradually being converted to growing rice in irrigated fields (see Map 60). Two major religious organizations competed for ownership of the new rice fields, and the maps served to establish their boundaries. In China, several hundred years later, the leadership of the Southern Song dynasty wanted better information on the boundaries of the administrative units it controlled. The resulting maps were printed so could be copied and distributed. Despite their prosaic purpose, some of these maps were the most exquisitely designed in the world at that time (see Map 61).

In Europe, written texts remained the rule for land surveys until the sixteenth century. Even England's famous *Domesday Book*, the remarkable survey of English landholdings after 1066, contains no maps but only text. In the sixteenth century, Englishmen began to produce maps based upon surveys of the land. These maps were printed and became so popular that some of them were even woven into giant tapestries to hang on walls of great houses (see Map 62). By the eighteenth century, land surveys had become commonplace in many different parts of the globe for a variety of different reasons.

Timeline of world history

after 200 CE
Spread of Buddhism to East Asia

618–906
Tang Dynasty, China

960–1279
Song dynasty, China

c. 1300
First Gyoki maps, Japan

1392–1897
Choson dynasty, Korea

1443
Invention of *hangul* alphabet, Korea

c. 1500
Development of Sikhism (India)

c. 1517
Beginning of Protestant Reformation

1644–1910
Qing dynasty, China

c. 1720–1790
European Enlightenment

c. 1750
Population boom starts in Europe, China, and the Americas

c. 1760
British industrialization begins

since 1782
Chakri dynasty, Thailand

1789–1797
French Revolution

1791
Creation of Ordnance Survey, England

60

Japan: The First Rice Field Surveys, Eighth Century CE

• ◆ •

Middle Section 14
Map of farmland owned
by Todai-ji Temple
Kusooki village, Asuka district,
Echizen Province
Dated October 21, end Year of
Tenpyojingo (766 CE)
SHOSOIN TREASURE
courtesy of the SHOSHOIN
TREASURE HOUSE, Nara, Japan

Japanese mapping began in the eighth century with the first surveys of the boundaries of rice fields. While rice can be grown during the rainy season, it can also be grown any time of the year by flooding fields with water. The crop from this second method of rice farming is known today as "paddy" rice, from the Malay word for rice, *padi*. This flooding technique dates back to 3000 BCE, with both China and Korea claiming to have been the first sites of paddy rice cultivation. However, the earliest maps of paddy rice fields did not appear until much later, and in Japan.

Around 400 BCE, paddy rice production was introduced to Japan. The system of land ownership of paddy fields remained chaotic for many centuries. However, during the eighth century CE, new areas began to be flooded in order to grow rice. Although Buddhism had arrived in Japan only a hundred and fifty years earlier (around 552 CE), by the eighth century the religion was rapidly gaining power and wealth. Buddhist monasteries claimed many of the newly irrigated rice-growing plots. But the monasteries encountered significant political opposition from the guardians of the traditional Japanese Shinto shrines that laid claim to the same fields. To resolve the conflict, the boundaries of paddy rice fields were redefined in the 740s, and a consistent system called *jori* was installed. Jori consisted of a square with sides of approximately 109 meters (357.6 feet), which was then subdivided into ten evenly sized rectangles. Often jori were separated from one another by irrigation ditches or walking paths. The first maps were therefore created to clarify ownership of the land between the competing religious organizations.

To ensure the precise boundaries of fields, extremely careful measurements were used to draft jori maps. The resulting maps, such as the one on the right, showing *jori* in a district in Echizen province, contain spare black lines on a cream-colored surface (usually cloth made from hemp) delineating the boundaries of each plot, with names or descriptions included on every square.

Although initially created to settle land disputes, government leaders soon realized that these maps could be used to establish the long-sought but unrealized goal of a national land register. Since jori maps inventoried the boundaries, ownership, and value of each plot, they also proved to be ideal for tax purposes. While the national register ceased functioning in the tenth century, joris remained in use in local taxation until the fifteenth century. Even after the system ceased to be the basis for tax revenue, some owners continued to use joris as a means of separating irrigated paddies from dry fields.

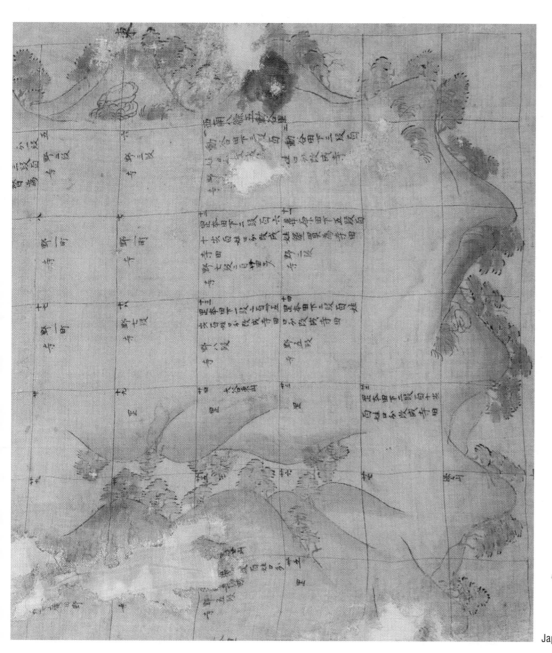

Hokkaido

Tohoku

Echizen ● Chubu Kanto

Chugoku Kinki

Shikoku

Kyushu

Japan

Japan, with Echizen province indicated on the country's western coast.

61

Chinese County Maps:
Dinghai County, 1226

• ◆ •

Ancient map of Ding Hai Xian Jing Tu
Southern Song dynasty, 1226 CE,
Woodblock printing

On the right is the finest example of an early printed map. It is, in fact, one of the oldest printed maps in existence. The printing technique, which was developed in China during the Tang dynasty (618–907 CE), allowed almost no leeway for error, as designs and characters were carved into wooden blocks. Any major mistake meant the chiseling of blocks had to begin all over again. The desired images were drawn on the flat surface of the wood and the area between them was carved away, so that the features of the map appear elevated. Ink was applied to the raised characters. Paper was then placed on top of the inked block of wood and rollers rubbed the ink into the paper.

This map of Dinghai County, China, dated from about fifty years after the first printed map (1177), originated in the Southern Song region of China, which extended south from the Yangzi River. The impetus for creating the woodblock maps stemmed from a desire to exercise better political control and to define the boundaries of administrative districts. To that end, the Southern Song government ordered the collection of all the names of the places in their domain so that maps could be produced. Most of the resulting maps showed counties with redefined administrative boundaries.

The map shown here is a detail of a map for Dinghai County that was included in a collection of names called *Gazetteer of Siming*, published between 1226 and 1228 CE.

The place shown on the right is Ningbo, which is now a provincial coastal town. Ningbo was one of the earliest seafaring regions in China, with evidence of sailing going back to at least 5000 BCE. At the time this map was drawn, it had been one of China's two or three principal seaports for more than six hundred years. That position would not last, for as these maps were being printed, the Mongol leader Genghis Khan (c. 1162–1227) had already turned the Northern Song region into a Mongol vassal state. The Southern Song held out longer, but it too eventually succumbed to the Mongols in 1279.

Unlike the first, simple printed wooden block maps, this map is densely carved. The entire page is filled with symbols, characters, and names, arranged with extraordinary clarity and precision. Remarkable artistic skill is displayed through the use of varied and sophisticated symbols for landscape features.

The China Sea on the right and top sides of the map features stylized waves drawn as humps, but with whitecaps topping the waves. When the water becomes that of the freshwater Yong River, the very fine lines on the ocean waves become smaller and smoother, but they are still recognizably water. Fine lines crossing the river may appear to be bridges, but in fact they are dams. The mountains, in contrast, are depicted with short sharp lines combined with sharp angles that indicate the elevation and angle of rise in height elevation. Along the top peninsula an undulating shape with short straight lines indicates a sandy area. Other features are equally skillfully rendered. A name with a ring at the bottom shows the location of a shipyard, four dark circular objects near the upper left are lakes, and to the right, protecting the region from flooding, is a seawall depicted as dashed lines of bricks or stones.

Following a convention employed on the first printed maps from several decades earlier, the names of all the features on this map are carefully enclosed within rectangles. The technique of placing text inside boxes continued to feature in printed maps for several centuries and ensured greater precision in identifying places and avoiding misreading. Names of temples and gardens appear in vertical boxes atop temple-like structures, while county names and boundaries appear in horizontal boxes, written from right to left, thus avoiding confusion when place names lie close to one another.

Map showing Ningbo on the East China Sea.

62

Elizabethan Tapestry
Map, 1580

◆ ◆ ◆

An Elizabethan Cartographical
Tapestry Fragment, Late 16th century
Sheldon Manufactory
Woven in wools and silks
74 × 48¼ in. (188 × 122.5 cm.)
The Bodelian Library,
University of Oxford

Tapestries are painstakingly constructed, using different colored threads that are hand-woven together to produce a picture. Unlike embroidery, in which colored threads are sewn on top of a cloth, a tapestry consists exclusively of colored threads. Because tapestries depend upon the arrangement of threads, they are easily damaged by tears and rips, or simply fall apart as the threads deteriorate. One of the most famous cloth designs, dating from the eleventh century, depicts the Norman conquest of England. Although it is called the *Bayeaux Tapestry*, it is in fact embroidery rather than a tapestry.

Many maps in the past may have been woven as tapestries, but because of their fragility only comparatively recent and well-preserved map tapestries have survived. Yet the technique of weaving colored threads to produce a map goes back at least two millennia. The historical record includes a description, from a Greek writer living in Rome, of a tapestry map of the world presented by an unnamed queen to the Roman emperor during the first century of the Christian era. The tapestry, of unknown size, is described as "a perfect copy of the harvest-bearing earth, all that the land encircling ocean girdles . . . and the gray sea too." The harvest-bearing earth is further described as the area "obedient to Caesar," suggesting that it illustrated the extent of the Roman Empire surrounded by an ocean. The map, however, has not survived.

Tapestries grew in popularity in Europe beginning in the fourteenth century, as looms became capable of weaving large drawings. In addition to serving as decoration, the thick weavings were hung on stone walls as a form of insulation. During the fifteenth century, Flanders (present-day Holland) became the most important center of tapestry weaving, but during the vicious Spanish repression of Protestants after 1559, many talented tapestry-makers fled to safety in England.

In 1570, William Sheldon set up a venture in Warwickshire, about 80 miles northeast of London, to train Englishmen as tapestry weavers. Over a decade later, his son Ralph Sheldon commissioned four tapestry maps that provided an immense panoramic view of the surrounding countryside. The tapestries decorated his newly constructed house in Weston, Long Compton.

To provide the weavers with guidance, Sheldon consulted the county maps recently created by surveyor Christopher Saxton (*c.* 1540–1610). In 1570, Queen Elizabeth's secretary William Cecil commissioned the 30-year-old Saxton to survey England and Wales, county by county. Over the next decade Saxton dutifully examined every county, and produced thirty-four colored maps. Designed to give Queen Elizabeth a comprehensive geographic overview of her dominions, the maps were also intended to assist her advisors (the Privy Council) in making judicial decisions regarding property and public administration.

Apart from their political functions, these maps proved popular with the English public in both their design and subject matter. Over the course of the next century they were repeatedly copied and reissued, sometimes under other people's names but employing Saxton's basic coloring and layout.

Sheldon's unusual choice of material for his version of the Saxton maps stemmed from his ownership of the tapestry workshop he inherited from his father. For his home in Warwickshire, Sheldon desired a tapestry that would depict his family's and friends' considerable agricultural holdings. Together these farmlands stretched across the four major counties of England's Midlands: Worcestershire, Oxfordshire, Gloucestershire, and Warwickshire.

The completed tapestries are ten times larger than Saxton's engravings. Each weaving measures 13 by 20 feet.

◄ **TOP RIGHT**
An Elizabethan tapestry, depicting the towns, rivers, and forests near the Bristol Channel on the west coast of England.

◄ **FAR LEFT AND**
▼ **BOTTOM RIGHT**
Close-up of the tapestry map showing a boat and a ferry crossing the Bristol Channel on the West Coast of England.

Map showing the location of the four counties shown on the map.

63

The Land That Windmills Made: A Dutch Polder Map, 1750

• ◆ •

Thooge Heemraedschap van
Delflant, 1750 CE
Nicolas Samuelsz Kruikius
Delft [Netherlands]:
Hoogheemraadschap van Delfland, 1985
Library of Congress Geography and
Map Division Washington, D.C.

The windmills for which the Netherlands is so famous created the land shown on this map. Without the help of windmills to pump out the water and dikes to hold it back, all of the territory shown on this map, including the famous city of Delft in its center, would be flooded. Of these two famous landmarks of the Dutch countryside, dikes have a much older history.

When humans first settled the Netherlands, they discovered the giant delta for two large European rivers, the Rhine and the Meuse. As these rivers drain out into the Atlantic, they deposit fertile silt at the entrance. Over the centuries, high sand dunes, some distance away from the mouth of the rivers, prevented the silt on offshore islands from being entirely washed out to sea. As a result, over the years, mounds of extremely rich soil developed, renewed annually by the flowing waters of the Rhine and Meuse. The first settlers established themselves on these fertile mounds and created basic dikes to protect the land from periodic flooding.

By the ninth century CE, many of these small mounds had become connected to each other, forming villages. Steadily rising sea levels forced the inhabitants to build higher and higher dikes, many of which were constructed by large landowners. The majority of the dikes consisted of mounds of earth, sliced vertically on the sea side and covered with a layer of seaweed, reeds, or wicker mats to prevent the earth from being washed away. This outward protective layer was anchored in place by poles. By 1250 nearly all of the coastline was reinforced by a long row of earthen dikes.

In addition to flooding from the sea, other places in the Netherlands faced a different problem during the Middle Ages. In areas covered with peat, farmers drained the water from the peat by means of ditches and then grew wheat on the ground left behind. The only problem was that a year or so after being drained the peat fields sank and the ground became soggy, rendering it useless for farming.

In the 1400s, the Dutch first began to use windmills as pumping stations to drain water from land that would otherwise flood. The windmills would first raise the level of the water by about a meter (a little over a yard), where it then would flow into elevated canals and waterways to be stored until it could be released into the sea. The farmland created by these windmills was called **polder land**.

In the following century, increased urbanization led to greater demand for peat as cooking and heating fuel. In order to reach peat that remained underwater, a "dredging bracket"—a long stick with a net on the end—allowed peat to be pulled up and dried. But removing the wet peat caused the surrounding land to sink.

Responsibility for maintaining the dikes originally rested with local landowners. But regulation of water flows was far more complicated. Eventually, water control boards (*hoogheemraadschappen*) took over responsibility for protecting the land against the sea, regulating the water levels of the various canals into which water was pumped from the polders. Maintaining waterways in the area that would eventually become the province of South Holland fell to an organization called *hoogheemraadschappen Schap van Delfland*, located in the city of Delft, and situated roughly in the center of the map.

In the middle of the eighteenth century the Delfland Water Board asked the local surveyor Nicolaas Kruik to undertake an overview of all the canals, dikes, and other waterways in the district. A perfectionist, Kruik not only sketched in all the polders (outlined in brown) but also added every field under cultivation in the entire area.

To this day the Delfland Water Board regulates the flow of waters throughout south Holland and maintains the peat mounds visible on Kruik's map.

THOOGE HEEMRAED SCHAP VAN DELFLANT

◀ **LEFT**
A polder map commissioned by the Delfland Water Board around 1750.

Map showing the Netherlands today.

Netherlands

Delft · Rhine · Germany

Belgium

Luxembourg

Rhine

64

Paris on the Eve of the French Revolution, 1789

• ◆ •

Carte de France / levée par ordre du
roy, 1756–[1818] CE
César-François Cassini
Library of Congress Geography
and Map Division

Between 1744 and the start of the French Revolution in 1789, César-Francois Cassini directed the first survey undertaken of France in its entirety. While regional governments as well as the military had produced small-scale maps for their own purposes, no one previously had mapped the entire country on a single scale. Doing so required establishing uniform methods of measurement and a common set of standards for recording and notating geographical information.

César-Francois Cassini (1714–1784), who created the map on the right, was the grandson of a prominent astronomy professor at the University of Bologna, Gian Domenico Cassini (1625–1712). Louis XIV (r. 1643–1715) invited the elder Cassini to France to serve as an advisor on the construction of the Astronomical Observatory in Paris, and Gian Domenico found life in France so agreeable that he moved his entire family there in 1671.

The central question preoccupying astronomers at the time was the width of a degree of longitude, which was essential for determining the shape and dimensions of the Earth. Isaac Newton (1642–1727) had proposed that the Earth was flatter at the poles rather than perfectly round. Since longitude degrees resemble upright orange slices, narrowing to a point at the top, a broader degree near the poles would indicate that Newton was correct.

Gian Domenico's grandson, César-Francois, tackled this problem by creating a grid in which a chain of triangles horizontally crossed France and intersected with the vertical degrees of longitude that traversed the country, creating a "geometric canvas" composed of 3,000 points. The map was centered on a longitude line that passed through Paris.

In 1744 CE, Louis XV (r. 1715–1774) authorized the creation of a group of surveyors, who, in addition to measuring distances, would develop the first comprehensive list of place names for the entire country. He had hoped that the information would help him develop additional sources of revenue, but 12 years later the king was forced to withdraw his patronage for financial reasons. To compensate for this lost funding, Cassini created a society of fifty members, the Society of the Map of France, whose members would help defray the costs of the project in exchange for copies of the completed map. Local municipalities, provinces, and prefectures (*pays d'états et generalités*) desiring better maps of their own environs, contributed approximately 40 percent of the costs of the project.

The resulting map of France consisted of 180 separate black and white sheets, 85 percent of which were large sheets (41 inches by 28.7 inches, or 104 cm by 73 cm) and the remainder smaller sheets of varying sizes. The most extensive and accurate map of France drawn up to that time, the Cassini map showed a wide variety of features: vineyards, forests, gardens, watermills, windmills, bridges, post offices, and mines. The immense amount of detail even depicted the streets in cities as large as Paris (see detail on the right).

Cassini's map was completed just as the French Revolution began. The close-up of Paris on the right includes the Louvre, where Marie Antoinette and Louis XVI were detained, and the Place de la Concorde, where the guillotine sliced off their heads. Printing of the map was delayed until after the Revolution, when engravers added topography and systemized the layout of the **toponyms**, thus ensuring overall excellence.

The Cassini map would remain the only officially commissioned civilian map of France for the next 150 years, as the military took over mapping functions. Not until 1942 did the army create a civilian mapping agency, the *Institut géographique national* (IGN), which remains in charge of producing official maps of France to this day.

▲ **TOP**
Paris on the eve of the French Revolution. This sheet from the Cassini map of France shows Paris and environs with the Seine winding through the center.

▼ **BOTTOM**
Close up showing Paris. The detail and meticulousness are extraordinary.

65

The Origins of the Ordnance Survey: Scotland's Loch Ness, 1747–1755

••◆••

A very large and highly finished colored military survey of the kingdom of Scotland, 1747–1755 CE
William Roy
The British Library
Image created by Sarah Lyons based on 11 sections of the map

This official military survey map from the mid-eighteenth century shows an area rich in history and legend. The long lake running through the middle of the map is Loch Ness, home to the legendary monster. Just east of where the River Ness empties into the sea lies Cawdor Castle, where Shakespeare set *Macbeth*. Near Cawdor is Culloden, where a famous battle indirectly led to the first countrywide survey in Britain. This Scottish survey would provide the impetus for subsequently undertaking a similar one in England, created under military auspices, and called the **Ordnance Survey**.

The events leading up to 1746 had their start more than half a century earlier. In 1688, the Catholic King of England, James II (*r.* 1685–1688) was forced into exile in France and replaced on the throne by his Protestant daughter. Supporters of James, known as Jacobites, maintained that he and his descendants remained the lawful rulers of England. While feeble attempts by James and his son to reconquer England failed, more strenuous efforts by his grandson got off to a more promising start. Charles Stuart, known as "Bonnie Prince Charlie" (1720–1788), set sail for Scotland in 1745. Despite early successes, he was soon forced to the relative safety of the Highlands. On April 16, 1746 at Culloden, Charles' forces and his strongest supporters, the clan leaders of the Scottish Highlands, were massacred by the English and the Jacobite uprising came to an end.

In order to consolidate their military victories against the resentful and well-armed surviving clan leaders, an English officer, Deputy Quartermaster David Watson, planned the construction of forts and roads to protect English troops and to deprive the Scots of their home field advantage. Watson hired the relatively unknown but very talented William Roy (1726–1790) to undertake a rigorous survey of the Scottish Highlands. From 1747–1755, assisted by other surveyors and then by mapmaker Paul Sandby, Roy created the basis for the first Ordnance Survey of Britain in 1791. Sandby (later famous for his watercolor landscapes) used brush strokes to show the pitch of each slope and differentiated steeper slopes by employing darker, more closely spaced strokes. In the Highlands, trees, grass, and dense Scottish heather concealed abrupt cliffs and deadly steep mountainsides. They also shielded more gentle inclines, where a chieftain could simply hide or lie in ambush. Surveying the angles of the mountainsides revealed both the safety and the dangers hidden beneath the seemingly innocuous vegetation.

Although Roy began the survey of Scotland in 1746, at around the same time as Cassini's group began working their survey in France (see Map 64), the motives for producing each survey were entirely different. Where the British military ordered the survey of Scotland in order to secure the victory over the Scots at Culloden by revealing concealed terrain, King Louis XV sponsored Cassini so that he might profit from taxes based upon information from a better map of his kingdom.

While Roy had borrowed his original techniques from Jacques Cassini, both William Roy and Cassini's son, César-Francois, employed similar techniques. However, each man was convinced his measurements were more accurate. In 1783, César-Francois proposed that competing French and English measurements of the exact locations of their respective observatories be put to the test through a cross-Channel measurement. Roy headed the English team, Cassini the French squadron—but, unfortunately, Roy died during the competition and the contest collapsed. The year after Roy died, the **triangulation** of Britain began; it would be completed in 1822, laying the framework for the first topographical survey of England.

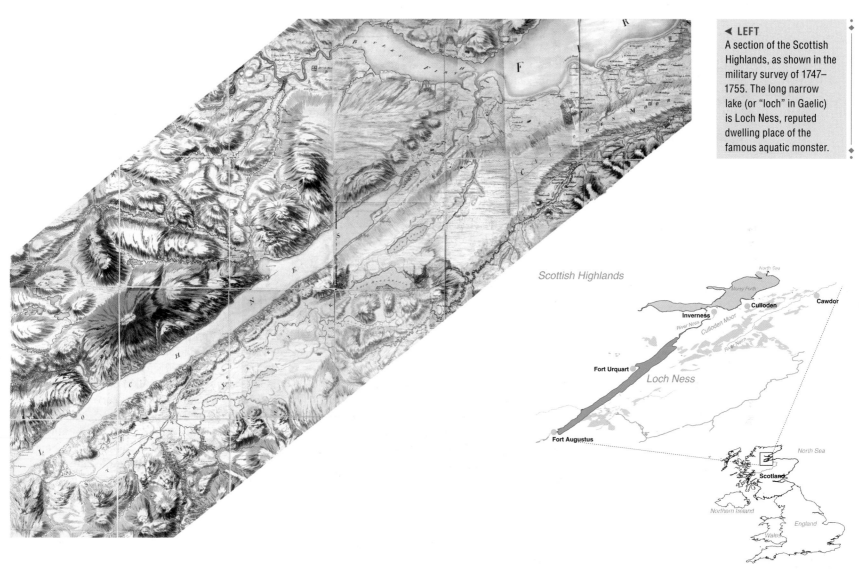

Scottish Highlands

North Sea

Moray Firth

Culloden

Cawdor

Inverness

River Ness

Culloden Moor

River Nairn

Fort Urquart

Loch Ness

Fort Augustus

North Sea

Scotland

Northern Ireland

England

Wales

Map showing Loch Ness, Scotland.

66

Thai Map, *c.* 1782

◆◆◆

Khmen Nai Ni
c. 1782–1824 CE
Used with permission of Her Royal
Highness Princess Maha Chakri
Sirindhorn of Thailand.
All rights reserved

Burma got Thai

gained independence

Burma never let it go

The only country in Southeast Asia to avoid European colonization entirely, Thailand (also known as Siam), was not always so successful in fending off invasion from neighboring Burma (Myanmar). In 1767 a Burmese army sacked the Thai kingdom, burning its capital city to the ground and destroying precious historical and religious records, including maps created during the Ayutthaya Kingdom (1351–1767). Hence, the earliest surviving Thai maps only date from after 1767 when Thailand successfully became independent of Burma.

After several turbulent years of transition following the ousting of the Burmese, a new Thai government materialized under the leadership of a former military chief, Lord Chakri, who became known as King Rama I (*r.* 1782–1809). Mindful of the vulnerability of the capital to invasion, he built a new capital on a readily defensible island at the site of the former village of Bang Makok (meaning "place of olive plums"). The shortened name for the new capital became Bangkok.

Despite ejecting the invaders from Thailand, King Rama I (the first ruler of the Chakri dynasty) had to contend with continuing incursions from the Burmese. They entered the country through the Three Pagoda Pass, which had been the main land route into western Thailand since antiquity. A series of inconclusive border wars with Burma were repeatedly fought over the next half century.

At the center of the map is the largest freshwater lake in Southeast Asia, Cambodia's Tonlé Sap, drawn using crescent-shaped symbols for bodies of water similar to those that appeared on Chinese maps from previous centuries (see Map 61). During the dry season, Tonlé Sap is a fairly small body of water with a river that flows southward until it joins the Mekong River at Phnom Penh. During the summer monsoon season, however, immense quantities of water flood the river as far south as Phnom Penh, where some of the water changes direction and flows back up into Tonlé Sap. This rare reversal of a river more than triples the size of the lake, flooding the adjoining fields with water needed to grow rice and pushing large quantities of fish (depicted on map) into the lake. When the rain stops, the waters drain and once again begin flowing downstream into the Mekong River through Vietnam and emptying into the South China Sea.

This map, like the others in a trove of recently discovered Thai maps, dates from the early years of the Chakri dynasty (which remains the ruling family of Thailand). The map depicts the countryside—trees, mountains, rivers and lakes—with such extraordinary and delicate detail that the viewer can envision himself stopping under the shade of a tree. It is also dashed with touches of humor: giant fish from the bountiful monsoon harvest cavort in Tonlé Sap. Religious structures called *stupas*, which guard Buddhist relics, are drawn with the same care. Yet, overlaid on this idyllic landscape are thin, almost delicate red lines tracing the major transport arteries for military movements. The precise distances are noted in black alongside the red lines with the same light hand, and population centers are drawn with simple circles, squares, and rectangles. With exceptional detail, the map conveys an extraordinarily beautiful and abundant natural world.

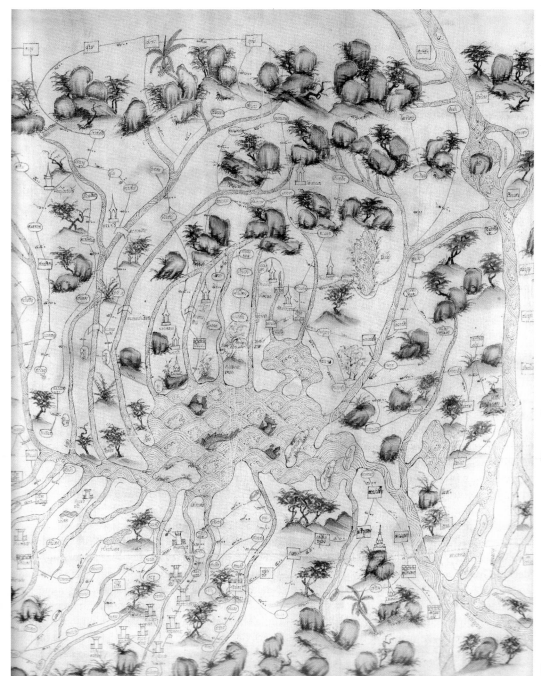

Mainland Southeast Asia.

67

The Vale of Kashmir,
1836

•◆•

Pictorial map on cloth of the Vale
of Kashmir, showing Srinagar
in detail, c. 1836
Library of Congress, Vault

In August 1836, a painted cloth map of the Valley of Kashmir, one of India's most spectacular regions, was presented to the military aide to the British Governor General of the region. Colonel Claude Wade was complimentary about the extraordinary detail but less appreciative of the map itself, whose general outlines he characterized as "extremely primitive." Indeed, the map failed to live up to the precise British standards for maps of India at the time (see Map 72), since it neither employed measurement nor included a scale, and it exaggerated the size of important cities. Furthermore, the painting was executed on burlap, a material usually employed as carpet backing.

However, as a cultural portrait of Kashmir the map is extraordinary. Its massive size—227 by 407 cm. (7 feet by 13.3 feet)—allowed for exceptional detail. Waterways, temples, mosques, and gardens, as well as various economic activities including saffron harvesting, are recorded with graceful precision. Roads lined with the famous Kashmiri poplar trees even show people walking. An enlarged view of the regional capital, Srinagar, clearly depicts its famous Shalimar Gardens and pleasure boating on Dal Lake. The map's creator employed color effectively, distinguishing land use by painting cultivated fields light green, village groves a darker green, bare earth brown, and settlements outlined in black or grey ink. Topography is conveyed via a similar color scheme: mountains are painted in purple and distant snow caps are white. Particular attention is paid to rivers, with the Jhelum River—the easternmost limit of Alexander the Great's conquest—carefully outlined (see Map 19).

At the time of this map a famous maharaja ("great king"), Ranjit Singh (r. 1801–1839), had successfully conquered huge swaths of the northwestern part of the Indian subcontinent. His rule included Kashmir and surrounding territories, extending into parts of modern Pakistan and Chinese Tibet. His empire became known as the *Punjab* from two old Persian words that mean "the land of the five rivers," namely, the major tributaries of the Indus: the Beas, Ravi, Sutlej, Chenab, and Jhelum rivers.

The first Sikh to rule an empire on the subcontinent, Maharaja Singh became known as the "Lion of Punjab." Although he displaced nearly a thousand years of Muslim rule, Ranjit Singh practiced religious toleration, appointing Hindu, Muslim, and Sikh officials in his government.

Several indications point to an Islamic cartographer as creator of Map 67. First, south lies at the top, as is customary in Muslim maps. Second, the individual who gave Colonel Wade the map had a traditional and very popular Kashmiri Muslim name, Abdul Raheem al-Bukhari. However, Wade knew little about Islamic genealogical naming practices, mistaking his surname "al-Bukhari" to mean that Raheem had personally come from the city in modern Uzbekistan. In reality, Muslims, mostly Sunni from present-day Uzbekistan and other adjoining Central Asian regions, moved in great numbers to Kashmir during the fourteenth and fifteenth centuries. "Al-Bukhari" thus likely indicated both his family's historic place of origin and the branch of Islam to which it owed allegiance and not the actual city where he was born. In a region with many Shiites, "al-Bukhari" also indicated the cartographer's Sunni faith, brought to the region from Uzbekistan. The final evidence that a Muslim drew the map are the numerous labels in a form of Persian known as *Dari*, for centuries the lingua franca of the Muslim Mughal empire in northern India (English inscriptions were added to the map later). Because of the amount of detail on the map, Raheem likely directed a team of cartographers.

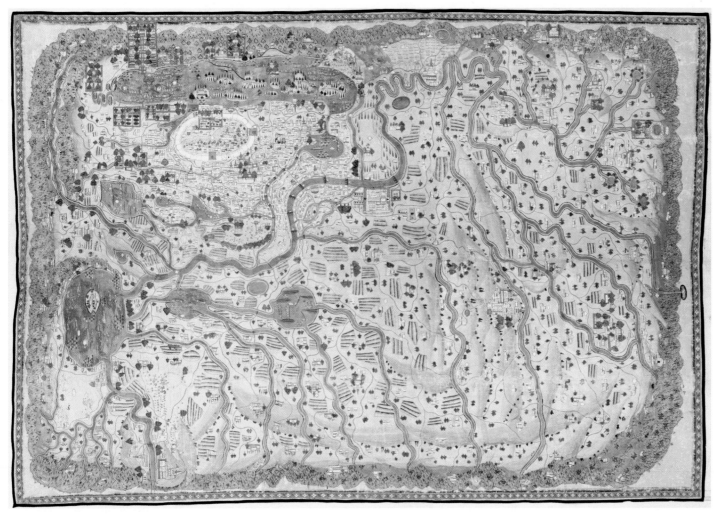

▲ **ABOVE**
Map of Kashmir, 1836.

Detail showing pleasure
boats on Lake Dal, Srinigar.

68

The Eight Provinces of Korea, *c.* 1850

● ● ●

Ch'onha chido
Pen-and-ink and watercolor
on rice paper
Library of Congress Geography
and Map Division

The Choson era of Korean history (sometimes spelled *Jaseon* or *Chosun*) lasted approximately five centuries, from the end of the fourteenth to the end of the nineteenth century (1392–1897). Several regional maps have survived from this period, such as the one on the right.

One of the most famous Choson rulers, King Sejong (*r.* 1419–1450) created *hangul,* the modern Korean alphabet. Interest in literacy had been strong in Korea even before the rise of the Choson state. In 1377, 62 years before Gutenberg in the West, Korea printed the first book with moveable metal type. Although the Korean language had always differed from Chinese, up until Sejong's reign it was written using Chinese characters. In addition to creating a new alphabet, King Sejong wanted to invent a form of writing that would allow more of his subjects to become literate. Writing Korean in Chinese characters (known as *hanja*) was so difficult that only privileged male aristocrats could read and write fluently. Hangul, created in 1443/1444, enabled commoners learn to read and write and soon allowed popular genres of writing to emerge. However, the elite continued to prefer the exclusivity of hanja and referred derogatorily to the new hangul as a children's script, or "writing you can learn in a morning."

Hangul is unusual in that each symbol constitutes a simplified diagram of the patterns made by the mouth, tongue and teeth when making the sound related to the character. The characters are then written in blocks of syllables and strung together. The script can be written either left to right, or more commonly top to bottom and right to left. While hangul became widely adopted for popular writing, official documents such as maps continued to be written in hanja through the end of the nineteenth century.

In Choson-era regional maps, mountains and rivers are the most important features. Settlements assume less importance. Twenty-three mountains are depicted in the map, sometimes lyrically. The countryside is also filled with rivers and includes three important ones: the Yeongsangang, Seomjingang, and Tamjingang, all of which flow into the Yellow Sea to the west (left on the map). Rivers are differentiated from bays or inlets by the presence of curving branches or forks. In many Korean regional maps, the mountains were drawn first and the rivers' paths wind at odd angles because they had to be fitted in between the mountains.

China influenced Korean mapmaking during the Choson era, but several Chinese map conventions were jettisoned. In Map 68, coastlines appear in overly broad wavy lines, as classically depicted in China (see Map 61). It follows the traditional Chinese style of indicating the names of settlements by using a red dot. However, Korean maps eliminated Chinese styles that were retained by other Asian societies to show water. Both Japanese and Thai maps of this same period retained Chinese semi-circular lines for oceans; Thai maps of this same era also employed Chinese rope-like lines for rivers (see Maps 66 and 69.) Korean maps instead use a single, simple blue color for rivers and oceans.

From 1910 to 1945 Korea was a Japanese colony (see Map 89), regaining its independence after the Second World War. Hangul is the national alphabet in both North and South Korea.

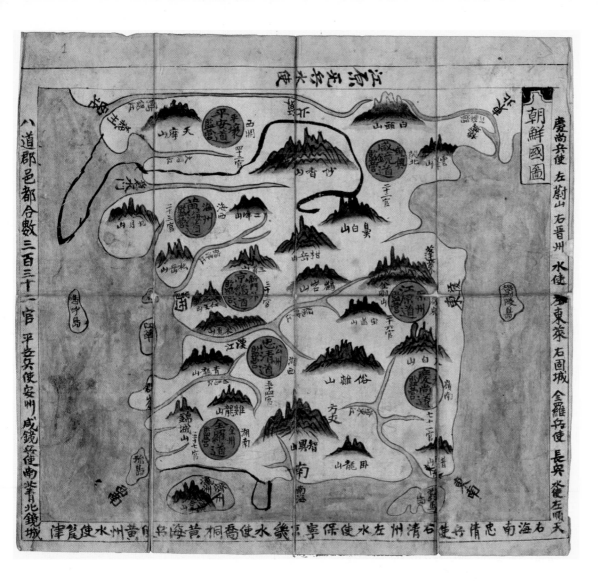

The names of the eight provinces in English (above) and Hanja (below).

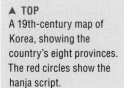

▲ TOP
A 19th-century map of Korea, showing the country's eight provinces. The red circles show the hanja script.

Transliteration of the stamp from Joella province, located at the bottom left of the map.

69

Japan: Gyoki Map on a Porcelain Plate, *c.* 1830

• ◆ •

Map of Japan, on a plate of Imari
ware, c. 1830–1843
Ceramic
30 × 33 cm
Library of Congress Geography and
Map Division Washington, D.C.

A new form of mapmaking began in Japan in the early fourteenth century. This new style of maps showed distinct regional boundaries within a complete outline of the country. Such maps appeared on a variety of materials, including popular porcelain plates such as the example shown at right. It would seem that such maps originated with secular political impulses; in fact, they were linked to annual religious rituals that exorcised evil spirits.

These maps are known as **Gyoki maps**, even though the influential Buddhist monk Gyoki (668–748) had nothing to do with their invention. Gyoki was, and still remains, the monk popularly associated with the widespread conversion of the country to Buddhism during the eighth century. But the maps and rituals associated with his name did not appear until more than seven hundred years after his death. Sometime in the early fourteenth century, Japanese began celebrating the annual end of the imperial court year with a festival called *Tsuina*. During the ceremony, evil spirits were driven from the kingdom and Gyoki's name was invoked. Interestingly, these rituals were performed at Shinto shrines; however, maps created for this event contained written praise for the Buddha, hence the association with the long-deceased monk.

Gyoki maps have two very distinct characteristics. First, they illustrate all the provinces with irregularly curved shapes. The irregular-shaped provinces contrast sharply with the regular, geometric semicircles that indicate the sea and that are modeled on Chinese motifs (see Map 61). Because Gyoki maps are associated with driving out evil spirits, boundaries between sea and land are important, a distinction reinforced by the contrasting use of color.

A second distinctive characteristic of Gyoki maps centers on their orientation. Most often, these maps exaggerate the shape of Japan in an east–west direction, with a slight upward curve on the eastern end of the country near Honshu island. But the angle of the maps is actually not that important. Among the earliest surviving Gyoki maps, two face east, two face west, another seven are oriented to the north and an equal number to the south.

As the Tsuina rituals spread among local Shinto shrines, the associated maps proved immensely popular. Gyoki maps were created for participants at the ritual casting out of evil spirits, and porcelain emerged as a popular and durable medium. Maps such as the one at the right were painted onto a white plate and outlined in a blue color, with the name of every province inscribed inside the country. Unless smashed or dropped, these maps could survive a long period of time without requiring upkeep or special handling.

The earliest Western maps of Japan (drawn in the mid-1400s) were based upon Gyoki maps. The Gyoki shape was used to depict Japan in European maps and atlases until 1600. Neither the large island of Hokkaido nor Okinawa appeared on these maps, since they did not become part of Japan until later in the nineteenth century.

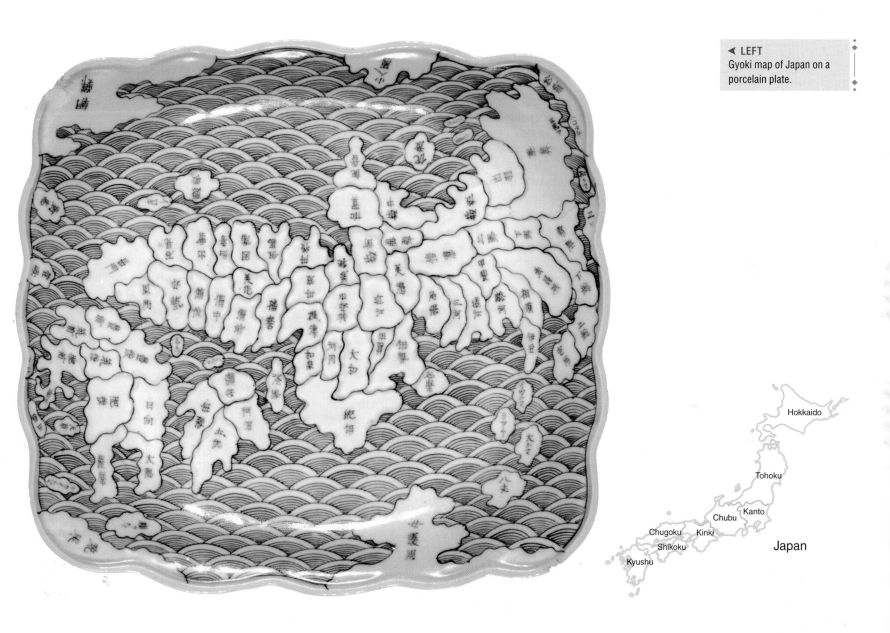

Hokkaido

Tohoku

Chubu

Kanto

Chugoku Kinki

Shikoku

Kyushu

Japan

155

70

Mongolian Land Survey, 1892

• ◆ •

Centre for Documentation and
Area-Transcultural Studies, Tokyo
University of Foreign Studies

Because they were a largely nomadic people, Mongolians tended not to draw maps. We do know that the famous thirteenth-century Mongol leader Genghis (Chinggis) Khan hired Chinese cartographers when he took up temporary residence in the Central Asian city of Samarkand. Unfortunately, none of these maps appear to have survived.

Although Mongols ruled China from 1271 to 1368, the situation was reversed during the eighteenth and nineteenth centuries when Mongolia was ruled by China (whose ruling dynasty, the Qing, was actually from Manchuria). The earliest surviving Mongolian maps appear to have originated with requests from officials in nearby China sent to quiz local princes about the nature of the terrain, the principal features of the landscape, and local boundaries. The degree and type of information supplied depended upon both the skill of the Chinese official and that of the local who wrote down the descriptions. The map on the right is the product of such a collaboration. It is a hybrid of Chinese and Mongolian elements, with Mongolian predominating.

Drawn in 1892, the map describes a central Mongolian "banner" (county) under the rule of "First Class Aristocrat" Jamiyan Khorloo. Place names are written in a highly distinctive Mongolian script called *bichig* (meaning "clear writing"), which was developed in 1648 CE. It is written from top to bottom and then from left to right. On the right-hand side of the map, from top to bottom, the year of the map's creation is inscribed in oversized letters. The red seal of the banner depicted on the map is inscribed in both Manchu (the official language of the Qing dynasty) and Mongolian.

The squares outlined in red employ a traditional Chinese pattern of representing area. But the apparent boundary, which is a straight red line, may be nothing of the sort. The long, often double, strings of bichig name the actual boundary points, which are marked by a red rectangle drawn at the top of the lines of script. Hence the actual border may weave in and out or up and down around the lengthy rows of Mongolian script perpendicular to the outside lines.

Each named rectangle stood for distinctive Mongolian cairn or stone piles called *ovoos* or *oboos* that marked the boundaries of the region. On the map, ovoos are distinguished by their color and shape. Mountains are colored brown, while ovoos are grey-blue. Ovoos often also have a tree branch at the top, often appearing schematically as a line with three smaller straight lines denoting smaller branches. In addition to marking borders, ovoos were religious sites used in traditional shamanistic worship of the mountains and the sky (hence the blue grey color—grey for the stones, blue for the sky). During summer sky-worshipping ceremonies, Mongolians place a tree branch or stick in the ovoo while tying it with a blue ceremonial silk scarf symbolic of the open sky and the sky spirit, Tengri. Traditionally, traveling wayfarers walked three times in a clockwise direction around the ovoo to ensure a safe journey. In modern times, this requirement has been modified by honking a car horn three times when passing by.

Other distinctive Mongolian features of the map are found in the drawings of the mountains. Mountain ranges seldom follow a straight line, but the Mongolian design places them as if they did. The hillsides and shapes of the mountains reflect the characteristic shapes of Mongolian script.

Some Mongolian maps from this period also depict Tibetan Buddhist temples (Buddhism was brought to Mongolia from Tibet in the seventeenth century). Many others show the traditional round Mongolian nomadic dwelling place made of felt. Called a *ger* in Mongolian, the structure is better known in the West as a *yurt*.

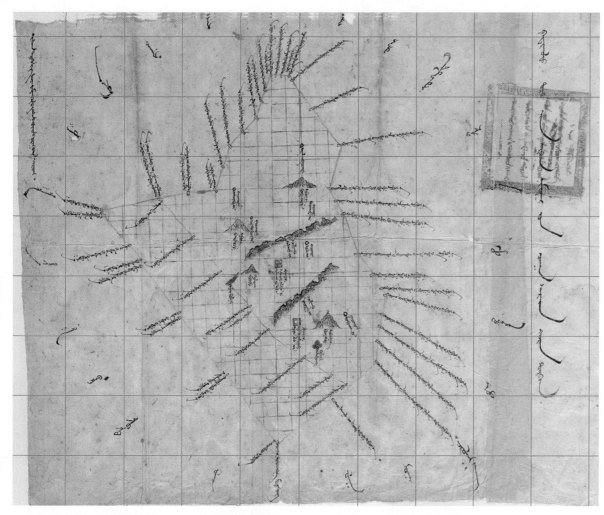

◄ TOP LEFT
1892 Mongolian map showing the eastern part of the current province (aimag) of Dundgovi (Dund Gobi) and the Iraha Uula Mountains. "Banner [county] of Jasak [first class aristocrat] Jamiyan [title of the living Buddha] Khorloo". *Jasak* is a political position, *Jamiyan* is the title given to a living Buddha, and *Khorloo* is the person's name. The vertical writing on the map is classic Mongolian script.

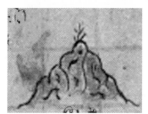

Detail showing a Mongolian ovoo

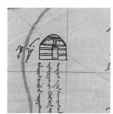

A Mongolian ger, or yurt, from from a 1913 map

A Tibetan temple from the same 1913 map

RUSSIA

KAZAKSTAN

Ulaanbaatar

MONGOLIA *Dundgovi*

CHINA

Part **7**

Mapping the Natural World, 1800–2010

Beginning in the eighteenth century, intense curiosity about the natural world accelerated. Questions about the islands of the vast, largely unexplored Pacific, the exact shape of the Earth, weather patterns, and the height of distant mountains intrigued government leaders, scientific communities, and adventurers.

This increased curiosity about the natural world led to heightened interest in the ways in which the inhabitants of many different parts of the world portrayed the environment around them. Since at least Roman times (see Map 18), travelers had gathered geographic information from the natives of the regions they visited. Yet, before the nineteenth and early twentieth centuries, they had shown little interest in the styles of mapping used by other cultures.

The nineteenth century, in contrast, marks a new respect for indigenous forms of knowledge and the belief that useful data often overlooked by mere visitors could be found on locally produced maps. One of the more spectacular examples of these was a driftwood map of a tiny set of islands on the edge of one of Greenland's major bays, drawn by a native Greenlander, Silas Sandgreen (see Map 78). The natural world began to be valued for itself as a separate field of study, instead of merely a means to achieving some other objective.

Other maps of the natural world created during this period served traditional political or commercial goals. The idea that maps could incorporate huge amounts of data began to be manifested in several major maps of the world's oceans, accumulating data from hundreds of voyages. Maps of the floor of the ocean were likewise the product of huge amounts of data collected over decades, and brilliantly assembled into a single map (see Map 82).

Confronted with a deluge of new information, mapmakers began to create markers that could be used to designate various natural phenomena. Since they were inundated with data from ever larger swaths of the world, the number and complexity of symbols on maps increased dramatically. For example, where earlier maps of the coastline only showed the location of small islands, sandbars, and rocks that posed a threat to navigation, the new coastline maps included information on the depth of the coastal shelf, shipwrecks that needed to be avoided, and deep versus shallow-draft ports.

To assist readers in understanding the greater and more diverse information increasingly recorded on maps, cartographers began to place a list of the symbols and signs alongside or inside the map, with annotations explaining what they stood for. These written explanations became so commonplace that a new word was devised: **legends**. Legends explained the colors, symbols, line patterns, shadings, and annotations used on maps. Eventually, the data represented in legends expanded to include the scale, origin, orientation, and other technical information about the map's composition.

71

Bali: Rivers and Temples, 1935

● ◆ ●

Koninklijk Instituut voor de Tropen
Batavia: Topografische dienst
Bali, 1935

The island of Bali, located in the Lesser Sunda Islands in the modern country of Indonesia, is the only province in Indonesia with a Hindu majority. Cascading down Balinese hillsides, brilliantly green rice paddies cover every inch of land. Alongside these fields run irrigation ditches that furnish the water for the plentiful fields of rice.

The source of the water lies upstream from the fields in a barrier that deflects nearby rivers into a maze of canals. Next to every such diversionary structure is a Hindu temple dedicated to the deity of the dam. The farmers whose lands are watered by a dam make up the congregation of the temple that adjoins the dam. They bring offerings to the temple to appease the god, but they also apportion maintenance tasks for the dams and canals and establish how and where the waters will flow in a manner not that dissimilar to the functions performed by water control boards in the Netherlands (see Map 63).

However, unlike most areas of the world where water rights are under the control of either private landowners or public officials, in Bali members of a Hindu temple are in charge. Water is sacred. Temple control rests upon the belief that the waters flowing through the fields contain the water goddess Dewi Danu, whose movement through the channels purifies the land and brings sustenance to the crops.

Hindu temples began to control water rights on the island of Bali around 900 CE, not long after similar water temples appeared on both the neighboring island of Java and the Southeast Asian mainland. The magnificent buildings of Angkor Wat in what is now Cambodia were Hindu water temples that sustained the Khmer kingdom for over 500 years (834–1431 CE). But only in Bali have these water temples continued to flourish, despite efforts by outsiders to alter the system.

Unlike Java and Angkor Wat, which experienced invasions and conquests, Bali remained relatively undisturbed for several centuries as encroachers from Asia and Europe bypassed the island in favor of places with better harbors and more lucrative agricultural products. Bali was not invaded by an outside force until the middle of the nineteenth century. The Dutch conquered the island in two stages, first conquering princely kingdoms in the north part of Bali, around 1849, followed by the conquest of the southern kingdoms in 1906. Coming from a society whose terrain was created by pumping water out from fields that lie below sea level, the Dutch were uniquely qualified to understand the significance of control over water.

The Dutch sought to wrest control of irrigation from the temples with the aim of organizing the water management system so that they could more readily control and tax its production. But in order to implement their own arrangements they first needed to document the existing system. Since local inhabitants were the best source of information, Dutch mappers quizzed them about place names and usually placed native names rather than Dutch ones on their maps.

Local input went beyond the toponyms. When Dutch cartographers began producing detailed topographic maps after 1904, they involved members of the local community in precisely measuring the heights of hillsides and mountains as well as in drafting maps. As a result, Dutch maps of Bali were grounded in native names, measurements, and sketches, but were translated into the increasingly international design standards for topography. Thus Dutch mapmakers, in collaboration with native informants, crafted a valuable series of maps documenting the island's water temple networks for the first time. While Dutch efforts to transform the Balinese water system ultimately failed, they did create a valuable historical record of the locations of the central water temples on the island.

BALI

◄ LEFT
The island of Bali. Many of the most important water temples are clustered along the sides of volcanoes, where rain collects during the rainy season.

Detail showing a volcano, with temples regulating irrigation water marked as red dots.

Closeup showing the islands of Java and Bali.

Southeast Asia, with the island of Bali colored in blue.

161

72

The Great
Trigonometric Survey
of India, 1802–1866

• ◆ •

Index Chart to the Great
Trigonometrical Survey
of India, 1885
Royal Geographic Society, London

1858 map to illustrate Col A.S.
Waugh's paper
on Mt. Everest & Deodanga
Royal Geographic Society, London

In 1802, a British army officer began a survey to establish the precise dimensions of the Indian subcontinent. While scientifically accurate survey methods had already been established and used in Great Britain (see Map 65), the subcontinent presented challenges unlike any that surveyors had previously faced. Only six countries in the world today are larger than India (Australia, Brazil, China, the United States, Canada, and Russia) and when the survey began in 1802, four of those countries were barely settled and neither China nor Russia had been surveyed. The area confronting the British surveyors measured 14 times the size of Great Britain, which required assembling a huge team and building a measuring device large enough for the task. The final challenge was the extreme variations in height, which ranged from sea level near the coast to the highest mountains in the world, the Himalayas.

The surveyors need to establish a baseline from which to measure, and under the direction of Sir George Everest (1790–1866), who headed the survey from 1830–1843, the team of surveyors established a baseline extending from central India north to Nepal, a distance of approximately 2,400 kilometers (1,491 miles).

The survey started with a baseline of two points, usually 7 miles apart. The surveying instrument, known as a **theodolite**, was a giant telescope mounted on a pivoting table. Weighing nearly 1,100 lbs. (500 kg), it required 12 men just to move it. The theodolite measured the angle between the ends of the baseline and a third point. Knowing both angles allowed calculation of the length of the other side of the triangle. That triangle formed the basis for calculating the next triangle, and so on, which resulted in the map at right.

When Everest retired, his successor undertook the survey's final challenge; namely, establishing the

elevation of the world's highest mountain chain. The most difficult work involved the numerous calculations of spherical trigonometry. Since the beginning of Everest's tenure, the most gifted mathematician working for the survey was a Bengali named Radhanath Sikdar. In 1852, Sikdar announced that his calculations had established that the mountain that was then called simply "Peak XV" was the highest in the world. Either due to caution or a reluctance to acknowledge Sikdar's achievement, survey head Colonel Andrew Waugh waited for four years before announcing that Peak XV was the highest in the world, at a then-recorded 29,002 feet (8,840 meters), and naming it for Sir George Everest, his predecessor as head of the survey. In subsequent years a more precise measurement of Everest has recorded its elevation at 29,035 feet (8,850 meters).

However, the survey of the Himalayas was incomplete without taking measurements from the northern side of the mountain chain. The British, though, were banned by the Chinese from entering Tibet. To verify the height of Himalayan peaks from the Tibetan side and establish the level of the plateau (the highest in the world), the British sent Indians as secret surveyors, in the guise of traders, to scientifically survey the Tibetan side. These disguised scientific emissaries of the Great Trigonometric Survey were called *pundits*, a Hindi word meaning "man of learning." From this origin, the word entered modern English. The most famous of these pundits, a Sikh schoolteacher named Nain Singh who masqueraded as a horse trader, entered Tibet in 1866 after a 1,200-mile journey from Kathmandu, Nepal. Singh became the first to correctly establish the latitude and longitude of Lhasa, Tibet's capital, as well as the height of the Tibetan plateau.

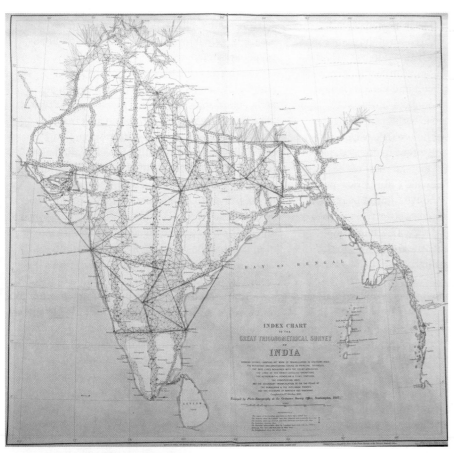

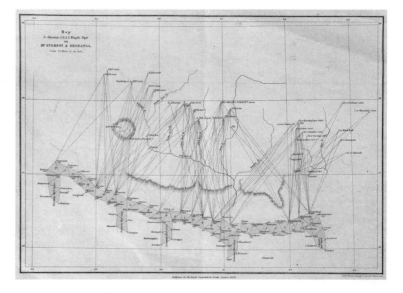

Mt. Everest, the highest mountain in the world.

◄ **LEFT**
Outline for the great trigonometric survey of India, showing how measurement was built by measuring triangles.

▼ **BOTTOM**
Trigonometric survey drawing for the height of Mount Everest and surrounding peaks in the Himalayas, a vast mountain range that stretches approximately 1,500 miles (2,414 kilometers).

73

Alexander von Humboldt's Map of Plants on Chimborazo, 1803

• ◆ •

Geography of Plants in Tropical Countries, A Study of the Andes
Drawn by Schoenberger & Turpin
Printed by Langlois, Paris
Baron von Friedrich Alexander Humboldt
(1769–1859)
Colour lithograph, 53.5 × 83 cms
Humboldt-Universitaet,
Berlin, Germany

[handwritten margin notes: map of plants; intensity note; Conditions as they go up; what plants there are]

164

German explorer Alexander von Humboldt (1769–1859) created this map of the plants growing on what was then believed to be the highest peak in the world, Chimborazo, in South America's Andes Mountains. Humboldt and his companion, French physician Aimé Bonpland (1773–1858), climbed to what was then a world record height of 19,286 feet (5,878 meters) before they became ill with altitude sickness and were forced to descend, just over a thousand feet (390 meters) short of the peak.

By today's measurements, Chimborazo in today's Ecuador is only the 17th highest peak in the world. However, it still holds a special claim to height. In this equatorial region of the world, the Earth bulges out from the center and so this mountain, the country's highest, may in fact be the highest point on the surface of the planet.

Humboldt understood that vegetation gradually changes the further one ascends a mountain. But he wanted to show how a different and wider range of vegetation characterized mountains in the tropics. Chimborazo lies practically upon the equator, at 1.5 degrees south.

On the right and left sides of Humboldt's map, the first column carefully establishes the height of the mountain in meters. Next to the meter columns are a series of other columns containing data on humidity and air pressure (on the left) and temperature and the height of the sun (on the right). To the right of the brilliantly colored mountain is a diagram that provides information about plant life on the mountain. The names of individual plants are written out as if aligned on a ruler, while the names of the categories appear in a larger italic font, often in an arc shape.

The drawing of vegetation on the left side of the mountain shows five zones of vegetation, beginning on the bottom with tropical palm trees, giving way to a greener band, followed by a partially snow-covered area, a largely snow-blanketed region, and finally perpetual snow.

In the text that accompanies the map, Humboldt groups the plants into 15 categories: herbs, palm trees, tree ferns, marshy plants, firs, dianthus, flowering plants and shrubs from the legume and caltrop families, flowering plants of the mallow family (including hibiscus and balsa), various climbing woody and tropical vines, orchids, cactuses, evergreen shrubs and trees, grasses, mosses, and finally lichens. While these categories are not those of a modern botanist, Humboldt was among the first to investigate the role of geography in impacting the interaction between plants and their environment, laying the foundations for modern biogeography, ecology, and ethology.

Humboldt decided to represent the information he gathered in Ecuador as a nature painting, and so he described the mountain and provided his data to two artists, Lorenz Schoenberger and Pierre Turpin, who had never seen it. Perhaps influenced by the knowledge that Chimborazo was an extinct volcano, the artists drew the mountain in a cone shape that they associated with volcanoes.

Two engravers then engraved the map using a new, relatively inexpensive color printing technique called **lithography**. Invented in 1796 in Bavaria, lithography drew an image in wax or other oily substance applied to a stone. Color adhered to the oil, which then transferred ink to the printed sheet.

During the four years he spent gathering information on the natural environment in Mexico, Cuba, and South America, Humboldt earned the affection of the people he met. As a result, he has remained better known and more popular in Latin America than in Germany.

GÉOGRAPHIE DES PLANTES ÉQUINOXIALES.

The coat of arms of Ecuador, showing Mount Chimborazo.

Venezuela
Colombia
Ecuador
Peru
Brazil
Bolivia
Paraguay
Uruguay
Chile
Argentina
Chile

74

Geological Map of Southwestern England, 1815

• ◆ •

Geological Map of Southwestern
England, 1815
William Smith, A Delineation of the
Strata of England and Wales with Part of
Scotland, London, 1815, sheet 11
Library of Congress, Vault

In the eighteenth century, European scientists became interested in how the Earth's surface had formed. After an earthquake destroyed Lisbon in 1755, interest grew in the dynamic nature of the earth's crust, particularly its quakes and volcanoes. This new study of rocks led to the creation of a new field of research: geology. In 1815, William Smith (1769–1839) portrayed his native Britain in the brightly colored map at right, the first ever geological map of an entire country.

Geologists soon discovered that they could discern certain types of rock layers that contained precious metals, such as gold and silver, in which more practical metals such as iron and coal were embedded. While gold and silver were far more glamorous minerals, coal and iron actually aroused greater interest, particularly in Western Europe where the science of geology originated. Beginning in the late eighteenth century, Western Europe underwent an Industrial Revolution, much of it fueled by coal and iron. The development of geology as a field meant that determining where to mine for coal and iron could be carried out scientifically. Geologists could pinpoint the location of previously undiscovered deposits of minerals that could be tapped and brought to the surface. Furthermore, geologists could also help planners make predictions as to which regions would be likely to furnish future quantities of iron, coal, and later, petroleum.

Smith's research originated with the search for coal. Coal lay buried beneath the ground but not in evenly shaped layers. Massive deposits could be found in great folds at subterranean depths, twisting and turning in seemingly unpredictable directions. In order for mine owners to exploit new coal fields, they needed to know where the formations were located. They also needed new modes of transport to bring coal to regions where it was needed.

Smith began his career as a surveyor of canals that transported coal to market. While working for the Somerset Coal Company, Smith lowered himself into the mines where he noticed different types of rocks spread across oddly tilted, separated layers. A layer of gently downward sloping red marl would suddenly give way to gray sandstone that plunged steeply but also appeared folded and shattered in places. The presence of these layers, and their odd comportment, raised questions in Smith's mind about the natural forces that led to the creation of such rock strata. Miners sought after the coal seams that were embedded between layers of different rock. In mine after mine, Smith discovered the same pattern: sandstone, siltstone, mudstone, non-marine band, marine band, coal—after which the entire pattern would repeat, beginning again with sand-stone. When the coal company sent him to survey canals in other parts of England, Smith had the opportunity to broaden his observations.

In 1799, Smith devised a way to definitively categorize one layer from one another by the types of different fossils found in each layer. Every layer of rock had a distinct collection of fossils that differed from those above or below it. He called this discovery the principle of *faunal succession*—the ability to identify separate layers of rock by the distinctive fossils found within them. While geologists today use radiocarbon dating to identify the age of rocks, many still rely on Smith's principle, which is now known as *fossil succession*.

This discovery laid the groundwork for other discoveries. Shifting focus from the age of rocks to that of the fossils embedded in them, a young Charles Darwin (1809–1882) puzzled over the changes across geological time. In 1859, after decades of research, he published *On the Origin of Species*. The world would never be the same.

75

1851 Whale Chart

• ◆ •

Whale Chart, 1851
Color lithograph
Matthew F. Maury
Washington, D.C., Naval Observatory

At first glance, this American whale chart seems to simply show where the great sea mammals tended to be found in the ocean. Many whales today are endangered, including most of the ones listed on this map. But during the eighteenth, nineteenth, and early twentieth centuries, maps like this one marked killing fields. Whales were hunted for their blubber, which was used for lamps and candles, and their bones, which were turned into umbrella ribs, corsets, and fishing rods. Even the discovery of kerosene in 1846 did not slow down the slaughter of whales. Whale oil continued to be used for decades in the manufacture of pencils and crayons, leather weatherproofing, rust-proofing materials, and as a lubricant for marine chronometers.

Whaling was an important part of the economy for coastal communities in England and the United States during the eighteenth and nineteenth centuries. In his 1851 classic, *Moby Dick*, published the same year as this map, Herman Melville describes the effect of whaling upon one small Massachusetts town: ". . . nowhere in all America will you find more patrician-like houses; parks and gardens more opulent, than in New Bedford. Whence came they? . . . Go and gaze upon the iron emblematic harpoons round yonder lofty mansion, and your question will be answered. Yes; all these brace houses and flowery gardens came from the Atlantic, Pacific, and Indian oceans. One and all, they were harpooned and dragged up hither from the bottom of the sea."

Because they showed the location of the most productive fishing grounds, for most of the nineteenth century maps such as the whale chart at right were closely guarded by merchants and pilots of whaling ships. This map, and Map 76, resulted from research conducted by the first Superintendent of the Navy, Matthew Fontaine Maury (1806–1873), who reviewed the logbooks that had been deposited at the Naval Observatory in Washington, D.C.

Up until 1870, the most frequently hunted whales belonged to the baleen group. These whales filter food through hanging curtains of fingernail-like keratin in their mouths. Among baleen whales, two were nicknamed *right whales* because they were the "right" ones to harpoon. Slow swimmers, they had large amounts of blubber and floated when killed. Since the cutting out of the blubber was done at sea, the task was easier when the carcass floated. These "right whales" are mostly found on the map within the swath of green that surrounds New Zealand; they are indicated by a whale symbol that has two spouts of water coming out its blowhole. If a square shows two whales it denotes particularly rich and active grounds.

In the mid-latitudes and tropics, the most sought after whales were the so-called *sperm whales*, which have teeth rather than filters. They dive deep into the oceans to catch giant squid. Their name comes from the enormous liquid wax–containing organ in their heads that was mistakenly thought to be sperm. A substance in their intestines used to digest squid is called *ambergris,* or grey amber, and is still used to extend the life of the most expensive perfumes. The fictional whale sought by Captain Ahab in *Moby Dick* was a sperm whale. On the map, sperm whales are found mostly inside the pink swath and are indicated by a whale symbol with a single spout coming out of its blowhole.

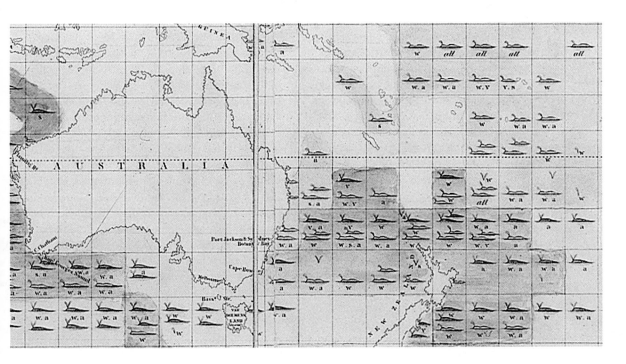

◀ **LEFT**
American whale chart, 1851. The section shown here was one of the most productive whaling grounds— the South Pacific.

▼ **BOTTOM**
Detail from the logbook of master sailor John D. Sampson, kept on board the whaling ship *Charles W. Morgan* during 1845–1848. Each whale stamp indicates a sighting at sea.

Detail showing whale sightings. The letters indicate the best fishing season: "w" for winter; "a" for autumn; "v" for spring; "s" for summer; and "all" for year-round.

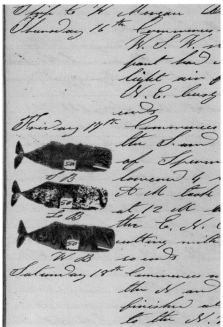

169

76

Monsoon and Trade Wind Chart of the Indian Ocean, 1859

• ◆ •

Monsoon and Trade Wind Chart of
the Indian Ocean, 1859
Color lithograph
Matthew F. Maury.
Washington, D.C., Naval Observatory

[handwritten note: followed winds to go to and from]

For millennia, sailors knew that winds and currents between the Horn of Africa and the west coast of India reversed themselves on a seasonal basis. While such regular and predictable changes in wind direction also occur in other places, such as the Caribbean, the Philippines, and West Africa, this particular seasonal shift has special significance because it is located along a major trade route that links northeast Africa, the Middle East, and India.

The advantage for merchants and travelers who operated in this trading zone was clear. Instead of being forced to cautiously follow the coast along the southern part of the Arabian Peninsula, paying fees at every port, merchants could follow a shorter and faster route that went direct from northeast Africa to India. Winds and currents moved toward India from northeast Africa and Arabia during the summer months of June, July, and August. During November, December, and January, winds and currents reversed and merchants could return following the same direct route in the opposite direction. In 1859, as steamboats were becoming more widespread, ships could still use these weather patterns for more efficient journeys.

Because this weather pattern was first intensely exploited toward the end of the first millennium CE, when Arabs dominated the trade between East Africa and India (see Map 26), the phenomenon became known by the Arabic word for season, *mawsim*, which became *monção* in Portuguese and in English was rendered as *monsoon*. For hundreds of years, sailors would gather information about the seasonal ("monsoon") changes and share this information with other pilots, usually through oral transmission and often in verse. Not until the middle of the nineteenth century would this information be collated in a systematic fashion and precise data on the best times and places to sail be made available.

In 1842, Matthew Fontaine Maury became the first superintendent of the United States Naval Observatory (see Map 75). His principal responsibility was to maintain the U.S. Navy's charts, timepieces, and other navigational equipment. In the course of his duties, Maury discovered a vast storage area containing thousands of old ships' logs and charts dating back to the founding of the Navy in 1775. Recognizing that these logbooks contained a treasure trove of information about winds and currents from all over the world, Maury and his staff of fourteen pored over these documents and grouped the information according to the ocean and time of year. His "Monsoon and Trade Wind Chart of the Indian Ocean" (at right) was based upon 16,914 separate observations. By synthesizing this extraordinary quantity of information cartographically, he showed U.S. sailors how to use the ocean's currents and winds to their advantage.

Since Maury aimed to improve the safety and efficiency of sea travel regardless of the season, his chart of the monsoon winds contains four separate maps. The two larger maps shown on the right cover the identical geographical area, but the map at bottom left is labeled "Winds in January," while the identical one on the right hand side is labeled "Winds in August." The January map shows northward-moving currents; the August map shows the same currents flowing south. Above these two charts are two equally important drawings that show zones where the ocean is always calm—areas that would stall or slow ships trying to make progress across the Arabian Sea and Indian Ocean.

By making this map available to pilots, Maury greatly improved the speed and reliability of shipping in the Indian Ocean basin. He performed no first-hand research himself, but showed great originality in synthesizing masses of data.

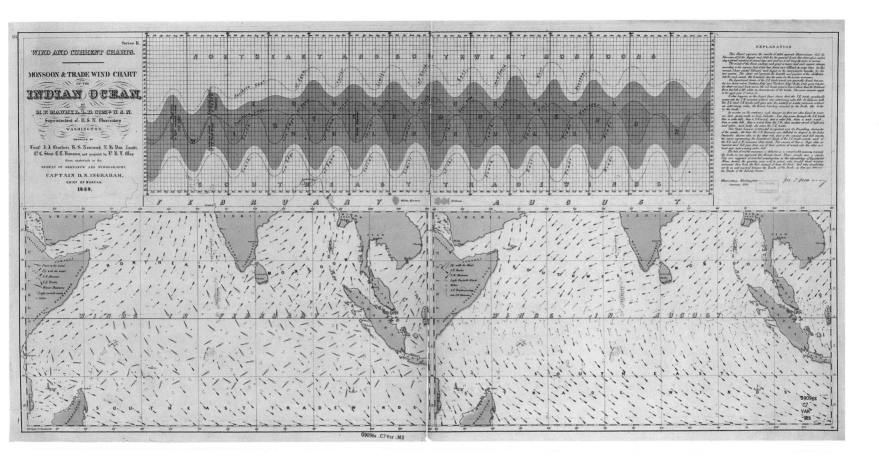

77

Marshall Islands Stick Map, 1870s

• • •

Stabkarte (Stick Chart), 1870s
Marshall Islands
© bpk / Ethnologisches Museum,
SMB, Berlin

Before setting out on journeys that would often cover over a thousand miles and last several weeks, navigators of the vast central Pacific memorized the positions of stars and the direction of far-off islands. As far as anyone knows, they carried these maps only in their heads. In 1769 when Captain Cook asked Tupaia, a local navigator he met in Tahiti, to locate Polynesian islands on a map, Tupaia astonished Cook by depicting islands spread across an area bigger than the continental United States. This was a knowledge he carried in his head without benefit of a map or guide (see Map 53).

Southeast of the Philippines are a group of islands called *Micronesia* (so named because of the many tiny-sized islands). Like other Pacific voyagers, Micronesians relied upon their memories for the location of stars and direction of islands. Yet, because they found the local equatorial currents both unpredictable and constantly shifting, Micronesians developed another unique form of mapping. In the late nineteenth century, German visitors discovered that inhabitants of the Marshall Islands, a small chain of islands in Micronesia, lashed sticks together to create maps to teach young sailors. These unique maps were based upon the exceptional characteristic of the Pacific, namely the pattern of swells that spread across the ocean.

Generated by storms off Antarctica, swells are giant waves that move north across all of the world's oceans. In the Atlantic, however, their path leads them toward the west coast of Africa, where they are blocked by the continent's massive width. In the Indian Ocean a similar path pushes the swells toward western Australia and north, where they are blocked by the large islands of western Indonesia. However, in the Pacific the swells encounter no large landmasses, only relatively small islands. As a result, swells cross the Pacific unimpeded as they move toward Hawaii and the western coast of the United States. These swells create giant waves,

making possible the sport of surfing first witnessed by members of Captain James Cook's expedition along the coast of Hawaii in 1778.

When the swells encounter the underwater shelf off the smaller islands of Polynesia and Micronesia, they slow down and are deflected back into the ocean. The different size of each island means that swells throughout the Marshalls ripple out to different distances, and larger islands reflect swells over a larger part of the ocean. Since these patterns can be detected ten, fifteen, and sometimes twenty nautical miles away, a navigator knowing the pattern of the swells around particular islands can identify an island from far off and determine whether he is traveling away from the island or toward it. The three outwardly curving coconut fronds on the **stick map** on the right represent the shape of the swells as they ripple back from an island on both sides. Marshall Islanders called these general maps for teaching about swells *mattang*.

Throughout the Marshall Islands, islands lie at different angles to each other; the swells coming from one island intersect with the swells coming from another island. When a navigator senses the motion of swells coming at him from an angle instead of straight ahead, he knows that he is near another island. This relationship between different swells forms the basis of two other types of stick charts called *meddo* and *rebbelib*. Meddo charts show the angle at which the swells intersect for a small group of islands. The map here, a rebbelib, shows the intersection of the swells from major islands throughout most of the chain. Along the top stick are three of the Marshall islands of Ujae, Wotho, and Bikini, each lying at the tip of a triangle. Bikini, at the top of the chart, lies at the intersection of two very large swells. It is to be remembered that stick charts, however, were used strictly for teaching purposes. The meddo might be used first to teach a young pilot to sail around a smaller group of islands, while the rebbelib would be reserved for the more skilled and experienced pilot who could navigate the entire chain. Once at sea, the navigator had to rely on memory, because the stick charts were left back at home to teach the next generation of Micronesian navigators.

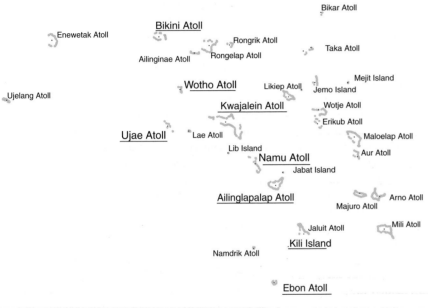

Map of the Marshall Islands. Islands and atolls that are underlined correspond to places indicated on the stick chart.

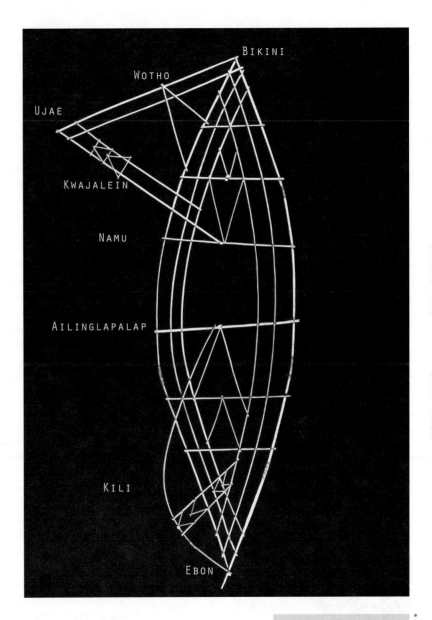

▲ ABOVE
Marshall Islands stick map.

78

Crown Prince Islands in Disko Bay, Greenland, 1926

• ◆ •

Map of the Crown Prince Islands,
Disko Bay, Greenland, 1926
Wood, mounted on sealskin base
89 × 61 × 4 cm.
Silas Sandgreen
Library of Congress Geography and
Map Division Washington, D.C.

1996
Egedesminde-Godhavn
Grønlands Vestkyst
Kort & Matrikelstyrelsen, Denmark
Ilulissat, Greenland, photograph
by author

Greenland, the world's largest island at over two million square kilometers (over 800,00 square miles), is almost entirely covered by giant glaciers. The only ice-free parts of the island are in coastal areas during the summer months. The natives of Greenland, the Inuit, live along the coast, where they grow crops during the brief summer season and hunt for food offshore. Naturally, the maps they draw focus upon the coastline.

Europeans first began to inquire about Inuit maps during the nineteenth century, when whaling ships and explorers probed Greenland's many bays and fjords. When they asked about mapping, Europeans received astonishingly detailed responses from the Inuit. Mapping was a widespread skill. In 1935, a Danish visitor to Ammassalik, on the eastern coast of Greenland, asked the town's young people to draw a map of the area. He received 157 drawings of the region, some from children as young as four years old, reflecting the fact that the children were taught to map from their earliest years. Adults, who drew maps only upon special request, sketched them with a speed that astonished outsiders. Inuit adults could map coastal regions in immense detail, using any material they had on hand—pen and paper, but also virtually any material including wood and, in the example at right, sealskin.

In 1926 a group of visiting Europeans and Americans asked an Inuit named Silas Sandgreen to draw a map of a small group of islands at the outer edge of Disko Bay, near the northernmost point along the coast that was habitable. Sandgreen picked up a piece of driftwood and proceeded to astonish the visitors with the speed and accuracy with which he selected the shapes to represent the islands and arrange them on the sealskin. Sandgreen then painted the driftwood to show how the islands—some just rocks—appeared when viewed from out in the waters of this large bay. The result is the map at right.

To understand why the Inuit placed such a premium on visualizing and memorizing the coastline, one needs to consider the unique features of Greenland's geography. The island consists of bedrock, gradually exposed as glaciers retreat and the ice cap melts, a process ongoing for millennia. The coastline is littered with rocks. The island's climate further complicates travel. Fog often blankets the coast during the morning hours, making it imperative for any traveler to have a visual image of exactly where the rocks lie scattered across the waters. Additionally, shards of ice ranging from a few inches to many feet often coat the surface of Disko Bay. Under these conditions, boats continually push against a hard, lumpy surface. Knowing the location of rocks determines different resulting sounds: the satisfying sharp snap of cracking ice filling the air or the muffled grinding of a boat scraping against rock.

In Disko Bay, knowledge of the precise location of rocks and islands matters for yet another reason, namely the presence of icebergs. A giant glacier on the edge of Disko Bay produces more icebergs than anywhere else in the Arctic. Gargantuan icebergs weighing over seven million tons regularly fall into Disko Bay, sometimes gliding smoothly into the water and at other times crashing and suddenly generating unsurvivable thirty-foot high swells. The *Titanic* is believed to have been sunk by ice from this glacier. The giant arched berg at right, photographed in Disko Bay, captures the immense size and spectacular varied shapes of icebergs off Greenland's coast.

◄ LEFT
Map of the Crown Prince
Islands of Disko Bay,
Greenland, created by
Silas Sandgreen, an Inuit,
in 1926.

Modern nautical map of the
Crown Prince Islands.

Iceberg in Disko Bay, Greenland, 2012.

79

Luba Mapping Device, Congo, 1930s

• • •

Luba mapping device, 1930s or 1940s
Carved wooden board decorated
with shells and beads
Democratic Republic of Congo
Courtesy Thomas Q. Reefe via Mary
Nooter Roberts

Mapping devices such as the one shown here have been used in the Congo since at least the nineteenth century. The example at right was created by the Luba Katanga, who number around 1.5 million and reside in the country's southeastern region, between the Lomani and Lualaba rivers.

Typically, the object consists of a carved hand-sized wooden board. Sometimes the panel consists simply of a rectangle, while other times the tablet might also possess both a carved head and a tail, symbolizing an animal such as a tortoise. As in the example at right, often the boards are decorated with beads, shells, bits of metal, and large cowry shells arranged in a row at the top and bottom.

The Luba-Katanga employ these boards to recount histories of past rulers, to retell their creation story, and to reaffirm principles of leadership. When and if geographic information emerges, it usually appears intertwined with information about other aspects of Luba society. The boards are created for and remain the property of the highest ranking local political organization, called the *Mbudye*.

The Mbudye is composed of members who, after they have been initiated, become the guardians of history and enforcers of good government with the power to remove a leader who abuses his power. The organization ensures the just exercise of political power, the preservation and transmission of history, and the sacred prohibitions of Luba royal culture.

After induction into this group, both male and female members are introduced to these carved and decorated wooden memory devices and are taught the meaning of the basic symbols and arrangements of carvings, beads, and shells. The boards, called *lukasas*, are often translated in English as **memory boards** because they are ritually used by Mbudye members to recount the history or political structure of the community. In this sense, they are less strictly cartographic devices than a means to stimulate

an oral account of places, histories, and practices. Lukasas contain a system of codified patterns, colors, and motifs that can be interpreted in many ways.

The geographic information appearing on the device at right refers to three political pillars of Luba society: the chief or king, the Mbudye, and the diviners who consult the guardian spirits.

The top half of the map depicts spaces connected to the chief, while the bottom half shows spaces belonging to Mbudye members and diviners. In between, a series of raised circles reminds interpreters of important proverbs that members of the Mbudye must memorize. In this way, cues for spoken words appear intertwined with geographical information.

The cowry shell placed in the middle of the top row of shells indicates the place where the chief is invested. Just below, a large blue button indicates the first royal court . The color is significant because in Luba history blue is associated with the arrival of the hero who rescued the community from tyranny. The shell in the upper left shows a location of historical significance, the spirit headquarters of the father of the first Luba king. On the top right of the board, another cowry shell shows the location of three important female spirit mediums. Paths between places appear as horizontal rows of small white beads.

Along the bottom, the cowry shell in the lower left corner represents the head of the Mbudye. To its right, a smaller bead indicates the association's secret meeting place. The central cowry shell in the bottom row locates the spirit capital of the Mbudye association, while the cowry shell on the bottom right indicates a similar place for the royal diviners, as well as the lakes into which they sometimes submerge themselves. The memory board thus maps the complex geography of power in a Luba community.

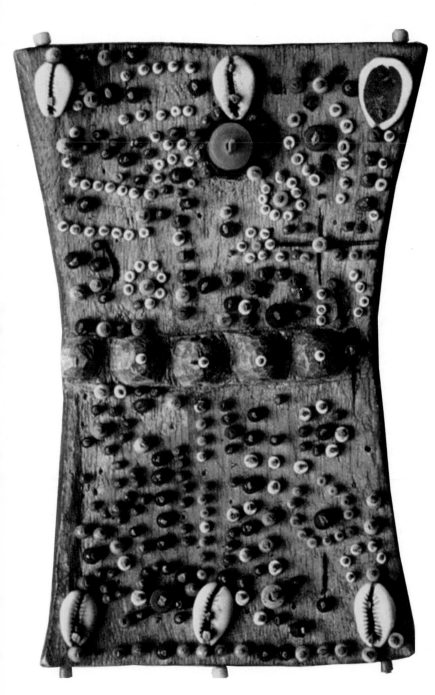

Congo River

Lomami River

Lualaba (Congo) River

★Makwidi

Democratic Republic of the Congo

Map of Africa showing the Democratic Republic of Congo and the Congo River Basin.

80

The Modern Zodiac,

1933

* ◆ *

Drawing by Tsvetelina Zdraveva
based on depictions from the
International Astronomical Union

In the early 1930s, the international organization of astronomers (International Astronomical Union) realized they had a problem. One of the founding principles of the Union, which was established in 1919, was to put astronomers from many different countries into regular contact with each other. Yet discussions quickly broke down when astronomers realized that they were referring to different stars. The source of the difficulty was the millennia-old problem of defining the sky by constellations. When referring to particular stars, many twentieth-century astronomers followed the custom first introduced by Johann Bayer (1572–1625) in 1603, in which the constellation was first named and then the stars within that constellation were designated by Greek letters. The problem was that astronomers were working with different definitions of the boundaries of constellations.

Once they identified the unnecessary confusion generated by these disparities, astronomers realized that they needed to create a single uniform system. In 1933, they divided the sky into 88 different constellations, fixing their boundaries with straight vertical and horizontal lines according to precisely defined mathematical coordinates. Drawings were then produced that showed the geometric pattern of these constellations.

The sky map at right shows the official boundaries of all the signs of the zodiac, as defined by the International Astronomical Union.

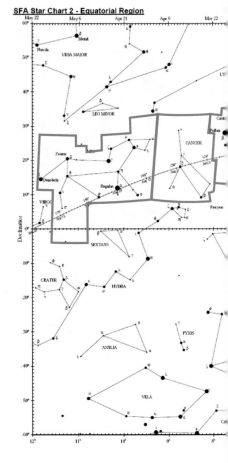

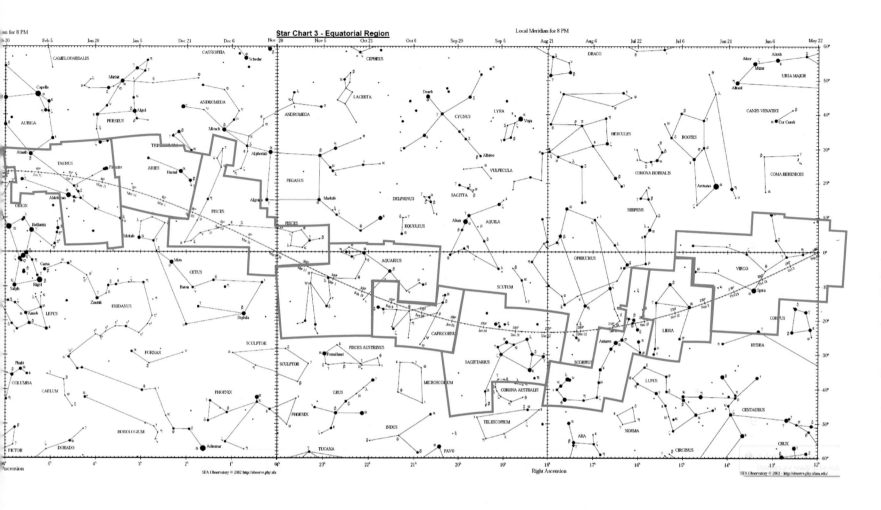

▲ TOP
Sky map showing constellations of the zodiac, as defined by the International Astronomers Union in 1933.

81

Maps into Art:
Aboriginal Map, 1987

• ◆ •

Water Holes at Jila Hapingka and
Pajpara with Parallel Sand Hills, 1987
Peter Skipper (Pijaju)
Arts Rights Agency

One of the few exceptions to the rule that only settled peoples produce maps comes from Australia, where nomadic aborigines drew maps on sand or bark during rituals and then swept over or burned the maps before moving on.

In the 1970s a European artist, Geoffrey Barton, introduced acrylic paints to a small, nearly extinct community living in the central part of the Northern Territory (Papunya). He asked them to preserve on canvas their tradition of dot-based painting. What began as a small exercise in cultural preservation soon spread throughout Australia as dozens of other indigenous communities recognized the utility of acrylic paintings in passing down traditional knowledge of the natural world. Today this experiment has become a major international art movement, with aboriginal acrylic paintings now hanging in major museums around the world.

While the aboriginal people of Australia speak 145 different languages and identify with different clans and tribal groups, they share a common approach to nature rooted in "the Dreaming." During the Dreaming, ancestral beings (usually half-human, half-animal) wandered over the country creating all the features on the landscape. Natural objects, such as hills, lakes, and trees, are considered marks of the ancestors' activities. Because passage along hills and water holes can also be associated with certain songs, the tracks of these ancestral beings are sometimes called "songlines."

All of these places visually represent important locations along nomadic paths—rock formations, waterfalls, and migratory patterns of the animals the aborigines pursued for food. Male members of each tribe were instructed in drawing these ephemeral maps, and the drawings were handed down over generations. As a result, many maps remained secret and could only be shown to initiated men. However, the Dreaming is further complicated by aboriginal beliefs about the time of the dreaming. The dreaming simultaneously represents both an ancestral past time and the present. Because aboriginal groups maintain that humans exist eternally, geographic and celestial representations are often thought to contain images of the dead who exist in the present through the Dreaming. Since these images of the deceased are potentially harmful, Australian law requires warnings and copyright restrictions for aboriginal paintings, especially of the sky and waters. But don't worry: The map at right can be shared with the uninitiated and is not known to contain representations of the dead.

The map depicts a typical landscape in the Kimberley region of northwestern Australia. It shows a large area of sandhills depicted as ladder-like green lines covering most of the canvas. Additional sandhills appear as two large semicircular lines on the right-hand side of the map. Also in the right-hand third of the painting are short arcs depicting clouds. Since the seasons in Australia alternate between a dry and rainy season ("the wet"), clouds are harbingers of rain. At the center of the clouds are four interconnected bulbs, each of which represents rain coming from different directions. The top bulb represents rains coming from the north, the right bulb rains from the east, the bottom rains from the south, and on the left, rains from the west. Thus the map represents both space and an event (the coming of the rains).

Since seasonal rains produce waterholes, the central circle joining the four bulbs is called *Japingka*, which is both a generic aboriginal word for water and a place in the Great Sandy Desert of Western Australia. The map was created by Peter Skipper (Pijaju) (1929–2007), a Wangkajunga speaker from the Kimberley region of western Australia.

◄ **TOP LEFT**
Aboriginal map of the
sandhills, Kimberley
region, northwestern
Australia.

Map of Australia.

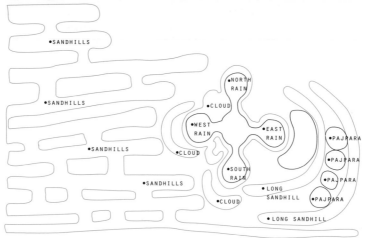

Diagram of the Sandhills map.

82

Map of the Ocean Floor, 1977

• ◆ •

Seismicity of the Earth 1960–1980
Alvaro F. Espinosa, Wilbur Rinehart,
and Marie Tharp
World Ocean Floor Panorama 1977
Bruce C. Heezen and
Marie Tharp, 1981

Photograph of Marie Tharp
by Bruce Gilbert

For thousands of years, sailors tested the depth of the water as they approached the shore, wanting to know if it was deep enough to continue closer without damaging the bottom of their ships. In very shallow waters, sailors simply placed a pole in the ground, but more often they tossed a rope over the side of the boat. Attached to the rope was a heavy object of some sort to ensure that the rope would sink. At the bottom of the weight, a sticky substance—resin, beeswax, or lard—would attract whatever kind of material lay on the sea floor below.

Over time, as the volume of sea trade grew, the exact depths of harbors were measured and underwater hazards mapped. But sea floors adjacent to coastlines could be mapped for other reasons as well. When Captain Cook landed in New Zealand in 1769, an old Maori chief named Toiawa drew a chart of the Coromandel Peninsula (on the east side of the North Island). In addition, he drew a chart of the sea floor around the tip of the North Island where spirits of the dead leaped out from this world and headed for the other world. The map correctly illustrated the Coromandel coast's varying depths, showing that the Maori had surveyed the sea floor.

But most of the ocean floor remained un-mapped until the nineteenth century, when the first submarines were built and mariners needed to acquire knowledge about depths far out in the ocean. In the 1840s, U.S. Navy commander W. F. Maury (see Maps 75 and 76) began compiling information from existing sea logs. In December 1872 a British ship, the H.M.S. *Challenger*, embarked on a 4-year voyage around the world equipped with 144 miles of hemp and a set of pulleys to drag the weights attached to the rope over the ocean floor. Obtaining a maximum measured depth of 26,850 feet, the *Challenger* collected enough information to produce the first map of the ocean floor in 1885. The science of **bathymetry** was born. The map that was produced from the data collected by the *Challenger* was very general, however.

Not until 1977 did the first detailed and accurate map of the ocean floor appear, based on 20 years of surveying at sea. The cartographer was Marie Tharp (1920–2006), who began working at the Lamont-Doherty Earth Observatory at Columbia University in 1948. Because women were not allowed on the ship, Tharp compiled the information at Colombia, painstakingly drawing the sea floor with pen and ink.

Onboard the Lamont-Doherty's exploratory ship *Vema*, Tharp's collaborator geologist Bruce Heezen (1924–1974) directed underwater photography, seismic studies, and the sampling of sediment cores. The *Vema*'s scientific team also employed a relatively new technique for measuring the depth of the sea floor: sonar. First developed toward the end of the First World War, sonar used sound waves to measure distance based upon the time it took the sound waves to bounce back. Sonar provided highly accurate information on the depth and contours of the ocean.

In creating the map, Tharp drew upon data collected from *Vema* and from the Woods Hole Oceanographic Institution. The result was the first map of the entire ocean floor. It confirmed the theories of plate tectonics and continental drift that were then gaining wide acceptance by the scientific community (in fact, the Americas is moving away from Europe and Africa at the rate of 1 inch per year).

While women may well have worked on maps in centuries past, Marie Tharp exemplifies an extraordinarily talented and original contributor to the history of cartography.

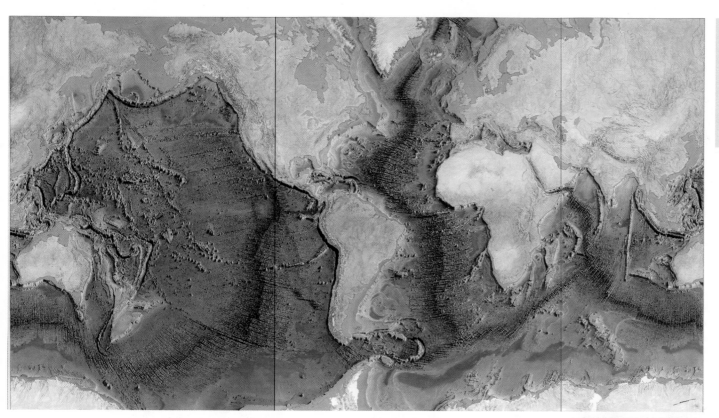

◄ LEFT
"World Ocean Floor," the first accurate global map of the sea floor, drawn by Marie Tharp in collaboration with Bruce Heezen and the painter Heinrich Berann in 1977.

Marie Tharp

83

Map of Antarctica,

2004

•◆•

Antarctica's topography, using data
collected from October 3 through
November 8, 2004
Digital rendering based on ICESat's
measurements
Christopher Shuman, ICESAT/NASA

At nearly 12 million square kilometers (4.6 million square miles), Antarctica is larger than the continental United States. No humans are indigenous to the continent, and only a small number (between 1,000 and 4,000) reside there on a temporary basis. There are good reasons for its lack of human occupation. Although covered by snow, very little water actually falls from the sky—less than an inch annually in most areas. Thus, the snow on the ground has resulted from small accumulations over thousands of years. So little snow falls, in fact, that the South Pole is technically classified as a desert. (A desert is any area that receives 9.75 inches of rainfall or less per year.) Since the humidity averages less than one percent, Antarctica qualifies as the world's driest desert. Other factors that make the continent difficult for humans to explore include the cold (average annual temperature of −56 degrees Fahrenheit) and the darkness. When the sun sets on March 22 it does not reappear again until six months later. If those difficulties were not great enough, there are also the winds that regularly reach up to 198 miles per hour along the coast. The winds pick up the accumulated snow and blow it around, creating frequent blizzards and white-outs.

Norwegian explorer Roald Amundsen (1872–1928) became the first person to successfully lead an expedition to the South Pole in 1911, borrowing survival techniques he had learned from the Inuit of Greenland when he had visited the island 8 years before. Sled dogs, like the ones the Inuit used in the Arctic, were a key reason he became the first to reach the Pole in 1911. After his triumph, he posed with his dogs for the picture at right.

A tragic end befell Amundsen's principal competitor. Robert Scott (1868–1912), an Englishman who led the second expedition to reach the South Pole in 1912, died along with his entire party on

their return trip. Even today, outsiders visit the Pole for only short periods of time.

It is far safer to explore Antarctica from the sky. Atmospheric conditions make it impossible for airplanes to fly over the continent except during the spring and summer. Even then, flights can be delayed by vicious storms. Hence, the safest place to study Antarctica is from high above the Earth. In 2003 NASA launched the Ice, Cloud, and Land Elevation Satellite to examine the depth of the ice sheets and to map the topography of the entire continent. The image at right shows the highest elevations (4,000 meters and above) in red, land that is 2,000 meters high in green, and coastal areas in blue. Atop the elevations are cross-hatching lines that contain information on the ice. White crossed lines indicate that ice sheets remain frozen, while the blue along the edges of the continent and along its western coast reveal considerable melting.

◄ LEFT
Map showing the elevations
of land in Antarctica.

84

Coastal Flooding in West Africa: Mapping the Future

•••

Patricia Seed
ESRI *Mapbook*

In 1989 the United Nations received a petition from the International Union for Conservation of Nature and Natural Resources to declare seemingly obscure wetlands on the west coast of Africa a World Heritage site. Previously, such status had only been granted to protect manmade sanctuaries—old Buddhist statues in Afghanistan, long-abandoned towns along the Tigris, ancient imperial citadels in Vietnam, and other cultural sites. The tidal flats, sand bars, and shallow bays of the Arguin Bank on the Atlantic Coast of Mauritania seemed like an unlikely candidate for such a nomination, especially since the local population, a mere 500 individuals, posed little threat to the ecosystem. But these wetlands lie just east of one of the richest fishing grounds of the West African coast. The combination of plentiful fish and thousands of kilometers of shallow waters in a warm climate attracts millions of fish-eating birds during the winter. More birds from Greenland, northern Europe, and Siberia migrate here to breed and feed their young than anywhere else in the Atlantic. If these grounds were degraded or destroyed, the fish-eating population of birds from Greenland to Siberia would be seriously depleted, with potentially serious results for the entire ecosystem of the Northern Hemisphere.

While industrial fishing in the region poses a potential threat to the bird population of this region, the more immediate danger comes from rising sea levels. Rising sea levels have already decimated one type of European spoonbill, which can no longer reproduce because its customary breeding grounds are now under water. In order to predict what would happen to these nesting and breeding grounds if sea levels were to continue to rise, the author of the book you are holding created a series of maps that showed the potential loss of nesting and breeding grounds that would result from different rises in sea levels. The resulting images show how maps can be used not only to think about the past but to predict the future.

CURRENT SEA LEVEL

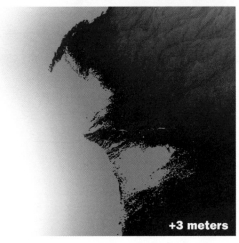

+3 meters

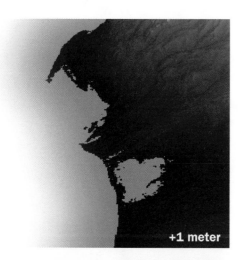

+1 meter

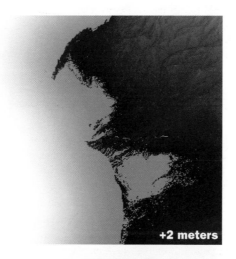

+2 meters

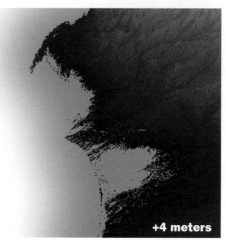

+4 meters

+5 meters

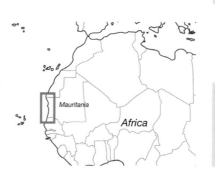

Mauritania

Africa

Part **8**

Empires, Wars, and Decolonization, 1884–1994

Maps in Part Eight

85. Cape to Cairo: The Scramble for Africa, 1884–1885
86. Territorial Claims in Central and Eastern Europe Prior to World War I
87. Trench Warfare: 1916 Artillery Map, Flanders
88. Soviet Georgia, from the First Russian Atlas, 1937–1939
89. Japanese Aviation Map, 1933
90. Royal Air Force Maps for Bombing Northern Germany, 1943
91. World War II Silk Escape Map
92. Post-War New World Map, 1942
93. Black Homeland Consolidation Proposals for South Africa, 1973
94. Peoples and Nations of the Soviet Union, 1991
95. Decolonization in Africa, 1960–1975

Over the course of the nineteenth and twentieth centuries, political and military mapping grew increasingly sophisticated as the impulses of empire and nationalism spread across the world. Accompanying the volatile geopolitics of this period was a surge of interest in mapping national borders.

From the end of the nineteenth century, the borders of countries around the world changed frequently as wars were won and lost, old empires collapsed and new ones arose, only to crumble as well. Although the roots of nationalism extend back to the eighteenth century, it reached its apex during the twentieth century, becoming a powerful force that pulled states together and pushed them apart, creating a fragmented world in which more independent nations existed than at any previous time in history. Fictitious countries could even be mapped (see Map 93). In Africa the speed of nation formation was dizzying, as seventeen separate countries became independent in just one year, 1960. Mapmakers were hard pressed to keep up.

Military mapping during this period also underwent dramatic changes as warfare became industrialized. Not long before World War I, Germans perfected an artillery technique called "indirect fire" that allowed the gunners to aim and fire without seeing their targets. While commanders had been sketching battlefields for centuries, the presence of hidden artillery in trenches meant that fighters had to know the location of their targets in order to attack. Battlefield maps quickly became indispensable (Map 87).

In the years leading up to World War II, air power increasingly played a pivotal role in combat. A variety of military aviation maps emerged as a result. By the 1930s, Japanese pilots during daylight hours were using visual flight rules and referred to long maps on a roller to help them follow the terrain below (Map 89). When launching nighttime bombing runs on Germany during World War II, the British Royal Air Force created a series of broadcast signals that pilots could follow in order to reach their destinations. The path of the signals was overlaid onto a map of the terrain that bombers would follow (Map 90). A final type of map related to military aviation was also invented during the Second World War: the escape map, or so-called "silk map" that pilots could easily conceal and use to escape out of enemy territory when shot down out of the sky (see Map 91).

The rise and fall of the Soviet Union was another political event of the twentieth century that was powerfully narrated through maps. In the Soviet Union, centralized economic planning required copious information about the natural resources and agricultural and industrial productivity of the entire country. Soviet leaders sponsored exhaustive statistical studies and produced immense atlases (see Map 88). The Cold War between the United States and the Soviet Union carved the world into two competing spheres of influence (Map 92). When the Soviet Union collapsed in 1991, it spun off fifteen separate countries, once again causing remaking of the maps with yet another set of boundaries (see Map 94).

Timeline of world history

1884–1885
Berlin Conference—Scramble for Africa

1894–1895
First Sino-Japanese War

1905
Korea becomes a protectorate of Japan

1914–1918
World War I

1920
Ottoman Empire abolished

1922
Soviet Union established

1929–1939
Great Depression

1937–1945
Second Sino-Japanese War

1939–1945
World War II

1945–1989
Cold War

1947–1999
Decolonization

1950
Apartheid legislation passed in South Africa

1973
Peters map projection

1991
Breakup of the Soviet Union

1994
First free elections in South Africa; end of apartheid

85

Cape to Cairo: The Scramble for Africa, 1884–1885

• • •

The Partition of Africa, 1911
William R. Shepherd
Norman B. Leventhal Map Center
Boston Public Library

Carta da Africa Meridional
Portugueza
National Library, Lisbon
1886

[handwritten: Europe powers met to try not to battle for land]

[handwritten: French claims]

[handwritten: British Claims]

[handwritten: railroad route]

While Portugal and Spain had controlled territory in Africa for centuries, by the 1880s both powers had long since been eclipsed by the economic and military might of Britain, France, and Germany. Leaders of these and other rapidly industrializing countries like Italy and Belgium saw enormous economic potential in colonizing African territory. Hoping to retain control of his possessions (shown in the "Pink Map" on the right), Luis I of Portugal (r. 1861–1889) called a summit of European leaders to discuss ways to avoid warring with each other over an unseemly "scramble" for African territory. The resulting conference, held in Berlin in 1884–1885 and organized by the German Chancellor Otto van Bismarck (1850–1898), set out the rules for partitioning Africa.

French leaders set their sights on much of the formerly Spanish and Portuguese territories in West Africa, including most of the former slave coast along the Gulf of Guinea (see Map 56). Britain's ambitions lay in a different direction. The English-born Prime Minister of South Africa, Cecil Rhodes (1853–1902), envisioned a grand scheme for British rule over Africa centered on a telegraph and a railway line that would run the length of the eastern side of the continent from Cairo to Cape Town.

The large map on the opposite page was drawn up in Britain after the Berlin Conference and represents the British understanding of what was agreed at the meeting. The map shows British claims to the entire pink-colored area, stretching from the Sudan down to South Africa and including much of the most productive agricultural land in Africa: Kenya, Uganda, and Zimbabwe. The map stakes out the Cape to Cairo route proposed by Rhodes.

Only Egypt, colored in yellow, is given semi-independent status as a British "protectorate."

Other powers received their shares as well. Belgian control of present-day Rwanda, Burundi, and the Democratic Republic of the Congo was reaffirmed, while Germany took over territory on the Gulf of Guinea and also secured the large territories of Namibia on the Atlantic and Tanganyika on the Indian Ocean. Even Italy gained possession of Eritrea, Somalia, and Libya. *[handwritten: Belgium]*

The only major power to object to the British-drawn map was the one that originally called for the conference. Portuguese officials affirmed their own version of territorial claims in the map they called the "Pink Map" (right). It showed the territory Portugal already controlled as stretching horizontally across southern Africa from Mozambique on the Indian Ocean to Angola on the Atlantic, including parts of Zambia, Zimbabwe, and Malawi, thus interfering with Rhodes' vision of the Cape to Cairo railroad. *[handwritten: Port]*

Two years after the conclusion of the Berlin Conference, Great Britain threatened a naval blockade of the port of Lisbon (whose import taxes constituted a major source of government revenue) should Portugal fail to remove its troops from forts throughout Zimbabwe and other areas of southeastern Africa sought by the British. Lacking naval forces to challenge the British, Portugal capitulated and removed its forces. Although British ambitions prevailed, the Cape to Cairo Railroad was never realized. However, a modern roadway called the Trans-African Highway (or the Cape to Cairo Highway) closely follows Rhodes' original plan.

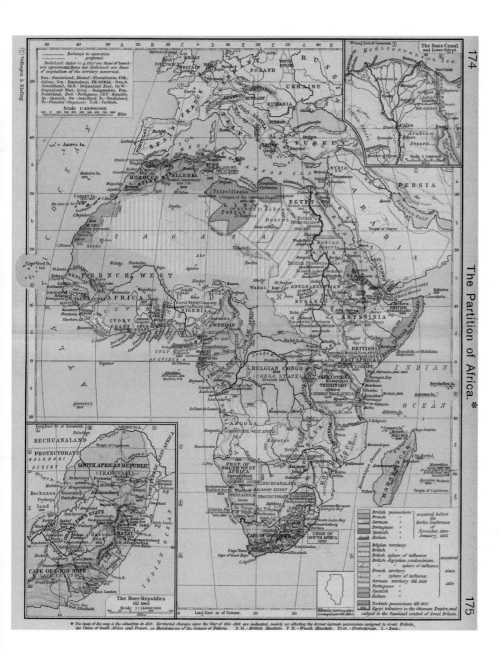

◄ **LEFT**
The "Scramble for Africa":
a British view.

▼ **BELOW**
The "pink map": the
Portuguese understanding
of the outcomes agreed to
at the Berlin Conference.

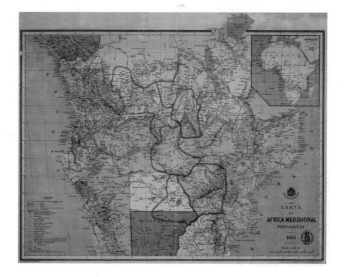

86

Territorial Claims in Central and Eastern Europe Prior to World War I

• ◆ •

Ethnographische Karte, 1868
Karl von Czoernig
ÖNB/Wien FKB O 18

Ottoman map, 1914:
author's collection

[handwritten margin notes: Fall of Austro-Hungary & Ottoman Empire ↓ countries declare independence; claims prior to war; attempted assassination]

On the eve of the First World War, two major empires were on the verge of collapse—Austro-Hungary and the Ottoman Empire. For hundreds of years, both had dominated large portions of Central and Eastern Europe and the Balkans, where a kaleidoscope of different ethnic groups spoke a hodgepodge of languages and practiced numerous distinct cultural traditions. The winds of nationalism swept through this region throughout the nineteenth century. Hungary was granted autonomous status by Austria in 1848, while other Eastern Europeans, including the Czechs, Slovaks, Slovenes, and Poles, were unsuccessful in shaking off Austro-Hungarian rule. Others were more successful in pushing out Ottoman forces. Greece won its independence in 1832. Romania gained its independence in 1877. The following year, Bulgaria gained autonomy even though formal independence would not take place for another 20 years.

The two maps in this section show Austro-Hungarian and Ottoman claims in the Balkans prior to the outbreak of World War I. Ottoman claims in the Balkans appear in pink on the smaller map, while the larger map depicts the multiple languages spoken within the Austro-Hungarian empire.

Both empires collapsed in the cataclysm of World War I. Serbian nationalists funded a team of seven assassins to kill the Habsburg crown prince, Archduke Ferdinand, hoping to destabilize the Austro-Hungarian empire and win Serbian independence. In June 1914, Ferdinand and his wife Sophia were visiting what was then the Bosnian capital of Sarajevo. At least one attempt—a bomb—failed to go off. One of the conspirators, Gavrilo Princip (1894–1918), then 19 years old, was heading toward

a coffee shop when the carriage with the archduke drove by on a road off the scheduled route. Seeing his opportunity, Princip shot Ferdinand and Sophia, killing both instantly. Austria-Hungary declared war on Serbia, joined by its ally Germany. Russia, a longtime Austro-Hungarian opponent and supporter of Serbia, retaliated by declaring war on Austro-Hungary. Further west, Great Britain and France were pulled into the widening conflict because of their alliance with Russia.

[handwritten margin notes: all t countries chose si]

The map on the facing page, showing the different language groups in Austro-Hungary, foreshadows the division of the empire over the twentieth century. German speakers appear in red, predominantly in Austria but also scattered in small pockets throughout the region. Hungarian speakers (here labeled by their Hungarian name, Magyars) are represented by the large white area. The yellow-green areas are Czech- and Slovak-speaking lands and include the formerly independent kingdoms of Bohemia and Moravia, which had long been conquered by outsiders. Just to the east lies the olive-colored Slovak-speaking region. The dark green area above Slovakia represents the Polish-speaking area of Austro-Hungary, a territory much smaller than present-day Poland. The light olive-colored group to the right is labeled *Ruthenian*, a generic word for Slavs but in this case referring to inhabitants of Belarus and Ukraine. Light orange marks the Rumanian-speaking area, while Slovene-speaking areas appear in blue. The remnants of Austro-Hungary's Italian possessions appear in bright yellow; the blue-green region below, extending down the Adriatic coast, is labeled Slovene- and Serbo-Croat, with the Bosnian Serb population outside the boundaries of the empire.

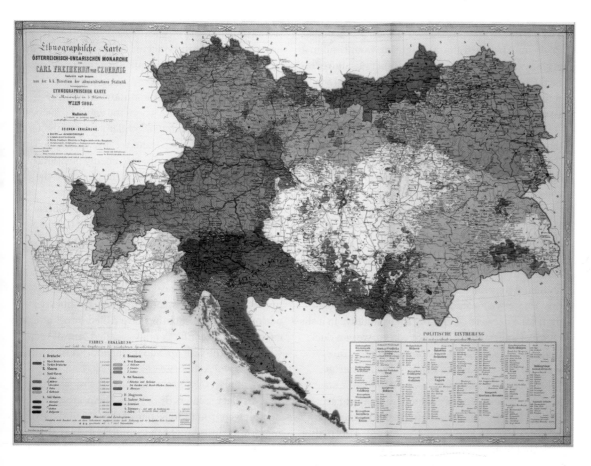

◄ **LEFT**
Austrian map of the
Austro-Hungarian Empire
in 1868.

▼ **BELOW**
Ottoman map of the
Balkans, 1914. Ottoman-
controlled territories are
shown in pink.

87

[handwritten: long war]

Trench Warfare:
1916 Artillery Map,
Flanders

[handwritten: trench warfare]

• • •

Map of No Man's Land created
by the 2ⁿᵈ Canadian Division
Blueprint, 1916
46 × 100 cm.
Library and Archives Canada,
NMC 21462

When the First World War began, most combatants believed that the fighting would end in a matter of weeks—instead, the conflict became measured in months and then years. Not only did the combatants expect a brief war, they also anticipated an entirely different type of conflict.

When British military planners deployed their troops against Germany in August 1914, the artillery commanders thought they would be fighting in open fields where they could see both where their artillery shells were landing and where the enemy's guns were placed. But beginning with the first battle of Flanders in October–November 1914, the two sides were hidden from each other by miles of trenches. British artillery commanders could neither see where their shells were landing, nor could they detect where the German artillery positions were located inside the trenches. "We lie under the network of arching shells and live in a suspense of uncertainty. If a shot comes, we can duck, that is all; we neither know nor can determine where it will fall," wrote Erich Maria Remarque (1898–1970) in *All Quiet On The Western Front*. Allied gunners clamored for a new means of accurately directing their fire onto German targets. An innovative solution was finally devised. Information collected from aerial balloon flights was rendered in the form of detailed battlefield maps and provided to the ground troops.

[handwritten: aerial balloons used to map out enemy trench]

World War I was the first war in which officers and enlisted soldiers thoroughly embraced battlefield mapping. At the beginning of the war, the British army map office included only two people. By the end of the war, the survey and mapping operation employed over 5,000 people and had produced more than 35 million sheets of maps.

The type of mapping done for the battlefields is called **topographic** mapping because it surveys and shows a region's surface features. Medium and heavy artillery units preferred maps like the one at right, drawn at a 1:2,500 scale, showing a wide area of German positions.

The new battlefield maps allowed artillery gunners to learn exactly where the enemy trenches were before firing commenced. This type of firing became known as "map shooting" because Allied forces used the maps to fire into enemy positions. To facilitate map shooting from the trenches, the maps were cut into squares and pasted to zinc plates, which became known as "artillery boards." Because the zinc remained perfectly flat, the map remained undisturbed during pasting and even during fluctuations in humidity. (Pasting the map to wood increased the potential for stretching and buckling later on. Hence, wood was only used in urgent circumstances, and only for very short periods of time.) Map shooting gave Allied forces a tactical edge in the conflict and was called "one of the wonders of the war" by Major General Franks of the British Royal Artillery.

Although GPS has eliminated the requirement that artillery soldiers draw maps themselves, mapping continues to be one of the first and most important skills taught to members of an artillery unit.

The war's most famous poem was composed in 1919 by a Canadian medical officer, Lieutenant Colonel John McCrae, not far from the trench mapped on the right. The first stanza of the poem reads:

In Flanders fields the poppies blow
Between the crosses, row on row,
That mark our place; and in the sky
The larks, still bravely singing, fly
Scarce heard amid the guns below.

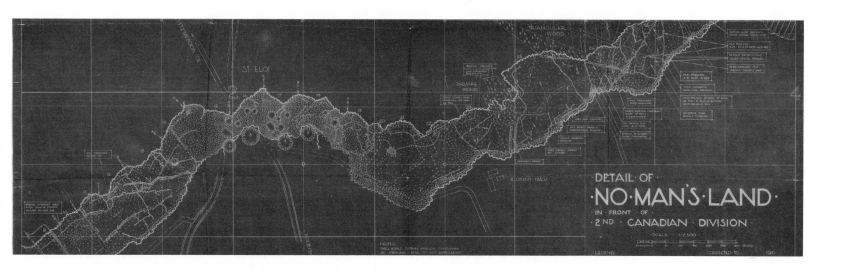

DETAIL OF
·NO·MAN'S·LAND·
IN · FRONT · OF
2ND · CANADIAN · DIVISION

88

Soviet Georgia, from the First Russian Atlas, 1937–1939

• ◆ •

Aleksandr Fedorovich Gorkin
Bol'shoĭ sovetskiĭ atlas mira,
1937–1939
Soviet Union, Glavnoe upravlenie
geodezii i kartografii

Geography and Map Division
Library of Congress

Prior to 1937, no original atlas had been created in either Russia or the Soviet Union. In that year, the Soviet Union produced the first volume of "The Great Soviet World Atlas" (*Bol'shoĭ sovetskiĭ atlas mira*) known simply as the *Atlas Mira*. The second volume appeared in 1939, but publication of a planned third volume was halted by the start of the Second World War. The government cancelled production because it feared that the atlas detailed information that the German military could use to attack targets inside the Soviet Union.

The Atlas covers an immense multitude of subjects ranging from the location of reindeer and goat herds to types of soil, climate zones, varieties of vegetation, and underlying rock formations. But its greatest contribution are the highly detailed and original economic maps.

Beginning in 1922, the Soviet Union underwent massive upheaval in an effort to transform the country into a world industrial power. Private ownership of land was eliminated and farms were transformed into collectives. Businesses with more than 20 employees were nationalized and put under state control. Governing authorities fixed the types and quantities of crops or industrial goods to be produced. In order to decide how resources should be allocated, the Soviet government required massive amounts of data, all of which was collected in the Atlas Mira.

The map at right graphically applies this data to the Soviet Republic of Georgia, a strategically important country located in the Caucasus. It shows the types of agricultural products that are harvested, the levels of industrial production for various products—automobiles, petroleum, timber, cement, silk, and wool manufacturing—as well as the energy capacity of each district. The design of the map is highly original, laying out industrial production in giant circles subdivided by color according to the type of industry, with the size indicating the amount of the output. Six-sided stars designate energy use; the size of each corresponds to an exact amount of energy output. The different colors of the stars indicate different types of energy sources—coal, petroleum, or hydroelectric. Since railroads were critical for transporting agricultural and industrial products, the map also designates the location of all existing lines, as well as ones under construction.

On the lower right, the map uses graphs to celebrate the agricultural and industrial successes of forced collectivization and economic planning. The top row illustrates increased agricultural output, the middle rows show improved industrial production, the bottom plots increases in educational levels and book production, key components in creating a modern workforce.

In each row, the left bar shows pathetically low levels of production prior to the 1917 revolution, with subsequent bars showing steadily increasing output. The message is clear: the command economy imposed from above by Soviet planners has created progress in all sectors of society, and this progress can be measured. It is an idealistic, even utopian vision.

The graph in the top center of the map serves as a reminder that even though Joseph Stalin (1878–1953), the despotic ruler of the Soviet Union, was a son of Georgia he did not grant it favored status. It shows the Georgian Military Highway, the principal route connecting Russia to Georgia, built by Russia at great cost in the nineteenth century as a key part of its imperial objectives in the Caucasus. It includes the distances between towns along the highway, the elevation of each town above sea level, and the height of the surrounding peaks of the Caucasus. So while, at one level, this map of Georgia from the Atlas Mira outlines a vision of utopian progress, on another level it unmistakably proclaims that this progress comes with a catch. The center—Russia—rules the periphery, Georgia. And it does so with iron and steel.

▲ **TOP**
1937 economic map of the
Georgian Soviet Republic,
showcasing agricultural
and industrial development.
The capital, Tbilisi, is
toward the bottom right,
surrounded by the largest
circle on the map.

Map of Georgia and surrounding region.

197

89

Japanese Aviation Map, 1933

● ◆ ●

Nippon Koku KK (Japan Air Transport Ltd.)
Dairen-Keijo Strip Map, 1933
Courtesy Col. Charles Quilter, USMC (ret.)

In the initial years of flight, pilots generally flew only during daylight hours, following the paths of roads, railroads, or coasts—a technique known as "contact flight". The earliest flight maps—such as the Japan Air Transport example shown here, from 1933, showing the air route between Seoul (Keijo), Korea and Dalian (Dairen), China—illustrated the land features—roads, rail lines, and coasts—that provided orientation while flying. On this map a railroad is clearly and sharply marked in alternate black and white rectangles, and readily distinguishable from the green and yellow background. For segments of the flight that lack a rail line or road for the pilot to follow, the clear outline of the coast, with a strong color contrast between the green land and the blue waters, serves as a useful marker.

When Japan Air Transport pilots suddenly encountered low ceilings, fog, or bad weather en route they could locate emergency landing fields, depicted on their maps by a double circle. Nearby airports along the way were symbolized by a staff with the letter "W". The radio operator on board could transmit information on the progress of the flight via Morse code, as well as receive weather reports warning of bad weather ahead.

The unusual shape of this map—a single long strip—represents the most convenient way for a pilot to follow a specific route. The map was meant to be mounted in a roller set on or near the instrument panel, so that a pilot could scroll it as he passed over various waypoints on his route. For ease of use, roller maps could be rotated so that the track of the flight was straight up. As the pilot unrolled the map, distances flown in kilometers would appear on the right hand side of the flight path, while the reverse scale indicated distances yet to go.

While Japanese pilots departing from Japan actually flew first to the northwest and then to the southeast, these conventional directions were only found in a small overview map (see middle photo on bottom row at right). The map the pilot actually used in flight depicted his path as a straight line—the way the pilot perceived his path from the aircraft. In this respect the earliest aeronautical charts resembled the route maps of the Roman Empire (see Map 18). Both represented the direction of the journey as a straight line, even though the travelers were actually moving north, south, east, and west. The straight line corresponded to how the traveler envisioned the journey.

Another important component of early aviation maps, such as this one, is topographical. Pilots needed to know the height of the terrain in order to fly around a mountain or over its peak. Rather than leaving pilots to guess at the height of nearby peaks, early aviation maps showed the elevation of mountain ranges that pilots could safely fly over. In the bottom right-hand corner the Japanese map shows elevations below 100 meters in green, those under 500 meters in light tan, and those under a thousand meters in a darker tan, with the heights of different mountains separated by a dotted line.

This map can also be viewed as part of Japan's imperial project in north and east Asia in the first half of the twentieth century, in which air transport played an important role. Lacking significant natural resources of its own, Japan sought to acquire coal and iron ore from the region's rich reserves. When this map was created, Japanese troops had already colonized Korea (1910) and ousted the Russians and Chinese from nearby Manchuria. By 1933, the air route shown in this map provided a crucial communication artery that linked Japan, its colonial capital in Korea (Seoul, known in Japanese as *Keijō*), and its major seaport on the Chinese mainland (Dalian, which the Japanese renamed Dairen). Not only was Dairen essential for the export of coal and iron to Japan, its capture by Japanese forces in 1905 represented Russia's loss of its only year-round ice-free port in the Pacific.

DAIREN 648哩(km) KEIJO
連大 ——— 城京
3時間約 35分(ʺ)

山ᵈ標識字ハ航空標識ノ路線地点・赤字ハᵈロギᵈレート示スᵈᵈロギᵈレート印ᵈ(ᵈᵈᵈ)

1933 Japanese aviation
map showing the route
from Seoul (Keijo) to
Dalian (Dairen).

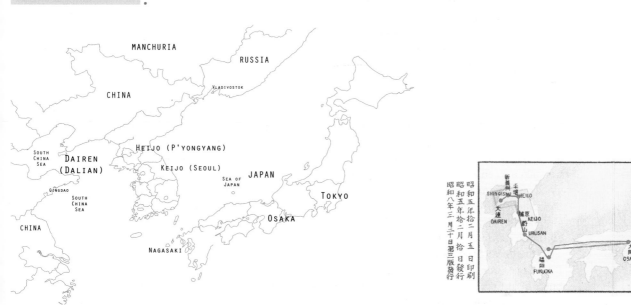

Map showing Japan, Korea, and northeastern China.

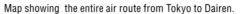

Map showing the entire air route from Tokyo to Dairen.

Map legend.

90

Royal Air Force Maps for Bombing Northern Germany, 1943

• ◆ •

Middlesbrough-Den Helder
Miniature Lattice 2nd ed.,
series 2, sheet 1
Amsterdam-Kiel
Miniature Lattice 2nd ed.,
series 2, sheet 2
February 1943
Courtesy Col. Charles Quilter,
USMC (ret.)

The map on the right, created for the Britain's Royal Air Force in 1943, appears plain and uninteresting. However, this seemingly unremarkable map marks one of the major transformations in cartography in the twentieth century.

Military necessity drove this change. In August 1941, RAF bombers attacked Germany's industrial Ruhr Valley. However, less than one in ten RAF bombers managed to come within even 5 miles of their intended target. By contrast, that same summer the German air force, the Luftwaffe, was accurately targeting London shipyards, armaments factories in Coventry, and tire plants in Birmingham.

The RAF's reliance upon navigational means unsuited to their missions was the root of the problem. Bombing raids had to be carried out at night in order to avoid being seen by German fighter planes (the Luftwaffe shot down and killed nearly 72,000 RAF airmen during the war). However, the RAF still relied upon traditional means of flying, using visual cues such as the ground, the stars, and a technique known as **dead reckoning**. Flying to Germany over darkened farms and fields at night provided little help for pilots trying to use the ground to locate their precise position. Using the stars to calculate their position required time-consuming calculations that were of little or no help at the speed of flight or when skies were overcast. Finally, dead reckoning (the technique used by Christopher Columbus when he sailed across the Atlantic) provided only approximate locations at best. Columbus had a far wider target to hit. In the dark over Germany, pilots were trying to find a much smaller object—a railroad yard or an industrial plant.

In order to hit their targets successfully, the RAF had to rethink the techniques it used to help pilots fly at night. In the process it transformed the way the skies are mapped. It shifted away from conventional sight-based methods and instead used unseen radio signals, a technique that the Luftwaffe was already using. Sending out pulses of radio energy from a central station located on a hilltop in Daventry, England, the RAF established a constellation of substations each located about 80 nautical miles away from Daventry and oriented roughly at 120-degree angles from the central station. Mathematicians and mapmakers plotted the time delays between sending and receiving these signals as three uniquely colored hyperbolas on a map. On a properly equipped aircraft the pulses appeared as spikes or blips on a cathode ray tube. By adjusting the synchronization of the pulses on the tube, a navigator could measure the time delay of each and plot them on the maps.

Using these signals and following the new maps, RAF pilots improved bombing accuracy to within one mile of their actual targets. In June of 1942, the new system of flight navigation helped the RAF execute first major large-scale successful bombing in German territory, hitting an important aircraft plant and shipyard in Bremen. In February 1943, the two radio navigation charts on the right helped bomber pilots fly from England to the Netherlands and from the Netherlands to Kiel, Germany, where they successfully destroyed a U-boat factory. The maps show little in the way of visual landmarks, identifying only populated towns and the distinction between water and land, both of which would often be visible to pilots at night.

The radio signals sent out from Daventry had an effective range of only 300 nautical miles, a distance that permitted RAF pilots to fly as far as the aircraft manufacturing plants in Bremen and the steel plants in Essex. Anything further east in Germany was beyond the reach of the radio signals. Nonetheless these RAF maps, created in the crucible of war, mark the beginning of the use of abstract, mathematical data instead of geographic features to chart the skies (see Map 99).

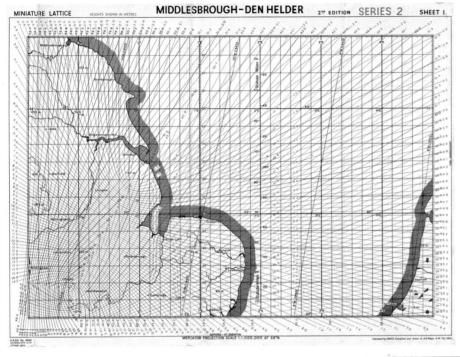

MINIATURE LATTICE · HEIGHTS SHOWN IN METRES · **MIDDLESBROUGH–DEN HELDER** · 2ND EDITION · SERIES 2 · SHEET I.

MERCATOR PROJECTION SCALE 1:1,000,000 AT 56°N.

◄ **TOP**
RAF navigational charts for the first major bombing of Germany in the Second World War.

Outline map showing the area depicted in the two RAF maps on the left.

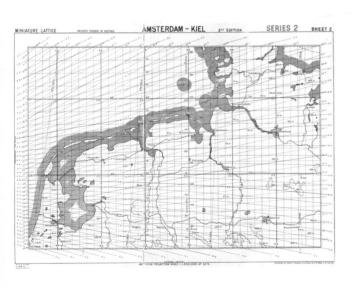

MINIATURE LATTICE · HEIGHTS SHOWN IN METRES · AMSTERDAM – KIEL · 2ND EDITION · SERIES 2 · SHEET 2

MERCATOR PROJECTION SCALE 1:1,000,000 AT 56°N.

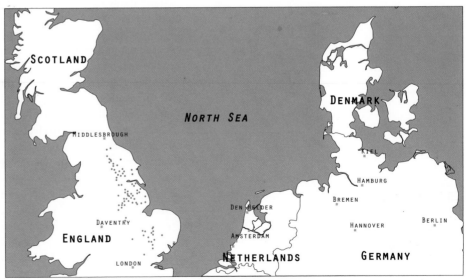

SCOTLAND

NORTH SEA

DENMARK

MIDDLESBROUGH

KIEL

HAMBURG

BREMEN

DEN HELDER

HANNOVER

BERLIN

DAVENTRY

AMSTERDAM

ENGLAND

NETHERLANDS

GERMANY

LONDON

91

World War II Silk Escape Map

• ◆ •

French Indo China (central) Siam
(Thailand) (east)
Silk Sheet J, c. 1944
Author's collection

paper didn't work

Whether shot down over enemy lines or captured on the field of battle, tens of thousands of soldiers during the Second World War often wound up in hostile territory. The main priority for combatants who found themselves on the wrong side of enemy lines was to ~~evade capture and get back to safety~~. Airmen who were shot down usually found themselves deep in enemy territory. They needed maps to show them the way out.

But ordinary maps could be dangerous. Paper maps crinkled when opened or folded, giving away a hidden position; if hurriedly crumpled, the paper could easily crease or tear, making it impossible to read. Moreover, paper's bulk made maps difficult to conceal. Downed airmen needed something thin yet strong and silent, which could be crumpled easily and remain concealed in a small space, such as the heel of a boot, where it could be readily retrieved and dunked in water, after which it dried quickly into its smooth original surface and could be easily read.

A British Army intelligence officer, Clayton Hutton (1893–1965), realized that the silk used to make parachutes possessed all the necessary qualities. His next challenge was finding an ink that would not dissolve in water. After many failed efforts, he found that adding pectin, a thickener used to firm jams, solved the problem, and escape maps began to be printed by the thousands. As parachute silk grew scarcer, mapmakers discovered that rayon could also be used to print escape maps.

The first **escape maps** featured regions in northern Europe where RAF airmen were likely to be shot down. The escape maps showed the main roads and detailed hundreds of side roads that could be taken in case of roadblocks or enemy troops marching along the main highways. Information on creeks, waterways, and other places also indicated hiding places. As the war expanded to other fronts, new maps were needed. When a large contingent of American bombers was sent to North Africa to pursue German forces there, American printers (with whom British intelligence had shared its techniques) began turning out escape maps first of North Africa and then of Italy, as Allied forces pursued Axis armies northward. In the Pacific theater, British intelligence produced silk maps for the war in Burma, the Marianas Islands, and other areas for pilots flying over China and Japan. A special series of rayon maps were produced for pilots fighting the air war in the Pacific. These maps showed the prevailing currents around Japanese-occupied islands and the direction in which they needed to row, steer, or swim to an area where they could be picked up by friendly naval vessels.

Soon thereafter, intelligence officials realized that escape maps would be useful to captured soldiers. Since the maps could not be openly brought into prisoner of war camps, they were hidden inside board games. A deck of playing cards, for example, would contain pieces of a map concealed between two sides of each card. Steam the cards open, and the assembled pieces would form a complete map. Monopoly games marked with special codes were a particular favorite. A tiny red dot on the "Free Parking" space meant the game contained escape materials—a map underneath the board, playing pieces that concealed compasses, and genuine German, Italian, and French currency mixed in the pile of seemingly worthless Monopoly money.

While it is impossible to say exactly how many Allied soldiers were saved by escape maps, some estimate that two out of every twelve downed airmen managed to make their way safely out of enemy territory. Luck and sympathetic strangers certainly helped many, but the airmen themselves considered their maps crucial. In 1942, when the U.S. Air Force surveyed downed crew members who had made it back to safety, 40 percent said that next to money, the maps had been the most crucial element of their escape and evasion kits.

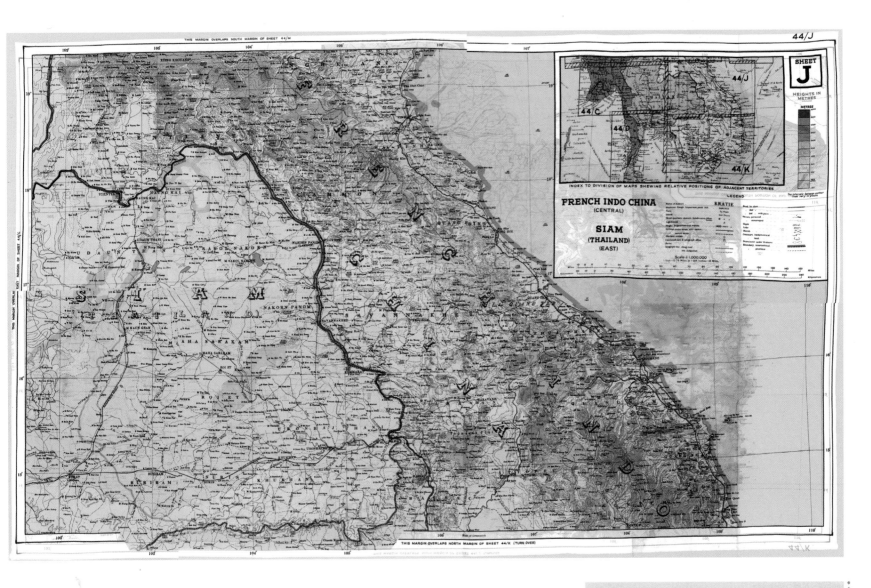

ABOVE
This American escape map shows Indochina, a French colony that included Cambodia, Laos, and Vietnam, and was invaded by the Japanese in 1940 and occupied until 1945. Escape maps were carried by U.S. pilots until the end of the Vietnam War.

92

Post-War New World
Map, 1942

• • •

Outline of post-war new world map
Color map, 1942
68 × 96 cm.
Maurice Gomberg
Library of Congress
Geography and Map Division
Washington, D.C.

204

The map at the right, created in the United States in October 1941 just before the country went to war against the Axis powers, was printed two months after war was officially declared. The map therefore only suggests what the world would look like if the Allies were to win, a fact that was by no means certain in 1942. Despite not having knowledge of what the future would bring, it made some surprisingly accurate predictions.

The inspiration for the "new world" map came from President Franklin D. Roosevelt's State of the Union address in January 1941. In that speech Roosevelt laid out the four freedoms—freedom of speech, freedom to worship, freedom from want, and freedom from fear. Roosevelt described his vision as one that opposed the "new order" sought by dictators like Hitler and Tojo, in favor of a cooperative effort to work toward guaranteeing human rights. "To that high concept there can be no end but victory," Roosevelt declared.

The map's creator laid out forty-one separate goals and predictions for the true new order that would follow the end of the Second World War. Among those proposed steps were an end to colonialism, the establishment of a United Nations ("League of Nationalities"), an International Tribunal ("World Court"), and criminal prosecutions of the war's perpetrators.

The map envisions unity across large swaths of the globe. The areas in blue are labeled "The United States and Protectorates" and show the United States completely dominating the Atlantic and Pacific oceans. Greenland, Canada , and all of Central America would become part of the United States; Iceland would become a U.S. protectorate. Similarly, the Madeira, Azores, and Cape Verde islands in the Atlantic would all become "security outposts" of the United States. In the Pacific these outposts would include all of Polynesia, Micronesia, and part of Melanesia—a forecast that was partly accurate.

The Soviet Union also emerges in the postwar new world as a major superpower. The map's creator increased the area under Soviet domination to include all of Eastern Europe and the Baltic States of Estonia, Latvia, and Lithuania. All of these predictions would come true. Only Finland and Iran, which the map shows as part of the Soviet Union, remained independent. The Soviets also gained only partial control of Germany.

The map's maker, a mysterious individual named Maurice Gomberg, also foresaw something like the European Union, which he labeled as "United States of Europe." The founding members of what would eventually become the EU were Belgium, France, Italy, Luxembourg, the Netherlands, and West Germany, all of which, with the exception of Germany, appeared on Gomberg's map. Two countries that he included in his European Union entered much later—Spain and Portugal only joined in 1986, and a third, Switzerland, still does not belong.

What Gomberg labeled the "Union of African States" did come into existence in 2002 as the African Union. The South American union that Gomberg envisioned has only been partially realized through a regional trade agreement, Mercosur, which went into effect in 1991.

In Asia and Southeast Asia, Gomberg's predictions were off the mark. According to his map, China's rule would expand to Korea, Laos, Cambodia, Vietnam, Thailand, and Malaysia. China never gained hegemony over any of these countries, and North Korea remains simply an ally. India, which in Gomberg's map includes Afghanistan and Burma, never achieved such territorial expansion; in fact, it suffered a bloody partition immediately after the war.

Perhaps Gomberg's most interesting proposition was that greater India would not be a part of the British Commonwealth; this prediction was wrong. In the Middle East Gomberg predicted an independent Israel and a united Arabian peninsula.

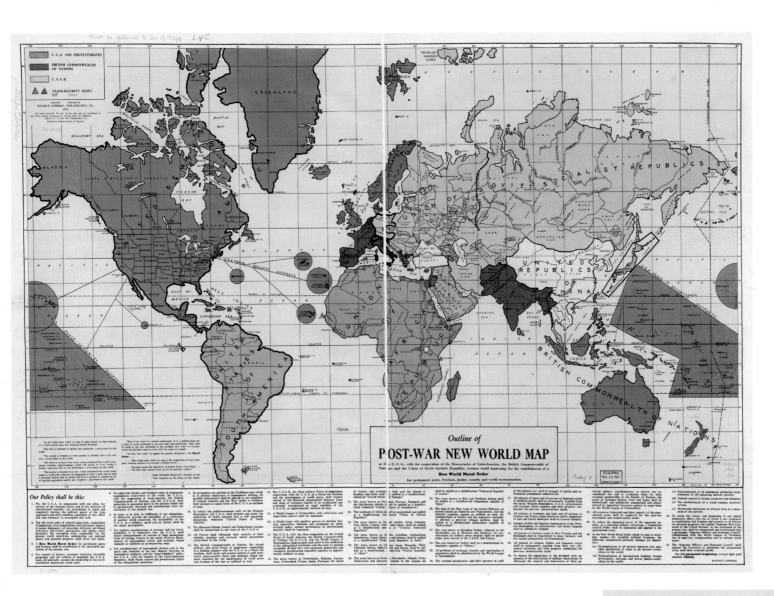

▲ **ABOVE**
An imagined postwar world with areas allied with the Soviet Union in pink, the United States and its protectorates in blue, and Britain and its Commonwealth shown in red.

93

Black Homeland Consolidation Proposals for South Africa, 1973

• ◆ •

R.S.A. black homelands consolidation
proposals
Color map, 1973
40 × 47 cm.
Created by Africa Institute
of South Africa
Library of Congress
Geography and Map Division
Washington, D.C.

Today's Republic of South Africa represents a successful union of formerly warring colonial domains and a wide array of distinct ethnic communities and languages. The country depicted on the right resulted from the union in 1910 of the British colonies of the Cape and Natal with the Boer (Afrikaaner) colonies of Transvaal and the Orange Free States. In addition to its complex colonial past, South Africa also includes large groups of speakers of mutually unintelligible native languages. In all of Africa, South Africa has the largest number of official languages—eleven in all—with two, Xhosa and Zulu, the most widely spoken.

However, until 1994 a racist policy known as apartheid dominated South African life. An extreme form of segregation, apartheid began to be implemented in 1950 when rightwing political parties won control of the country. Representing many of the descendants of the original seventeenth-century Dutch settlers of the country, these parties were called *Afrikaaner* because their members spoke a distinct variety of Dutch called *Afrikaans*. In 1950 they passed legislation, the Group Areas Act No. 41, which required South Africans to reside only with members of their own race.

At that time, the South African government recognized four racial groups: black, white, "colored," and Indian (South Asian). "Colored" encompassed mixed-race people, as well as immigrants from Malaysia. Prior to 1950 many people lived in predominantly black, white or "colored," areas, but mixed residential areas existed—including a vibrant area of Cape Town called District Six, which was razed to the ground and its nonwhite inhabitants forcibly removed. After the passage of Group Areas Act No. 41, an estimated three million people were involuntarily moved to segregated areas.

Twenty years later proponents of apartheid had a new agenda: to create a white political majority.

To do so, they needed to deprive millions of black South Africans of their citizenship by making them citizens of another political entity. Employing the political myth that the country's black population was not indigenous to South Africa but had only immigrated from other regions, the apartheid government created "homelands" that it claimed represented their actual place of origin and citizenship. These fictitiously independent black-only "homelands" were run by black leaders willing to cooperate with Afrikaaner authorities.

The map at right shows the South African government's 1973 redefinition of these boundaries primarily along linguistic lines. From top to bottom, the colored rectangles on the upper left list the following homelands: Basotho Qwaqwa for Southern Sotho language speakers, Bophuthatswana, Ciskei for Xhosa speakers, Gazankulu for the Tsonga, Lebowa for Northern Sotho, South Ndebele for the language of the same name, Swazi also for the language of the same name, Transkei for Xhosa speakers, and Venda for speakers of the language of the same name.

In 1961 the Union achieved full independence from Great Britain and became the Republic of South Africa. However, independence brought no change in the apartheid policies, as this 1973 map demonstrates. In the cities, blacks, who were supposedly citizens of "homelands," were forced to live in wretched suburban areas called townships.

International boycotts and increasing domestic political opposition eventually led to apartheid's abolition. In 1990 an Afrikaaner president, Frederik W. de Klerk (1936–), began winding down the apartheid era policies, including the release of the anti-apartheid activist Nelson Mandela (1918–) from jail. In 1994, free elections were held with universal suffrage, electing Mandela president and creating genuine independence for South Africa.

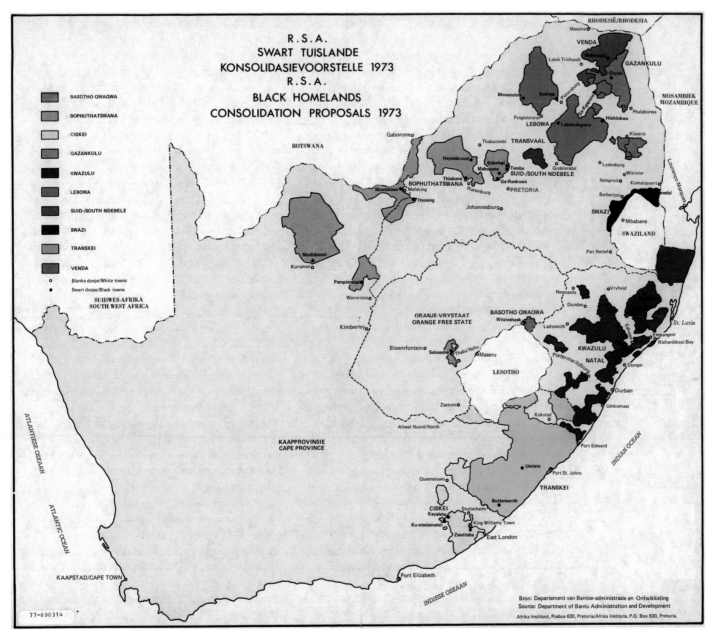

R.S.A.
SWART TUISLANDE
KONSOLIDASIEVOORSTELLE 1973
R.S.A.
BLACK HOMELANDS
CONSOLIDATION PROPOSALS 1973

BASOTHO QWAQWA
BOPHUTHATSWANA
CISKEI
GAZANKULU
KWAZULU
LEBOWA
SUID-/SOUTH NDEBELE
SWAZI
TRANSKEI
VENDA
○ Blanke dorpe/White towns
● Swart dorpe/Black towns

SUIDWES-AFRIKA
SOUTH WEST AFRICA

ATLANTIESE OSEAAN
ATLANTIC OCEAN

KAAPSTAD/CAPE TOWN

Port Elizabeth

INDIESE OSEAAN

BOTSWANA

Gaborone

Montshiwa   Mafeking
BOPHUTHATSWANA
Thlabane
Itsoseng

Mothibistat
Kuruman

Pampierstad
Warrenton

Kimberley

Bloemfontein
Seloseshe   Thaba'Nchu
Zastron

Aliwal Noord/North

KAAPPROVINSIE
CAPE PROVINCE

Queenstown

CISKEI
Kayaletu
Ku-ntselamanzi
Zwelitsha
East London

Stutterheim
King Williams Town

Butterworth
TRANSKEI
Umtata
Port St. Johns

Port Edward

Kokstad

ORANJE-VRYSTAAT
ORANGE FREE STATE

BASOTHO QWAQWA
Witzieshoek
Ladysmith

LESOTHO
Maseru

RHODESIË/RHODESIA
Messina

VENDA
Makwarela
Louis Trichardt
Giyani   GAZANKULU

Mmamelets   Seshego
Pietersburg   Ga-Kgapane
Potgietersrus
LEBOWA   Lebowakgomo   Hlohlokwe
Phalaborwa

MOSAMBIEK
MOZAMBIQUE

Thabazimbi
TRANSVAAL   Klaserie

Heystekrand   Lydenburg
Babelegi   Groblersdal   Witrivier
Temba   Nelspruit   Komatipoort
Mabopane   SUID/SOUTH NDEBELE   Barberton
Ga-Rankuwa
PRETORIA   SWAZI

Johannesburg   SWAZILAND   Mbabane

Piet Retief

Newcastle   Vryheid
Dundee
St. Lucia
KWAZULU   Empangeni
NATAL   Richardsbaai/Bay
Pietermaritzburg   Stanger

Durban
Umkomaas

INDIAN OCEAN

Lourenço Marques

Bron: Departement van Bantoe-administrasie en -Ontwikkeling
Source: Department of Bantu Administration and Development
Afrika-Instituut, Posbus 630, Pretoria/Africa Institute, P.O. Box 630, Pretoria.

77-690314

◄ LEFT
Map of revised boundaries
of segregated black "homelands" in South Africa,
1973. The title of the map
is in both Afrikaans and
English.

94

Peoples and Nations of the Soviet Union, 1991

● ◆ ●

Soviet Union Nationalities
Soviet Union – Comparative Ethnic
Groups, 1989
U.S. Central Intelligence Agency, 1995

In 1991, the Soviet Union, which had been founded nearly 70 years earlier, splintered into fifteen independent countries. The boundaries for these new countries followed previously established administrative units called Soviet Socialist Republics (SSRs). During the Soviet era each SSR possessed some autonomy, although ultimate authority rested with Moscow. In the years immediately preceding 1991, the leader of the Soviet Union, Mikhail Gorbachev (1931–), had inadvertently paved the way for secession by permitting greater openness and transparency in government (*glasnost*) and granting the republics increased political and economic autonomy (*perestroika*).

Drawn by the US Central Intelligence Agency just before the collapse of the Soviet Union, but based on a 1979 census, the map shows a kaleidoscope of nationalities spread across the Eurasian landmass. As recent historians have convincingly argued, "becoming national" is the condition of our times. When the great multinational states of the nineteenth century fell apart in the turmoil of World War I, the landscapes of Eastern Europe, Central Asia, and the Middle East were transformed. But though the Habsburg and Ottoman Empires were dismantled, the Soviet Union, established in 1922 as the world's first Communist state, inherited the lands of the former Russian Empire largely intact.

As shown on Map 94, scores of "nationalities" inhabited the vast spaces of the Soviet Union. The world's first worker state was also the first to classify all citizens according to biological nationalities. The metaphor of a "communal apartment" has been used by historians of the Soviet Union to describe this seemingly paradoxical phenomena of separateness and communalism.

In Map 94 these nationalities are categorized according to their language groups. Despite disagreements about how best to classify the many peoples (*narody*) of the Soviet Union, Communist party officials, ethnographers, and policymakers all fell back on language as the most dependable indicator. Stalin himself made language central to his definition: "A nation is a historically evolved, stable community based on common language, territory, economic life, and psychological makeup manifested in a community of culture." The Central Intelligence Agency appears to have agreed.

The map categorizes nationalities into four color-coded, language groups, many of which are further subdivided into subgroups: Caucasian, Indo-European, Uralic and Altaic, and Paleo-Siberian. Less populous nationalities, such as Koreans and Germans, are indicated by letters. Like colonial outposts, red dots represent the many Russian communities located far beyond the confines of their homeland.

The complexity of the Soviet Union's cultural landscape clearly comes through in Map 94, but it also suggests a reality far less complicated than it actually was. While the color codes effectively show the distribution of language families, they give no clues as to whether the speakers of related languages did, in fact, share a "community of culture". For example, the category "Caucasus Peoples" (light blue color) includes two groups, the Georgians and the Abkhaz. The Georgians and the Abkhaz intermarried and lived side by side for centuries. But in 1992–93 they fought a vicious, still unresolved war that included massive ethnic cleansing, over 15,000 fatalities, and the wholesale expulsion of 250,000 Georgians from Abkhazia. Diametrically opposed nationalisms fueled the conflict.

It would have been impossible for the analysts of the CIA to predict the outcomes of the Soviet Union's collapse in 1991. And while Map 94 offered a glimpse of what was to follow, it certainly was unable to chart the elemental, even primordial forces of nationalism that would be unleashed. The great nineteenth-century French historian Ernest Renan (1823–1892) famously said that a "nation is a soul, a spiritual principle." You cannot plot that on a map.

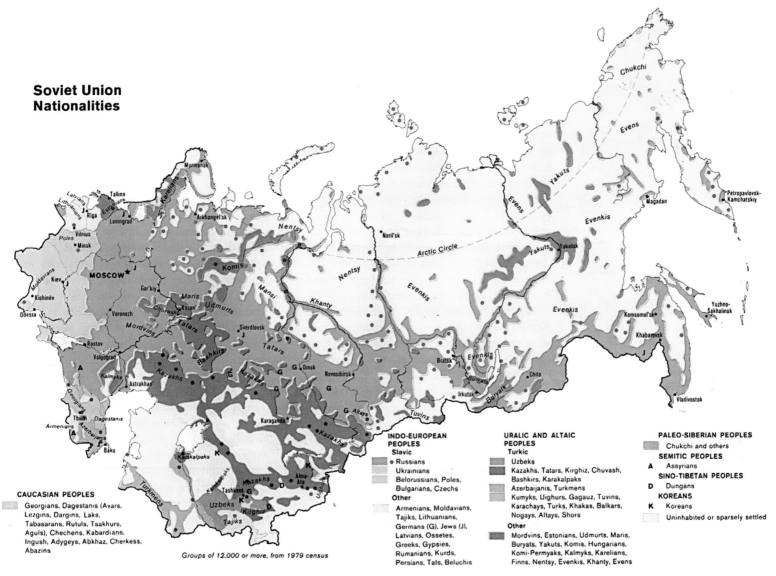

Soviet Union Nationalities

Chukchi

Evens

Yakuts

Evenkis

Evens

Petropavlovsk-Kamchatskiy

Murmansk

Magadan

Latvians
Lithuanians
Tallinn
Riga
Estonians
Karelians
Poles
Vilnius
Minsk
Arkhangel'sk
Nentsy
Noril'sk
Arctic Circle
Yakutsk
Komsomol'sk
Yuzhno-Sakhalinsk

Moldavians
Kiev
Kishinëv
Odessa
MOSCOW
Gor'kiy
Komi
Maris
Mansi
Khanty
Nentsy
Evenkis
Yakuts
Evenkis
Khabarovsk

Voronezh
Kazan'
Chuvash
Udmurts
Sverdlovsk
Tatars
Evenkis

Rostov
Mordvins
Tatars
Bashkirs
Omsk
Novosibirsk
Bratsk
Buryats
Chita
Vladivostok

Volgograd
Kalmyks
Astrakhan
Kazakhs
Kazakhs
Irkutsk
Buryats

Georgians
Tbilisi
Dagestanis
Karaganda
Kazakhs
Altays
Tuvins

Armenians
Azerbaijanis
Baku
Karakalpaks
Kazakhs

Turkmens
Karakalpaks
Tashkent
Uzbeks
Alma-Ata
Uzbeks

Uzbeks
Kirghiz
Tajiks

CAUCASIAN PEOPLES
Georgians, Dagestanis (Avars, Lezgins, Dargins, Laks, Tabasarans, Rutuls, Tsakhurs, Aguls), Chechens, Kabardians, Ingush, Adygeys, Abkhaz, Cherkess, Abazins

Groups of 12,000 or more, from 1979 census

INDO-EUROPEAN PEOPLES
Slavic
• Russians
Ukrainians
Belorussians, Poles, Bulgarians, Czechs
Other
Armenians, Moldavians, Tajiks, Lithuanians, Germans (G), Jews (J), Latvians, Ossetes, Greeks, Gypsies, Rumanians, Kurds, Persians, Tats, Beluchis

URALIC AND ALTAIC PEOPLES
Turkic
Uzbeks
Kazakhs, Tatars, Kirghiz, Chuvash, Bashkirs, Karakalpaks
Azerbaijanis, Turkmens
Kumyks, Uighurs, Gagauz, Tuvins, Karachays, Turks, Khakas, Balkars, Nogays, Altays, Shors
Other
Mordvins, Estonians, Udmurts, Maris, Buryats, Yakuts, Komis, Hungarians, Komi-Permyaks, Kalmyks, Karelians, Finns, Nentsy, Evenkis, Khanty, Evens

PALEO-SIBERIAN PEOPLES
Chukchi and others
SEMITIC PEOPLES
A   Assyrians
SINO-TIBETAN PEOPLES
D   Dungans
KOREANS
K   Koreans
Uninhabited or sparsely settled

505173 6-82

▲ ABOVE
The nationalities of the Soviet Union just prior to the country's collapse.

209

95

Decolonization in Africa, 1960–1975

• • •

Patricia Seed
ESRI ArcMap 10.0

Europe's late–nineteenth century scramble for Africa unraveled with stunning speed. In a single year, 1960, seventeen nations shed colonial rule. By 1970, fifteen more African nations had become independent; in nearly all cases colonial powers, faced with political or economic pressures at home, hastily packed up, leaving behind countries without a new generation of properly trained officials to assume leadership. Spain, France, and Britain each fought unsuccessfully to retain some of their colonial possessions. Portugal refused to cede any of its colonies peacefully, but the refusal backfired. In 1974, military officers sent to fight against independence movements instead overthrew the government, resulting in almost immediate independence for Angola, Mozambique, Guinea-Bissau, and Sao Tomé and Principe.

As they withdrew from Africa, however, the former colonial powers sought to maintain a measure of control. French President Charles de Gaulle (1890–1970) in particular was adamant that France should exert power over its former colonies. The *Communauté Française* (French Community) allowed former colonies some political and economic independence in exchange for continuing French control over defense and the currency. Drastic consequences followed for those who refused to agree to these conditions.

Decolonization did not always bring anticipated benefits, such as political freedoms or enhanced standards of living. Some countries, such as South Africa, prospered. But at least a dozen African states were consistently ranked at the top of the list of the world's poorest countries. The reasons for this are hotly disputed. However, the cultural and linguistic heritage of colonial rule is much less controversial. As of 2007, a total of 115 million people spread across 31 African countries speak French as a first or second language. Along Cecil Rhodes' envisioned Cape to Cairo railway (see Map 85), English is also spoken as either the official language or one of a handful of official languages.

In 1973, a cartographic controversy erupted over the representation of independent African states on world maps. That year, a German historian named Arno Peters (1916–2002) developed what he claimed was an original **equal area map** purporting to show that the geographic size of the African continent was underestimated on maps that used a Mercator projection (see Map 47). Professional cartographers soon pointed out that Peters had simply appropriated the well-known hundred-year-old Gall-Orthographic projection but had executed it far more poorly. Peters, however, succeeded as a propagandist, creating a straw man out of the widely used Mercator map that shows the correct direction between places. A side effect of the original Mercator projection was that the size of a landmass increased the farther it was from the equator, making countries located in northerly or southerly latitudes appear larger than they actually were. Peters, however, neglected to mention that increasing size applied equally to colonizing and colonized countries alike. As the example on the next page shows, Africa's major colonizers (Britain and France) were shrunk on his projection just as were their former colonies in northern and southern Africa. Latitude, not politics, lay behind the sizes of states on the Mercator map. For a misleading contrast, Peters targeted a landmass unconnected to African colonization and usually deemed to be part of the Americas not of Europe: Greenland, which was itself a colonized territory struggling to achieve home rule at a time when African countries had already succeeded in gaining independence.

Maps that preserve the relative size of land masses are useful in a variety of ways, including comparing the spread of urban areas or grazing areas for animals. On a map of Africa, an equal area projection will preserve the relative sizes of Egypt and Uganda, but it will be useless when undertaking a journey from Cairo to Khartoum because a travel map requires correct direction, which equal area maps are unable to provide.

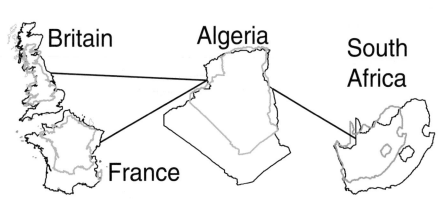

MERCATOR PROJECTION

GALL ORTHOGRAPHIC ("PETERS") PROJECTION

Part 9

Mapping Transport and Communication Networks 1884–2006

The seismic shifts in society and culture that marked the late nineteenth and twentieth centuries included the invention of entirely new forms of transportation and communication. In the skies, airplanes and rockets traveled at previously unimaginable speeds. On the surface of the Earth, a new mode of transport—the automobile—led to changing maps of roads, while deep underground, new networks of railways (called subways, undergrounds, and metros) spread from England to cities all around the globe.

Two of these new forms of transport required maps that maintained connections to the Earth's surface: the railroad and the automobile. Before any railroad could be built, surveyors had to establish the basic heights of areas where tracks could be laid. After construction, shippers, farmers, and ranchers needed railroad maps to know when and where to go to pick up goods and to ship their products. Similarly, automobile maps, like nautical charts, consolidated knowledge of travel from many different regions. And here, a new approach to organizing roadways—namely, the numbering of highways—emerged, first in Europe and then in the United States, before spreading to other parts of the globe.

But maps of other new forms of transportation soon cut their connections to topography. As examined in Part 8, airplanes initially followed rivers, railroads, and coastlines on the Earth below for direction, but they soon came to depend upon an invisible network of radio signals, first from land-based stations and then increasingly from satellites (see Maps 89 and 90). Maps of subways also soon broke away from showing real distances and actual geographic locations of stations, through the

innovative diagrams of a London engineer (see Map 98). Both types of new maps proved successful: pilots took to the skies with maps increasingly disconnected from the terrain below, and commuters around the world embraced the new maps of the underground mass transit.

At the same time, a fundamental shift in the means of communication, from fixed phone and telegraph lines at the beginning of the twentieth century to the Internet today, has led to hundreds of experiments in representing these entirely different networks. As with airplanes and subways, maps of the Internet are increasingly virtual, leading to innovative representations of space that are completely divorced from reality (see Map 100).

A countervailing impulse involves mapping the physical world more closely than ever before. Satellites each year collect millions of pieces of information from teeming metropolises as well as remote corners of the earth—the Amazon, the Sahara, the Gobi desert—to provide a picture of humanity and its impact on the planet that would have been unimaginable a few decades ago. Each hour, millions of people make use of such popular programs as Google Maps and Google Earth, or applications like geographical information systems (**GIS**) and global positioning systems (**GPS**) to situate themselves in our increasingly complex world (see Appendix). In this regard, these new maps bear an uncanny resemblance to the cosmographical drawings and mappamundi from earlier centuries (see Part 3). Though they use computer code instead of ink, today's world maps evince the same intense desire to find one's place in the universe.

Timeline of world history

c. 1825
First railroads

c. 1850
Electricity

1863
First underground railway, London

1884
First gasoline powered automobile

1893
First patent for a radio

1903
First successful airplane flight

since 1905, 1918, 1930
Relativity—quantum mechanics

cc. 1920
Development of international air travel

1956
Creation of Interstate Highway System, US

since 1960s
Development of GIS

since mid-1990s
Widespread use of Internet, GPS

since mid 2000s
Google Maps, Google Earth

96

Brazilian Railway
Map, 1884

◆ ◇ ◆

Planta geral das estradas de ferro das provincias do Rio de Janeiro
Alexandre Speltz, publisher
Rio de Janiero, 1884
Library of Congress
Geography and Map Division
Washington, D.C.

Prior to the development of a railway system, Brazil's agricultural products were transported to market on the backs of mules. Mules can carry large loads (up to 90 kg; 200 lbs.) over relatively long distances. Early in the nineteenth century an estimated 200,000 mules annually arrived at the port of Santos bearing sacks of coffee, sugar, and other products bound for markets in the United States and Europe.

As long as world market prices for coffee remained relatively depressed, the low-tech mule remained the most efficient means of transporting sugar and coffee from the plantations to the ports. In the 1840s, however, the price of coffee began to rise on the international market. Consequently, coffee production in Brazil increased and extensive tracts in the western part of the state of São Paulo were gradually converted into plantations. With the rising price of coffee, Brazilian entrepreneurs began to consider the advantages of investing in a faster means of transporting coffee from the plantations in the interior to the ports on the coast.

The benefits of railroads had been appreciated in Brazil long before they became practical. In 1828, only three years after the construction of the first successful railroad for carrying heavy freight in England, Pedro I, the emperor of Brazil, recognized their potential usefulness and authorized the construction of the first railroads in Brazil. But despite official support for this and several subsequent railroad projects, no Brazilian investor was willing to invest in railroad construction, fearing that they would be unable to make a profit. A run-up in coffee prices in the 1840s changed that attitude.

One of the country's leading entrepreneurs, Irineu Evangelista, traveled to England that decade where he observed the construction of railroad cars and railroads. He would later buy Brazil's first steam locomotive from an English company. Not long after his return from the United Kingdom, Evangelista received a contract from the state of Rio de Janeiro to build a railroad from the fertile agricultural lands of Petropolis, just outside the city of Rio, down to the city's beach at the entrance of Guanabara Bay. Construction began in 1852 and was finished two years later. In April 1854, the steam locomotive *Baroness* began carrying passengers and seven months later began hauling freight.

Soon railroads were being built by private companies throughout Brazil. In coffee-rich São Paulo, no fewer than eighteen different railway lines were built between the plantations and the coast, many over a thousand miles long, each with tracks of different widths. As a result, trains had to be bought separately for each individual line.

While nearly all railroad lines were built to carry agricultural goods bound for export, one line built in 1877 connected the country's two largest cities, São Paulo and Rio de Janeiro. By 1889, when Brazil underwent a transition from a monarchy to a republic, more than 10,000 kilometers of working railroad lines existed, nearly all carrying goods for export. In the early part of the twentieth century the first railroad penetrated the Amazon region, connecting the eastern edge of landlocked Bolivia with the Amazon River and providing Bolivia with an outlet to the Atlantic Ocean. The trans-Amazon railway also supported an increasingly important export—rubber for the making of tires—from deep within the interior.

On the map at right, railroads appear as thin red lines; thicker lines mark political boundaries between states. On the left side of the map, railway lines extend from the coffee fields in the interior toward São Paulo. From São Paulo one railroad line continues to the port of Santos, while another runs parallel to the coast at some distance inland and heads to Rio de Janeiro, marked by its large harbor.

(handwritten margin note) coffee price ↑ in new trade broom or investors

(handwritten margin note) before rr were built but no one saw its usefulness

(handwritten margin note) rend Amazon re

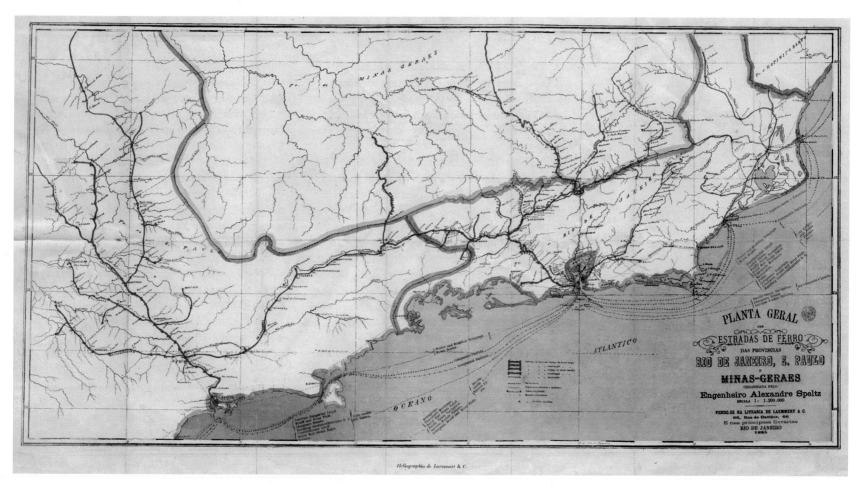

Close-up of the rail lines (shown in red) in the state of Rio de Janeiro. The large harbor of the city of Rio de Janeiro is visible at the bottom center.

97

French National
Automobile Map,
1902

• ◆ •

De Dion-Bouton, c. 1902
Carte Routière de France Spéciale
pour Automobiles 2nd ed.

Carte Michelin France en 47 feuilles
No. 40 Nimes-Avignon
University of California, Berkeley

Automobile road maps appeared in the first decade of the twentieth century, sponsored by four independent sectors: (1) mapmakers for older means of transportation, such as railroads; (2) tire manufacturers; (3) car makers; and (4) automobile enthusiasts.

The first national automobile maps appeared in 1900 in both France and Germany at the request of automakers and car enthusiasts. In France, the world's then largest car manufacturer, De Dion-Bouton, produced the first automobile map of that country, as shown on the right. In Germany that same year, the newly founded Automobile Club commissioned the country's leading bicycle mapmaker to create Germany's first national automobile road map. The following year, competing French bicycle mapmaker Cartes Taride followed suit and produced another automobile road map of France.

In both France and Germany other bicycle tire manufacturers, all of whom started manufacturing tires for cars, sponsored or created automobile maps to encourage people to buy their new products. In Hanover, Germany, the bicycle tire producer Continental Caoutchouc und Gutta Percha Compagnie published a road atlas in 1907. The French tire company Michelin, which began publishing road maps in 1910, included information on roadside attractions and restaurants, encouraging the public to take auto trips—the precursor of the famous Michelin Guides.

At the same time, French carmaker De Dion-Bouton's major German competitor, Mercedes Benz, also started sponsoring road maps. By 1909 Mercedes Benz had produced automobile maps of Germany, Switzerland, Austria, northern Italy, and Czechoslovakia.

In both Germany and the United States, railroad mapmakers soon joined the ranks of automobile mapmakers. German Wilhelm-Karl Koch began

publishing rail maps in 1897, but in 1901 joined with Carl Optiz to issue combined road and rail maps for all of Germany. Just 7 years later they printed a road map of all of Central Europe. The same evolution from railway to road maps also took place in the United States. William Rand and Andrew McNally owned a successful Chicago print shop that turned out railroad tickets and timetables. In 1872 they printed their first map of the rail lines that fanned out from Chicago. In 1904 they produced their first road map for New York City—an area with an already dense network of roads.

The greatest innovation in national auto maps was the introduction of a numbering system. Initially, road maps simply showed the names of the towns along the route, a tradition of mapping going back to at least the fourth century CE (see Map 18) and practiced across the globe. But in an era of rapidly proliferating roads, when choosing among different potential routes was becoming increasingly complicated, ad hoc solutions soon proved insufficient. Names of roads shifted from town to town, causing confusion. Numbering highways was first proposed in 1910 by the Michelin Tire Company. By 1919 French officials had established a numbering system for French roads—a hub and spoke system (like a bicycle rim).

Related schemes developed much later elsewhere in Europe and the United States. A prewar numbering system in Germany was replaced in 1974 with cross-country or international roads numbered A1 through A9. In the United States, roads were originally marked with colored bands tied to telephone poles. In 1926, numbered U.S. highways replaced the bands. In 1956 the interstate numbering system was created, then revised in 1973. As in Germany, north–south U.S. highways have odd numbers; east–west highways have even numbers.

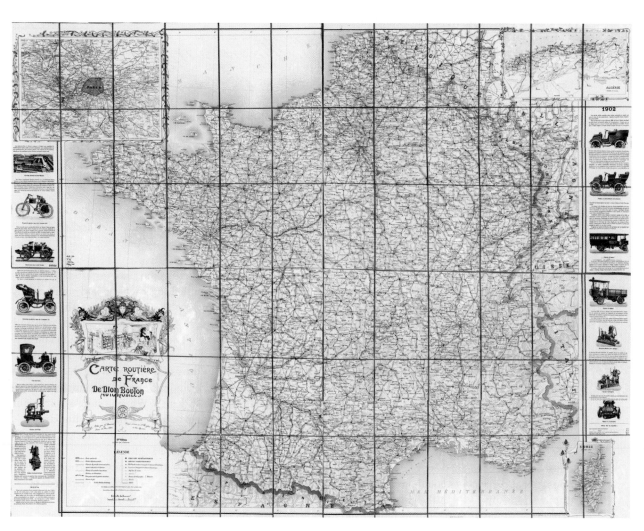

A Michelin road map from about 1910. The shaded box shows the area of France that is covered in the road map.

◀ LEFT
French Automaker De Dion-Bouton's 1902 auto map of France.

98

Harry Beck's 1933 Map of the London Underground

• ◆ •

H.C. Beck's London
Underground Map, 1933
Image 1991–247
226mm, Height: 154mm
London Transport Museum

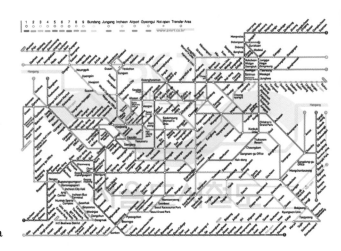

From Beijing to Tokyo, from Cape Town to Cairo, from New York to San Francisco, and from Mexico City to Buenos Aires, all the world's subway maps follow an almost identical design, first created by Harry Beck (1902–1974) in 1933 for the London Underground.

Beck worked for the London Underground in the 1930s as an engineer. Up until 1931, the year of Beck's first proposed design, maps of the Underground were overlaid on top of a simplified map of the city. However, this combination of aboveground information and subterranean paths created maps that were confusing to read. It was often hard to tell whether a place showed a location above ground or a subway stop.

These first Underground maps showed the distances between the stops more or less correctly, as well as the direction in which the tracks were laid. However, the users of the Underground were interested only in very limited information: they wanted to know the sequence of stops and the approximate direction in which the train traveled. In this sense, they required minimal information—like those on journeys along the ancient Roman roads (see Map 18).

Beck simplified the map of the subway so that it indicated direction in very general terms, and showed the sequence of stops along the route. He also did away with the need to accurately show the distance between stops. Instead, he spaced the stations so that their names could be clearly and distinctly labeled. As a result, the map exaggerated the length of distances between stops in the center of London, and dramatically decreased the distances between stops outside the city center.

Beck also depicted the Underground tracks with straight lines, while in reality the tracks often curved back and forth around subterranean obstacles. His straight line design was inspired by the electrical diagrams that he had used as an engineer. In order for electrical cables to be accessible to workers in the Underground, they needed to be bundled together and laid out in clearly accessible pathways. To simplify access, the cables were often fixed in straight lines or at 45-degree and 90-degree angles. Their locations were then laid out in diagrams for the mechanics and engineers who worked on the rail lines. Applying this principle to his map of the Underground, Beck employed a similar schematic design. Where a subway car might weave back and forth under a road, the line drawn on Beck's map appeared completely straight, or at 45-degree or 90-degree angles.

Beck's map, with its simplicity, diagrammatic lines, and clear labels perfectly suited the needs of commuters. It became not only popular in London; it immediately set the international standard for subway maps. To this day, Beck's map of the Underground is one of the most instantly recognizable drawings of the twentieth century and remains an enduring icon of modernity. While Beck's map cannot be used to repair tracks or gain access to a stalled train in a tunnel, it is the most successful transportation map ever designed for popular use—an outstanding example of consumer-oriented design.

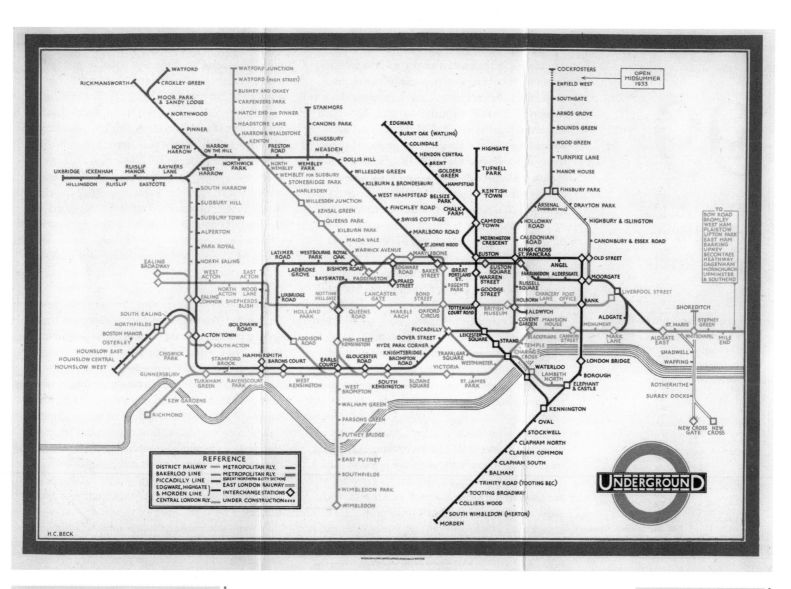

99

Landing on 27R: London's Heathrow Airport, 2006

● ◆ ●

Instrument Approach Chart–ICAO
London/Heathrow, 2006
Civil Aviation Authority (UK)
Crown Copyright
Courtesy Col. Charles Quilter,
USMC (ret.)

The map on the right shows a landing path for one of the busiest airports in the world: London's Heathrow International Airport. An elegant yet abstract image, the map appears scarcely recognizable to the uninitiated. Little more than a shadow, the Thames and its tributaries barely scratch the surface. London—its parks, its roads, its many squares—has vanished. Instead of terrestrial features, airspace dominates the map, which jet pilots consult in the cockpit as they approach runway 27R at London's Heathrow airport.

Only a few types of flight still use the older style of aviation maps (see Map 89). Pilots who fly at low altitudes in light aircraft or in helicopters, such as those used in search and rescue missions, still prefer to have maps with detailed images of the terrain. For nearly all passengers arriving at major international airports, their pilots will likely be using a map like the one at the right to land safely.

This dramatic change in mapping came about because of the introduction of instrument flight rules. The process of instrument landing became perfected during the late 1970s and early 1980s as pilots came to rely upon electronic signals from beacons. After the 1980s these signals were frequently displayed electronically in the cockpit. As a result, maps began to gradually eliminate ground information. The only place names that appear on Map 99 are those of the airports served and the names of radio navigation aids or intersections of their bearings. Even latitude and longitude only appear in very faint lines on the edge of the chart, clearly designed only to be used in an emergency.

Another innovation involves the way the height of objects in the area surrounding the airfield are measured and mapped. In contrast to the more general elevation information included in earlier flight maps, Map 99 shows the heights for specific places and objects. Wavy orange shapes indicate several regions of higher elevation, bounded by contour lines indicating feet above sea level. In addition, towers, buildings, or other objects more than 200 feet high are noted by a stylized dark blue arrow with the precise height in feet noted on the side. Those blue arrows, which at first appear to be windmills, have flashing lights on the top.

The city of London itself is transformed on this map from a place of streets, highways, and parks to a giant irregularly shaped pink mass. The pink color represents the restricted airspace above the city that can only be entered with specific permission from the control tower. Numbers in the pink space indicate the range (in feet) of restricted airspace, transforming the city of London into simply another geometrically defined elevation point along the path to runway 27R. The giant blue arrow cutting through the pink shape indicates the only way to this runway, following a 272-degree magnetic compass course once permission has been granted and the plane is cleared for landing. The procedures for landing and how to abort a landing also appear—the solid line for landing, the dashed line for an aborted landing.

Charts such as this one register an unseen world of radio and radar impulses, transforming the electromagnetic world into numbers and geometric shapes. With most information about the ground (except for elevation) removed, the maps appear far clearer and the pilot's attention can focus exclusively upon the most important features. Thus, a map composed almost entirely of geometric shapes and numbers enables millions of safe landings annually at Heathrow.

Aeronautical charts represent a different kind of transformation in mapmaking than that of the similarly geometric subway maps pioneered by Harry Beck in 1933. The simplicity of the subway map does not function to guide its engineer, but rather allows the passengers to find their way. By contrast, aviation maps guide pilots along the landing path. By transforming sound and signals into visual representations, aeronautical maps represent a profound shift in the way physical reality is depicted. Subway maps are triumphs of design; aeronautical maps are breakthroughs in data visualization.

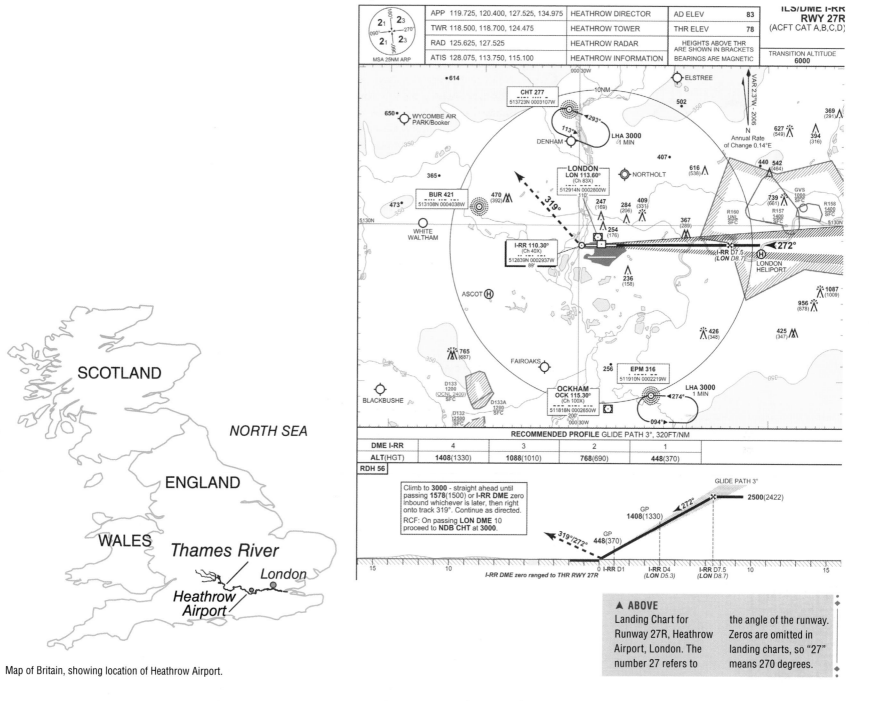

Map of Britain, showing location of Heathrow Airport.

SCOTLAND

NORTH SEA

ENGLAND

WALES

Thames River

London

Heathrow
Airport

ILS/DME I-RR
RWY 27R
(ACFT CAT A,B,C,D)

APP 119.725, 120.400, 127.525, 134.975	HEATHROW DIRECTOR	AD ELEV	**83**
TWR 118.500, 118.700, 124.475	HEATHROW TOWER	THR ELEV	**78**
RAD 125.625, 127.525	HEATHROW RADAR	HEIGHTS ABOVE THR ARE SHOWN IN BRACKETS	
ATIS 128.075, 113.750, 115.100	HEATHROW INFORMATION	BEARINGS ARE MAGNETIC	

MSA 25NM ARP

VAR 2.3°W - 2006
Annual Rate
of Change 0.14°E

TRANSITION ALTITUDE
6000

•614

ELSTREE

CHT 277
513723N 0003107W

10NM

502

369
(291)

WYCOMBE AIR
PARK/Booker
650•

293°

113°

LHA 3000
1 MIN

627
(549)

394
(316)

DENHAM

407•

365•

LONDON
LON 113.60°
(Ch 83X)
512914N 0002800W
110°

NORTHOLT

616
(538)

440 542
(464)

739
(661)

GVS
1000
SFC

BUR 421
513108N 0004038W

470
(392)

319°

247
(169)

284
(206)

409
(331)

R160
UNL
SFC

R157
1400
SFC

R158
1400
SFC

473•

WHITE
WALTHAM

5130N

254
(176)

367
(289)

272°

5130N

I-RR 110.30°
(Ch 40X)
512839N 0002937W
89'

236
(158)

I-RR D7.5
(LON D8.7)

LONDON
HELIPORT

ASCOT Ⓗ

1087
(1009)

956
(878)

426
(348)

425
(347)

765
(687)

FAIROAKS

256

EPM 316
511910N 0002219W

LHA 3000
1 MIN

274°

BLACKBUSHE

D133
1200
(OCNL 2400)
SFC

D133A
1200
SFC

OCKHAM
OCK 115.30°
(Ch 100X)
511818N 0002650W
200°

094°

D132
12500
SFC

000 30W

RECOMMENDED PROFILE GLIDE PATH 3°, 320FT/NM

DME I-RR	4	3	2	1	
ALT(HGT)	**1408**(1330)	**1088**(1010)	**768**(690)	**448**(370)	

RDH 56

GLIDE PATH 3°

Climb to **3000** - straight ahead until
passing **1578**(1500) or **I-RR DME** zero
inbound whichever is later, then right
onto track 319°. Continue as directed.
RCF: On passing **LON DME** 10
proceed to **NDB CHT** at 3000.

GP
1408(1330)

272°

2500(2422)

319°/272°

GP
448(370)

15   10   I-RR D1   I-RR D4   I-RR D7.5   10   15
                                                     (LON D5.3) (LON D8.7)

I-RR DME zero ranged to THR RWY 27R   0

▲ **ABOVE**

Landing Chart for
Runway 27R, Heathrow
Airport, London. The
number 27 refers to

the angle of the runway.
Zeros are omitted in
landing charts, so "27"
means 270 degrees.

100

Map of the Internet,

2003

• ◆ •

Map of the Internet, 2003
Opte Project
Retrieved September 2010

Early humans transmitted messages from person to person via direct face-to-face interaction. With the advent of writing, the necessity of firsthand contact diminished. But writing required transmission of a physical object—a clay tablet, a scroll, a book. Beginning with the invention of the telegraph in the late nineteenth century, people began to transmit messages with great precision over large distances using only electrical pulses sent through a wire. Today, however, messages travel around the world by almost invisible means, often in the form of electromagnetic signals such as radio waves or microwaves. These new forms of transmitting words, sounds, or images require electronic devices to both encode the information digitally in order for it to be sent, and to decode the same digital signals as information when they are received by the recipient.

As a result, cartography has come face to face with one of its most interesting recent challenges, the task of representing the transmission of invisible pulses through a physical space. Unlike aeronautical visualizations (see Map 99), maps of the Internet are not linked to localized geographic spaces. To send an email to my next door neighbor, my message is routed from Irvine, California to Los Angeles to San Francisco and then back to my neighbors' computer next door.

Sounds, text, and images are all transmitted on the Internet via packets of binary numbers, with the destination defined by a combination of numbers called an IP (Internet Protocol) address. IP addresses contain four sets of numbers separated by a dot or period, such as "166.70.10.23." Sometimes the transmission of packets is verified through a Transmission Control Protocol (TCP), resulting in messages sent through TCP/IP.

When packets have to be switched from one portion of the network to another on the way to their destination, the traffic directors on the route are called "network routers"; that is, they route the data to the appropriate sections of the network based upon the destination's Internet Protocol address. The network router reads the address information in the incoming packet and uses that information, plus dynamically established tables, to decide on the nearest available working network and other information that determines the fastest path.

Barrett Lyon (1978–), the creator of this 2003 map of the Internet on the right, chose to show the connections between network routers using straight lines to visualize the paths. The result is a schematic or diagrammatic representation, similar to the map of the London Underground created by Harry Beck 70 years earlier. But unlike subway lines, where trains travel to and from a single destination creating clear single lines, packets can follow multiple paths between routers.

While earlier route maps such as the Roman road map from antiquity indicated stopping points with a short line, the Internet map shows hundreds of lines fanning out from each of the network routers. The crucial question for Lyon was how to connect the routers to physical places. He decided to replace geographical space entirely with colors— with directions indicated by the path of the line. Asia/Pacifica is colored red, Europe/Middle East/Central Asia/Africa is green, North America is blue, Latin America and the Caribbean are yellow, and private Internet routers are blue-green. The white clusters represent unknown locations, mostly indicating government and private networks. For security reasons, these networks deliberately conceal their geographical locations.

This map of the Internet sufficiently impressed the curators of the Museum of Modern Art in New York that they made it part of their permanent collection of contemporary art. While the image is based upon visualization of large quantities of data, it is indeed a work of art.

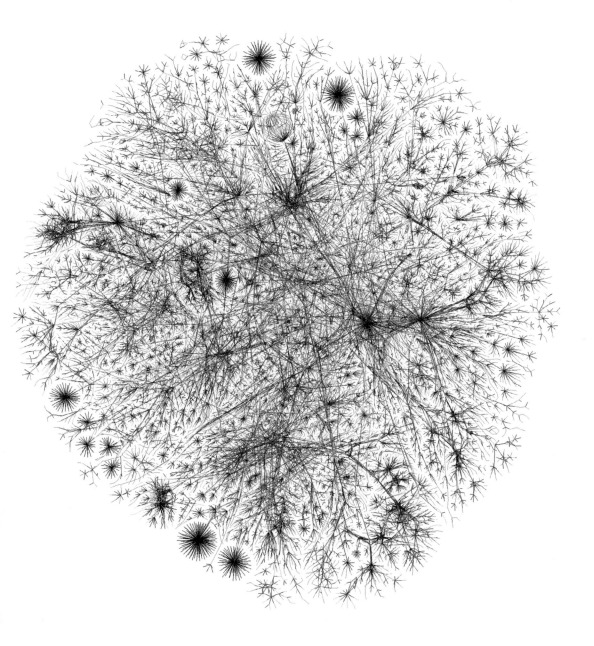

Appendix: Google Earth and Google Maps

• • •

Zooming in from outer space to the roof of your apartment or house and seeing familiar cars parked in the driveway on the street amazes nearly everyone who uses Google Earth. Click on "street view" in Google Maps and the world outside your front door appears on the screen. When visiting a distant city, or even just an unfamiliar neighborhood in your hometown, you can use Google Maps street view to see what well-known landmarks look like as you search for an unknown location. No longer do you need to constantly stop to ask strangers for directions. With a Google Map on your smart phone, you can call up the location instantly to find out how lost you are or how close you are to your destination. But Google Earth goes beyond the familiar. Googlers have bicycled on dirt paths capturing the appearance of some of the most remote places on Earth, from the Amazon to the Sahara to coral reefs under the sea. Google has transformed the world, or at least most of it, from a large and unfamiliar place to a warp-speed travel machine that can be summoned up in the palm of one's hand. Anyone with access to a computer or a smartphone can zip across the globe instantly.

All of this wealth of new information has come at some cost. Privacy advocates have expressed concerns about the information that Google collects. In some instances, Google has captured information on wi-fi networks in private houses and apartments, and has failed to delete this information from its records.

How Google manages to make you think that you can travel from outer space to the street beside you is the product of massive computer processors that sort thought billions of gigabytes of data to locate the exact image and location you are requesting. Powerful computers—requiring vast amounts of electricity—store the images that Googlers have collected; when someone wants to explore or navigate a city, it produces them upon demand.

However, Google relies upon more than its own data. It also acquires information from private companies and governments that operate giant satellites orbiting the sky. If you carefully examine the lower right hand corner of any Google map, you will see a series of unfamiliar names next to the copyright: Tele-Atlas, Geo-Basis DE/BKG, INVA-Geosistemas SRL, and Map-Link. These companies (and sometimes government organizations) maintain satellites that orbit the Earth, and relay images of the planet from hundreds of miles above. These satellites can see remote locations that are inaccessible to most people. They can identify regions where warfare has made travel impossible, or areas deep within the rainforest that might take weeks or months to reach. Google licenses the data from these companies, who hold the copyright to the pictures that appear on Google Earth.

When you zoom into your front door or to the mouth of the Amazon River, you are relying upon data from dozens of satellites, from billions of images collected on streets and paths around the world, all summoned at the click of a mouse. What you are watching as you seem to zoom from outer space to your own front door is similar to a movie or a flip book, composed of hundreds of individual snapshots flashing in front of you so quickly that it appears as though you are actually moving through space.

You cannot manipulate the Google Earth images as they flash by from outer space, any more than you can change the frame or direction of a movie camera in a particular scene to see what is happening elsewhere on the set or behind the camera. For this reason, professionals in fields as diverse as oil and gas prospecting to humanitarian relief organizations often bypass Google Earth and turn to the satellite operators themselves to focus their eyes in the sky toward untapped natural resources or on unseen trouble spots. But in their everyday life, both the energy prospectors and the relief workers will turn to a Google Map to find their way to a local hangout.

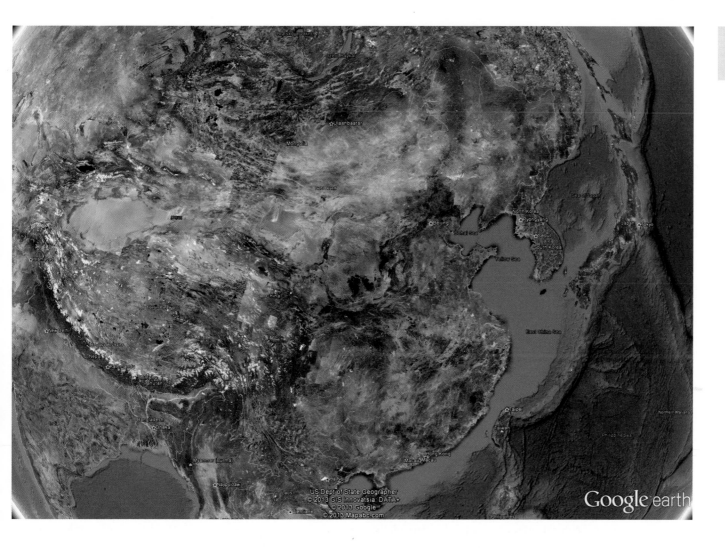

Glossary

A

atlas: a book of maps or charts.

B

bathymetry: an instrument used to measure the depth of water in seas or lakes.

C

cartogram: a map on which statistical information is shown in diagrammatic form.

compass: an instrument containing a magnetized pointer which shows the direction of magnetic north and bearings from it.

compass rose: a graduated circle printed on a map or chart from which bearings can be taken.

cordiform: heart-shaped.

cosmographer: one who studies the branch of science which deals with the general features of the universe, including the earth.

cosmographies: the branch of science which deals with the general features of the universe, including the earth.

cuneiform: denoting or relating to the wedge-shaped characters used in the ancient writing systems of Mesopotamia, Persia, and Ugarit, surviving mainly on clay tablets.

D

dead reckoning: the process of calculating one's position, especially at sea, by estimating the direction and distance traveled rather than by using landmarks or astronomical observations.

E

escape map: maps, made either of silk or rayon, that were produced by Great Britain and the United States during World War II to help downed airmen evade capture.

equal area map: a map in which a square kilometer in one portion of the map is equal in size to a square kilometer in any other portion. Equal area maps of the whole globe tend to be elliptical in shape, and severely distort the shapes of regions far from the equator.

G

GIS: Geographic Information System, a system for storing and manipulating geographical information on computer.

GPS: Global Positioning System, an accurate worldwide navigational and surveying facility based on the reception of signals from an array of orbiting satellites.

Gyoki maps: a Japanese Buddhist priest who lived in the late 7th century CE, devised a rough outline map of the country containing 66 "kunis" or provinces. These maps were subsequently referred to as "Gyoki-maps." They were the dominant map style in Japan until the middle of the Tokugawa Era and continued to be created until the Meiji Period.

H

hieroglyphics: a stylized picture of an object representing a word, syllable, or sound, as found in ancient Egyptian and certain other writing systems.

L

legend: the wording on a map or diagram explaining the symbols used.

lithography: the process of printing from a flat surface treated so as to repel the ink except where it is required for printing.

lunar mansions: a lunar mansion is a segment of the ecliptic (often called a station, or house) through which the moon moves in its orbit around the Earth, often used by ancient cultures as part of their calendar system. In general, though not always, the zodiac is divided into 27 or 28 segments relative to fixed stars - one for each day of the lunar month, which is 27.3 days long - and the position of the moon is charted with respect to those fixed segments. Since the position of the moon at given stage will vary according to the position of the earth in its own orbit, the mansions of the moon are an effective system for keeping track of the passage of seasons.

M

mappamundi: a medieval European map of the world. Such maps range in size and complexity from simple schematic maps an inch or less across to elaborate wall maps, the largest of which was 11 ft. (3.5 m.) in diameter. The term derives from the Medieval Latin words mappa (cloth or chart) and mundi (of the world).

marine chronometer: a timekeeping device that is used to determine longitude at sea by means of celestial navigation.

Memory board: a mapping device employed by the Luba people of the present-day Democratic Republic of the Congo. Memory boards typically consist of a carved, hand-sized wooden board on which various objects—shells, beads, bits of metal, and so forth—are arranged to recount, in symbolic fashion, the histories of past rulers, creation stories, or principles of leadership.

N

nautical astrolabe: an instrument used to determine a ship's latitude at sea by measuring the sun's altitude at noon or the meridian altitude of a star. The development of the nautical astrolabe, also known as a mariner's astrolabe, or sea astrolabe, is credited to Abraham Zacuto (1452–1515), a Portuguese-Jewish astronomer and mathematician.

O

Ordnance Survey: In the United Kingdom, an official survey organization, originally under the Master of the Ordnance, that prepares large-scale detailed maps of the whole country.

P

papyrus: a material prepared in ancient Egypt from the stem of a water plant, used in sheets throughout the ancient Mediterranean world for writing or painting on and also for making articles such as rope.

planisphere: a map formed by the projection of a sphere or part of a sphere on a plane, especially an adjustable circular star map that shows the appearance of the heavens at a specific time and place.

polder: a piece of low-lying land reclaimed from the sea or a river and protected by dykes, especially in the Netherlands.

portolan: a book of sailing directions with charts and descriptions of harbors and coasts.

projection: the representation on a plane surface of part of the surface of the earth or a celestial sphere.

S

stick map: stick charts made and used by the people of the Marshall Islands to navigate the Pacific Ocean. The charts represent major ocean swell patterns and the ways the islands disrupted those patterns. Stick charts are typically made from the midribs of coconut fronds tied together to form an open framework.

T

theodolite: a surveying instrument with a rotating telescope for measuring horizontal and vertical angles.

T-O maps: a "T and O map" or "O-T" or "T-O map" (*orbis terrarum*, orb or circle of the lands; with the letter T inside an O), is a type of medieval world map, sometimes also called a Beatine map or a Beatus map because one of the earliest known representations of this sort is attributed to Beatus of Liébana, an 8th-century Spanish monk.

topographic: relating to the arrangement or accurate representation of the physical features of an area.

toponym: general term for any place or geographical entity.

triangulation: (in surveying) the tracing and measurement of a series or network of triangles in order to determine the distances and relative positions of points spread over an area, especially by measuring the length of one side of each triangle and deducing its angles and the length of the other two sides by observation from this baseline.

V

vellum: fine parchment made originally from the skin of a calf.

Z

zodiac: a belt of the heavens within about 8° either side of the ecliptic, including all apparent positions of the sun, moon, and most familiar planets. It is divided into twelve equal divisions or signs (Aries, Taurus, Gemini, Cancer, Leo, Virgo, Libra, Scorpio, Sagittarius, Capricorn, Aquarius, Pisces).

Bibliography

General Introduction: Two recent books—Jerry Brotton, *The World in Twelve Maps* (2012) and Peter Barber and Tom Harper, *Magnificent Maps* (2012)—are as enjoyable as they are informative. For those interested in specific areas or time periods, the multivolume *History of Cartography*, started by the late David Woodward, contains many useful essays.

PART 1: MAPPING THE SKIES: PREHISTORY - 1515 CE

1. **Lascaux, France: the Pleiades, *c.* 17,000 BCE** Georges Bataille. *Lascaux, Or, the Birth of Art: Prehistoric Painting*. Lausanne: Skira, 1955.
2. **Polynesian Constellations, 300 BCE–1200 CE** Ben R. Finney. *Voyage of Rediscovery: A Cultural Odyssey Through Polynesia*. Berkeley: University of California Press, 1994.
3. **African Star Lore** Jarita C. Holbrook, Rodney Medupe, and Johnson O. Urama. *African Cultural Astronomy: Current Archaeoastronomy and Ethnoastronomy Research in Africa*. Berlin: Springer, 2008.
4. **The Emu, Australia** Bruce Chatwin, *The Songlines*, New York: Penguin, 1988. Ray Norris and Cilla Norris, *Emu Dreaming: An Introduction to Australian Aboriginal Astronomy*. Sydney, Australia: Emu Dreaming, 2009
5. **The Origin of the Zodiac, Ancient Mesopotamia: 1130 BCE** Alex A. Gurshtein, "On The Origin of The Zodiacal Constellations." *Vistas in Astronomy*, Vol, 36, Part 2:171–190. R. Watson and W. Horowitz. *Writing Science before the Greeks: A Naturalistic Analysis of the Babylonian Astronomical Treatise MUL.APIN*. Leiden: Brill, 2011.
6. **Greek Constellations and Arabic Stars: The *Almagest* (150 CE) and Arabic Star Lists (1065 CE)** Ptolemy and G J. Toomer. *Ptolemy's Almagest*. London: Duckworth, 1984. Emilie Savage-Smith. "The Book of Curiosities: An Eleventh-Century Egyptian View of the Lands of the Infidels." In: K. A. Raaflaub and R. J. A. Talbert, eds. *Geography and Ethnography: Perceptions of the World in Pre-Modern Societies*, pp. 291–310. Oxford: Wiley-Blackwell, 2010. David A. King. *Islamic Mathematical Astronomy*. London: Variorum Reprints, 1986.
7. **First Maps of the Greek Constellations, Persia, 964 CE** Paul Kunitzsch. *The Arabs and the Stars: Texts and Traditions on the Fixed Stars, and Their Influence in Medieval Europe*. Northampton: Variorum Reprints, 1989. Abu-'l-Husain Sufi, A.-R. I.-U, and Fuat Sezgi. *Kitab Suwar Al-Kawakib: The Book of Constellations*. Frankfurt: Institute for the History of Arabic-Islamic Science, 1986.
8. **The Hebrew Zodiac, 1361 CE** Y. Tzvi Langermann. "Hebrew Astronomy: Deep Soundings from a Rich Tradition." In: Helaine Selin, ed. *Astronomy Across Cultures: The History of Non-Western Astronomy*, pp. 555–584. Dordrecht: Kluwer Academic Publishers 2000.
   ___. *The Jews and the Sciences in the Middle Ages*. Brookfield, VT: Ashgate Varorium, 1999; especially "The Hebrew astronomical codex MS Sasson 823."
9. **Dunhuang Star Map (Tang Dynasty), 618–907 CE** Sun Xiaochun and Jacob Kistemaker. *The Chinese Sky During The Han: Constellating Stars and Society*. Leiden: Brill, 1997.
10. **Chinese Constellations (Song Dynasty), 1193 CE** Sun Xiaochun and Jacob Kistemaker. *The Chinese Sky During The Han: Constellating Stars and Society*. Leiden: Brill, 1997.
11. **From Sky to Land: Directions in China, 3000 BCE – Present** Suzanne E. Cahill. *Warriors, Tombs and Temples: China's Enduring Legacy*. Santa Ana, CA: Bowers Museum, 2011. Ann Paludan. *The Chinese Spirit Road: The Classical Tradition of Stone Tomb Statuary*. New Haven: Yale University Press, 1991.
12. **Albrecht Dürer, Map of the Constellations, 1515 CE** Giulia Bartrum, Albrecht Dürer, Günter Grass, Joseph L. Koerner, and Ute Kuhlemann. *Albrecht Dürer: The Graphic Work of a Renaissance Artist*. Princeton, NJ: Princeton University Press, 2002. For the following centuries see Nick Kanas, *Star Maps: History Artistry, and Cartography*, 2nd ed. New York: Springer Praxis, pp. 151ff.

PART 2: ROADS, RIVERS, AND ROUTES: 3000 BCE – 1360 CE

13. **Ancient Mesopotamia: The Town of Nippur, *c.* 2300 BCE** Joan Aruz and Ronald Wallenfels. *Art of the First Cities: The Third Millennium B.C. from the Mediterranean to the Indus*. New York: Metropolitan Museum of Art, 2003.
14. **Map of the Route to Paradise, Egypt, 1985–1795 BCE** John H. Taylor, *Spells for Eternity: The Ancient Egyptian Book of the Dead*, London: British Museum, 2010.
15. **Road Map to the Egyptian Quarries, 1150 BCE** James A. Harrell. "Turin Papyrus Map from Ancient Egypt." Department of Environmental Sciences, University of Toledo, online. James A. Harrell and V. Max Brown. "The World's Oldest Surviving Geological Map: The 1150 B.C. Turin Papyrus from Egypt." *Journal of Geology*, Vol. 100, No. 1 (1992): 3–18.

16. **Rivers and Roads: The Oldest Map in China, *c*. 239** BCE Mei-Ling Hsu, "The Qin Maps: A Clue to Later Chinese Cartographic Development." *Imago Mundi*, Vol. 45 (1993): 90–100.

17. **Rome Mapped in Marble: The Severan Marbles, 203–211** CE Emilio Rodríguez Almeida, *Formae Urbis antiquae: le mappe marmoree di Roma tra la Repubblica e Settimio Severo.* Roma: Ecole française de Rome, 2002.

18. **All Roads Lead To Rome: The Peutinger Table, *c*. 350–400** CE Talbert, Richard J. A. *Rome's World: The Peutinger Map Reconsidered.* Cambridge, UK: Cambridge University Press, 2010.

19. **River Maps: The Indus River, *c*. 1065** CE Yossef Rapoport and Emilie Savage-Smith, "The Book of Curiosities and a Unique Map of the World." In: Richard J. A. Talbert and Richard W. Unger, eds. *Cartography in Antiquity and the Middle Ages.* Leiden: Brill, 2008.

20. **Cairo to Constantinople: A Nautical Route along the Mediterranean, *c*. 1065** CE Emilie Savage-Smith, "Maps and Trade" In: M. Mango, ed. *Byzantine Trade (4th–12th centuries): The Archaeology of Local, Regional and International Exchange*, pp. 15–29. Farnham: Ashgate, 2009.
Jeremy Johns and Emilie Savage-Smith. "The Book of Curiosities: A Newly Discovered Series of Islamic Maps." *Imago Mundi*, Vol. 55, No. 1 (2003): 7–30.

21. **Crusader Jerusalem, *c*. 1200** CE John Wilkinson, Joyce Hill, and William F. Ryan. *Jerusalem Pilgrimage, 1099–1185*. London: Hakluyt Society, 1988.
Christopher Tyerman. *Chronicles of the First Crusade, 1096–1099.* London: Penguin, 2012.

22. **Gough Map of Britain: Rivers and Routes, *c*. 1360** CE Nick Millea, *The Gough Map: The Earliest Road Map of Great Britain.* Oxford: Bodleian Library, 2007. See the excellent website with the restored map and more information.

PART 3: MAPPING THE WORLD, 600 BCE – *c*. **1450** CE

23. **Babylonian World Map, 600** BCE Irving L. Finkel, M. J. Seymour, and John Curtis. *Babylon: Myth and Reality.* London: British Museum, 2008.

24. **Medieval Christian T-O Map, *c*. 600** CE David Woodward, "Medieval Mappaemundi." In: J. B. Harley and David Woodward, eds. *Cartography in Prehistoric, Ancient, and Medieval Europe and the Mediterranean;* Vol. 1, *The History of Cartography.* Chicago: University of Chicago Press, 1987.

25. **World Climate Map, *c*. Fifth Century** CE Alfred Hiatt, "The Map of Macrobius before 1100." *Imago Mundi*, Vol. 59, No. 2 (2007): 149–176.

26. **Medieval Islamic Map of the World, *c*. 1300** CE Ibn Khaldun, *trans.* Franz Rosenthal. *The Muqaddimah: An Introduction to History.* New York: Pantheon Books,1958, 2nd Prefatory Discussion.
Fuat Sezgin, Mazin Amawi, Carl Ehrig-Eggert, and E Neubauer. *Studies on Al-Wat wat (d. 1318), Ad-Dimasqi (d. 1327), Ibn Al-Wardi (d. C. 1446) and Al-Bakuwi (15th Cent.).* Frankfurt: Institute for the History of Arabic-Islamic Science at the Johann Wolfgang Goethe University, 1994.

27. **First Map of Turkish Central Asia, 1072** CE Kashgari Mah mud and Robert Dankoff. *Divanu Lugat-it-Turk.* Cambridge, MA: Basıldıgı yer Harvard Universitesi Basımevi, 1982.

28. **Hereford Mappamundi, 1300** CE P. D. A. Harvey, *The Hereford World Map: Medieval World Maps and Their Context.* London: British Library, 2006.
Scott D. Westrem. *The Hereford Map: A Transcription and Translation of the Legends with Commentary.* Turnhout: Brepols, 2001.

29. **Idrisi's Circular Map of the World, 1165** CE Jeremy Johns and Emilie Savage-Smith. "The Book of Curiosities: A Newly Discovered Series of Islamic Maps." *Imago Mundi*, Vol. 55, No. 1 (2003): 7–30.
Henri Bresc and Annliese Nef, editors and translators. *Idrisi: La premiere geographie de l' Occident.* Paris: Flammarion, 1999.

30. **Earliest Known Ptolemaic Map of the World, *c*. 1300** CE O. A. W. Dilke. "The Culmination of Greek Cartography in Ptolemy." In: B. Harley and David Woodward, eds. *Cartography in Prehistoric, Ancient, and Medieval Europe and the Mediterranean.* Vol. 1, *The History of Cartography.* Chicago: University of Chicago Press, 1987.

31. **Fra Mauro's Map of the World, 1448–1459** CE Piero Falchetta, *Fra Mauro's World Map: With a Commentary and Translations of the Inscriptions.* Turnhout: Brepols, 2006.
Angelo Cattaneo, *Fra Mauro's Mappa Mundi and Fifteenth-Century Venice*. Turnhout: Brepols, 2011.

32. **Buddhist World Map from Japan, 1710** CE Hugh Cortazzi. *Isles of Gold: Antique Maps of Japan.* Weatherhill, 1983.
Nobuo Muroga and Kazutaka Unno, "The Buddhist World Map in Japan and Its Contact with European Maps." *Imago Mundi*, Vol. 16 (1962): 49–69.

33. **Jain World Map** James Laidlaw. *Riches and Renunciation: Religion, Economy, and Society Among the Jains.* Oxford, UK: Clarendon Press, 1995.

PART 4: AN EXPANDING WORLD, 1300–1570

34. **Catalan World Map, 1375** Abraham Cresques and Georges Grosjean. *Mapamundi, the Catalan Atlas of the Year 1375*. Dietikon-Zurich: Urs Graf, Abaris Books, 1978.

35. **Arabic Portolan, *c.* 1300** J. Vernet-Gines, "The Maghreb Chart in the Biblioteca Ambrosiana." *Imago Mundi*, Vol. 16 (1962): 1–16.

36. **Nautical Chart of the Mediterranean and the Atlantic Coasts of Europe and Africa, 1511** Tony Campbell. "Portolan Charts from the Late Thirteenth Century to 1500." In: J. B. Harley and David Woodward, eds. *Cartography in Prehistoric, Ancient, and Medieval Europe and the Mediterranean;* Vol. 1, *The History of Cartography*. Chicago: University of Chicago Press, 1987.

37. **Which Way Is North: An Introduction to the History of Directions in the West** Heinrich Winter. "On the Real and the Pseudo-Pilestrina Maps and Other Early Portuguese Maps in Munich." *Imago Mundi*, Vol. 4 (1947): 25–27.
_____. "A Late Portolan Chart at Madrid and Late Portolan Charts in General." *Imago Mundi*, Vol. 7 (1950): 37–46.
Armando Cortesão. *History of Portuguese Cartography*, vol. 2. Lisbon: Junta de Investigações do Ultramar,1969–71.

38. **Map of the Known World, by Martellus, *c.* 1489** Alexander O. Vietor. "A Pre-Columbian Map of the World, circa 1489." *Imago Mundi*, Vol. 17 (1963): 95–98.

39. **First Map of America: The Cantino Map, 1502** Ernesto Milano and Alberto Cantino, *La Carta Del Cantino E La Rappresentazione Della Terra Nei Codici E Nei Libri a Stampa Della Biblioteca Estense E Nei Universitaria*. Modena: Il Bulino, 1991.

40. **Latitude and Longitude: The Keys to Expanding the World** The best accessible history of longitude is available online at the National Maritime Museum, Greenwich, England. For latitude (also online) see Seed, "Latitude: The Art and Science of Fifteenth-Century Navigation."

41. **Waldseemüller Map of the World, 1507 CE** Alfredo Pinheiro Marques. *Origem e desenvolvimento da cartografia Portuguesa na Epoca dos descobrimentos* [The Origins and Development of Portuguese Cartography at the Time of the Discoveries]. Lisbon: Imprensa Nacional – Casa da Moeda, 1987.

42. **The Indian Ocean Mapped by Pedro Reinel** Richard Uhden. "The Oldest Portuguese Original Chart of the Indian Ocean, A. D. 1509." *Imago Mundi*, Vol. 3 (1939): 7–11.
Francisco Bethencourt and Diogo R. Curto. *Portuguese Oceanic Expansion, 1400–1800*. Cambridge, England: Cambridge University Press, 2007.

43. **A Heart-Shaped Map: 1534** Jean-Jacques Brioist. "Oronce Fine and Cartographical Methods." In: Alexander Marr, ed., *The Worlds of Oronce Fine: Mathematics, Instruments and Print in Renaissance Franc*, pp. 137–155. Lincolnshire, UK Shaun Tyas, 2009.

44. **Magellan's Circumnavigation of the Globe, 1519–1522** Antonio Pigafetta and T J. Cachey. *The First Voyage around the World, 1519-1522: An Account of Magellan's Expedition*. Toronto: University of Toronto Press, 2007.

45. **Abraham Ortelius, The Atlas, 1570, Part A** C. Koeman. *The History of Abraham Ortelius and His Theatrum Orbis Terrarum*. New York: Elsevier, 1964.

46. **Abraham Ortelius, The Atlas, 1570, Part B** Thomas Horst, *Le monde en carte: Gérard Mercator (1512-1594) et le premier atlas du monde*. Antwerp: Mercatorfonds, 2011.

47. **Mercator's World Map, 1569** Nicholas Crane, *Mercator: The Man Who Mapped the Planet*. New York: Henry Holt, 2003.
Mark S. Monmonier. *Rhumb Lines and Map Wars: A Social History of the Mercator Projection*. Chicago: University of Chicago Press, 2004.

PART 5: WORLDS COLLIDING, 1550 – *c.* 1800

48. **Native Towns of Spanish Mexico** Barbara E. Mundy. *The Mapping of New Spain: Indigenous Cartography and the Maps of the Relaciones Geográfica*. Chicago: University of Chicago Press, 1996.
Robert Wauchope, Howard F. Cline, eds. *Handbook of Middle American Indians*, Volume 12: *Guide to Ethnohistorical Sources, Part 1*. Austin: University of Texas Press,1972.

49. **Guaman Poma, Mappamundi as Satire, 1615** Felipe Guaman Poma de Ayala. *El primer nueva corónica y buen gobierno*. Mexico: Siglo Veintiuno, 1992.
Rolena Adorno. *Guaman Poma: Writing and Resistance in Colonial Peru*. Austin: University of Texas Press, 2000.
Patricia Seed. "Failing to Marvel: Atahualpa's Encounter with the Word." *Latin American Research Review*, Vol. 26 (1991): 7–34.

50. **Northeast Coast of North America, 1607** Marcel Trudel. "Samuel de Champlain." In: *Dictionary of Canadian Biography*. Toronto: University of Toronto Press, 1966.
Marc Lescarbot and William L. Grant. *History of New France*, Vol. 1. Toronto: Champlain Society, 1907.

51. **East and Southeast Asia, c. 1625** Information on line at the Bodleian Library, Oxford, on the "Selden Map of China."

52. **Nagasaki Harbor, Japan, 1764** For background see Leonard Blusse, "No Boats to China: The Dutch East India Company and the Changing Pattern of the China Sea Trade, 1635–1690." *Modern Asian Studies*, Vol. 30, No. 1 (1996): 51–76.

53. **Tupaia's Map of Tahiti for Captain Cook, 1769** Ben Finney, "Nautical Cartography and Traditional Navigation in Oceania." In: David Woodward and G. Malcolm Lewis, eds. *Cartography in the Traditional African, American, Arctic, Australian, and Pacific Societies;* Vol. 2, Book 3, *History of Cartography*. Chicago: University of Chicago Press, 1998.

54. **North American Buckskin Map, 1774–1775** G. Malcolm Lewis. "Maps, Mapmaking, and Map Use by Native North Americans." In: David Woodward and G. Malcolm Lewis, eds. *The History of Cartography* Vol. 2, Part 3, pp. 51–182. Chicago: University of Chicago Press, 1998.

55. **Powder Horn Maps, 1750s–1780s** Dan Trachtenberg. "Map Powder Horns or Powder Horn Maps." *Portolan* (2003): 17–20.

56. **Slavery on the Gold Coast of Africa, 1729** Paul E. Lovejoy. *Transformations in Slavery: A History of Slavery in Africa*. Cambridgeshire: Cambridge University Press, 1983.

57. **The Niger River Described by a Fulani Ruler, 1824** E. W. Bovill, Frederich K. Hornemann, and Alexander G. Laing. *Missions to the Niger*, Vol. 4. Cambridge, UK: Published for the Hakluyt Society by the Cambridge University Press, 1964.

58. **Cedid Atlas, 1803** Donald Quataert, *The Ottoman Empire, 1700–1922*. Cambridge, UK: Cambridge University Press, 2005.

59. **Napoleon's Advance and Retreat from Moscow, 1812–1813** Edward R. Tufte, *The Visual Display of Quantitative Information*. Cheshire, CT: Graphics Press, 1983.

PART 6: LAND SURVEYS
c. **800–1900**

60. **Japan: The First Rice Field Surveys, Eighth Century** CE Kazutaka In Unno. "Cartography in Japan." In: J. B. Harley, David Woodward, et al., eds. *Cartography in the Traditional East and Southeast Asian Societies*, pp. 346–477; Vol. 2, Part 2, *The History of Cartography*. Chicago: University of Chicago Press, 1994.

61. **Chinese County Maps: Dinghai County, 1226** CE Lucille Chia and Hilde De Weerdt, eds. *Knowledge and Text Production in An Age of Print: China, 900-1400*. Leiden and Boston: Brill, 2011.
Frances Wood and Mark Barnard. *The Diamond Sutra: The Story of the World's Earliest Dated Printed Book*. London: British Library, 2010.

62. **Elizabethan Tapestry Map, 1580** Hilary L. Turner, "The Sheldon Tapestry Maps: their Content and Context." *The Cartographic Journal*, Vol. 40, No. 1 (2003): 39–49.
Christopher Saxton and W. L. D. Ravenhill. *Christopher Saxton's 16th Century Maps: The Counties of England & Wales*. Shrewsbury: Chatsworth Library, 1992.

63. **The Land That Windmills Made: A Dutch Polder Map, 1750** Walter W. Ristow. "Dutch Polder Maps." *The Quarterly Journal of the Library of Congress*, Vol. 31, No. 3 (1974): 136--149.
Paul Wagret, *Polderlands*. London: Methuen and New York: Barnes and Noble, 1968.

64. **Paris on the Eve of the French Revolution, 1789** Jerry Brotton. *A History of the World in Twelve Maps, Allen and Lane, 2012*. Monique Pelletier. *La Carte De Cassini: L'extraordinaire Aventure De La Carte De France*. Paris: Presses de l'Ecole nationale des ponts et chaussées, 1990.

65. **The Origins of the Ordnance Survey: Scotland's Loch Ness, 1747–1755** Rachel Hewitt, *Map of a Nation: A Biography of the Ordnance Survey*. London: Granta, 2010.

66. **Thai Map, c. 1782** Narisa Chakrabongse and Henry Ginsburg. *Siam in Trade and War: Royal Maps of the Nineteenth Century*. Bangkok: River Books, 2006.

67. **The vale of Kashmir, 1836** Susan Gole. *Early Maps of India*. New York: Humanities Press, 1976.
_____. *Indian Maps and Plans from Earliest Times to the Arrival of Europeans*. New Delhi: Manohar Publications,1989.

68. **The Eight Provinces of Korea, c. 1850** Han Young-woo, Ahn Hwi-Joon, and Bae Woo Sung. *The Artistry of Early Korean Cartography*. Choi Byonghyon, trans; Alexander Akin, ed. Larkspur, CA: Tamal Vista Publications, 2009.

69. **Japan: Gyoki Map on a Porcelain Plate, c. 1830** Kazutaka Unno. "Maps of Japan Used in Prayer Rites or as Charms." *Imago Mundi*, Vol. 46 (1994): 65–83
_____. "Cartography in Japan." In: J. B. Harley and David Woodward, eds. *Cartography in the Traditional East and Southeast Asian Societies*, pp. 346–477; Vol. 2, Part 2, *The History of Cartography*. Chicago: University of Chicago Press, 1994.

70. **Mongolian Land Survey, 1892** Hiroshi Futaki and Akira Kamimura. *Landscapes Reflected in Old Mongolian Maps*. Tokyo: Honbu, 2005.

PART 7: MAPPING THE NATURAL WORLD, 1800–2010

71. **Bali: Rivers and Temples, 1935** John S. Lansing. *Priests and Programmers: Technologies of Power in the Engineered Landscape of Bali.* Princeton, NJ: Princeton University Press, 1991.

72. **The Great Trigonometric Survey of India, 1802–1866** Matthew H. Edney. *Mapping an Empire: The Geographical Construction of British India, 1765–1843.* Delhi: Oxford University Press, 1999.

73. **Alexander von Humboldt's Map of Plants on Chimborazo, 1803** Gerard Helferich. *Humboldt's Cosmos: Alexander Von Humboldt and the Latin American Journey That Changed the Way We See the World.* New York: Gotham Books, 2004. Caroline Schaumann, "Who Measures the World? Alexander von Humboldt's Chimborazo Climb in the Literary Imagination." *German Quarterly,* Vol. 82, No. 4 (2009): 447–468.

74. **Geological Map of Southwestern England, 1815** Simon Winchester. *The Map That Changed the World: William Smith and the Birth of Modern Geology.* New York: HarperCollins, 2001.

75. **1851 Whale Chart** Eric J. Dolin. *Leviathan: The History of Whaling in America.* New York: W.W. Norton & Co., 2007.

76. **Monsoon and Trade Wind Chart of the Indian Ocean, 1864** Matthew F. Maury, *The Physical Geography of the Sea.* New York: Harper & Brothers, 1856. G. R. Tibbits. *Arab Navigation in the Indian Ocean before the Coming of the Portuguese: Being a Translation of "Kitab al-Fawaid fi usul al-bahr wa'l-qawa'id" of Ahmad b. Majid al-Najdi* London: Royal Asiatic Society of Great Britain and Ireland, 1971.

77. **Marshall Islands Stick Map, 1870s** Ben Finney. "Nautical Cartography and Traditional Navigation in Oceania." In: David Woodward and G. Malcolm Lewis, eds. *Cartography in the Traditional African, American, Arctic, Australian, and Pacific Societies;* Vol. 2, Book 3, *The History of Cartography.* Chicago: University of Chicago Press, 1998.

78. **Crown Prince Islands in Disko Bay, Greenland, 1926** Hans Christian Gulløv, "Introduction," *Arctic Anthropology,* Vol. 23, No. 1/2 (1986): 1–18. Robert A. Rundstrom, "A Cultural Interpretation of Inuit Map Accuracy." *Geographical Review,* Vol. 80, No. 2 (1990): 155–168. John Spink, *Eskimo Maps from the Canadian Eastern Arctic.* **Toronto:** B. V. Gutsell, 1972.

79. **Luba Mapping Device, Congo, 1930s** Mary N. Roberts, Allen F. Roberts, and S T. Childs. *Memory: Luba Art and the Making of History.* New York: Museum for African Art, 1996.

80. **The Modern Zodiac, 1933** International Astronomical Union, Adriaan Blaauw. *History of the IAU: The Birth and First Half-Century of the International Astronomical Union.* Dordrecht: Kluwer Academic Publishers, 1994.

81. **Maps into Art: Aboriginal Map, 1987** Peter Sutton, "Aboriginal Maps and Plans." In: David Woodward and G. Malcolm Lewis, eds. *Cartography in the Traditional African, American, Arctic, Australian, and Pacific Societies;* Vol. 2, Book 3, *The History of Cartography.* Chicago: University of Chicago Press, 1998.

82. **Map of the Ocean Floor, 1977** Bruce C. Heezen, Marie Tharp, Heinrich C. Berann, and Heinz Vielkind. *World Ocean Floor.* Washington: U.S. Navy, 1977. Ronald E. Doel, Tanya J. Levin, and Mason K. Marker. "Extending modern cartography to the ocean depths: military patronage, Cold War priorities, and the Heezen–Tharp mapping project, 1952–1959." *Journal of Historical Geography,* Vol. 32, No. 3 (2006): 605–626. Cathy Barton. "Marie Tharp, oceanographic cartographer, and her contributions to the revolution in Earth Sciences." In: David Oldroyd, ed. *The Earth Inside and Out: Some Major Contributions to Geology in the Twentieth Century.* London: Geological Society, 2002, pp. 215–250.

83. **Map of Antarctica, 2004** Stephen R. Bown. *The Last Viking: The Life of Roald Amundsen.* Boston: Da Capo Press, 2012. Caroline Alexander, *The Endurance: Shackleton's Legendary Antarctic Expedition.* New York: Knopf, 1998.

84. **Coastal Flooding in West Africa: Mapping the Future** Ellen J. Prager and Sylvia A. Earle. *The Oceans.* New York: McGraw-Hill, 2000. R. Vernet. *Le Golfe d'Arguin de la préhistoire à l'histoire: littoral et plaines intérieures.* Nouakchott: Parc National du Banc d'Arguin, 2007.

PART 8: EMPIRES, WARS, AND DECOLONIZATION, 1884–1999

85. **Cape to Cairo: The Scramble for Africa, 1884–1885** Thomas Pakenham, *The Scramble For Africa: White Man's Conquest of The Dark Continent From 1876 to 1912.* New York: Perennial, 2003. Eric Axelson. *Portugal and the Scramble for Africa, 1875–1891.* Johannesburg: Witwatersrand University Press, 1967.

86. **Territorial Claims in Central and Eastern Europe Prior to World War I** Samuel R. Williamson, *Austria-Hungary and the Origins of the First World War.* Houndmills, Basingstoke, Hampshire: Macmillan, 1991. Mustafa Aksakal, *The Ottoman Road to War in 1914: The Ottoman Empire and*

the First World War. Cambridge, UK: Cambridge University Press, 2008.

87. Trench Warfare: 1916 Artillery Map, Flanders Peter Chasseaud, "British Artillery and Trench Maps on The Western Front 1914–1918." *Map Collector,* Vol. 51 (1990): 24–32.
Army War College. *Maps and Artillery Boards.* Washington, DC: G.P.O., 1917.

88. Soviet Georgia, from the First Russian Atlas, 1937–1939 Ronald Gigor Suny, *The Making of the Georgian Nation.* Bloomington: Indiana University Press in association with Hoover Institution Press; Stanford University, Stanford, CA, 1988. For a wider treatment of the Caucaus, see Charles King, *The Ghost of Freedom: A History of the Caucasus* (New York: Oxford University Press, 2008) is indispensable, as is Thomas de Waal's *The Caucasus: An Introduction* (Oxford University Press, 2010).

89. Japanese Aviation Maps, 1933, Yoshihisa T. Matsusaka, *The Making of Japanese Manchuria, 1904-1932.* Cambridge, MA: Harvard University Asia Center, 2001.

90. Royal Air Force Map for Bombing Northern Germany, 1943 M. Kirby and R. Capey, "The Area Bombing of Germany in World War II: An Operational Research Perspective." *The Journal of the Operational Research Society,* Vol. 48, No. 7 (1997): 661–677. and Charles Quilter. PhD Dissertation, University of California Irvine, 2010.

91. World War II Silk Escape Map Barbara A. Bond. "Silk Maps: The story of MI9's excursion into the world of cartography 1939–1945." *The Cartographic Journal,* Vol. 21, No. 2 (1984): 141–144.

92. Post-War New World Map, 1942 Susan Schulten. "Richard Edes Harrison and the Challenge to American Cartography." *Imago Mundi,* Vol. 50 (1998), 174–188.John L. Gaddis. *The Cold War: A New History.* New York: Penguin, 2005.

93. Black Homeland Consolidation Proposals for South Africa, 1973 Laura Evans. "South Africa's Bantustans and the Dynamics of 'Decolonisation': Reflections on Writing Histories of the Homelands." *South African Historical Journal, Vol.* 64, No. 1 (2012): 117–137.

94. Peoples and Nations of the Soviet Union, 1991 Valery A. Tishkov. "The Soviet Empire before and after Perestroika." *Theory and Society,* Vol. 20 (1991): 603–629.

95. Decolonization in Africa, 1960–1975 Dhananjayan Sriskandarajahj. "Long Underwear on a Line? The Peters Projection and Thirty Years of Cartocontroversy." *Geography,* Vol. 88, No. 3 (2003): 236–244.John D. Hargreaves. *Decolonization in Africa.* **London:** Longman, 1988.

PART 9: MAPPING TRANSPORT AND COMMUNICATION NETWORKS, 1884–2006

96. Brazilian Railway Map, 1884 William R. Summerhill, *Order against Progress: Government, Foreign Investment, and Railroads in Brazil, 1854-1913.* Stanford, CA: Stanford University Press, 2003.

97. French National Automobile Map, 1902 *France, Routes Historiques: Villes et pays d'art et d'histoire.* Paris: IGN, 1994.

98. Harry Beck's 1933 Map of the London Underground Ken Garland and Henry C. Beck. *Mr Beck's Underground Map.* Harrow Weald, Middlesex: Capital Transport, 1994.

99. Landing on 27R: London's Heathrow Airport, 2006 P. T. Sherwood. *Heathrow:2000 Years of History.* Stroud, Gloucestershire: The History Press, 2009.

100. Map of the Internet, 2003 Andrew Blum. *Tubes: A Journey to the Center of the Internet.* New York: Ecco, 2012.

Credits

CHAPTER 1
Rock painting of a bull with long horns, the Hall of Bulls, c.17000 BC, . / Caves of Lascaux, Dordogne, France / The Bridgeman Art Library

CHAPTER 2
© 'Imiloa Astronomy Center

CHAPTER 3
Courtesy of the South African Astronomical Observatory

CHAPTER 4
© Serge Brunier

CHAPTER 5
Alfred Jeremias, Handbuch der altorientalischen Geisteskultur (Leipzig: J.C. Hinichs'sche Buchandlung, 1913), courtesy of Robert Harry van Gent via http://www.staff.science.uu.nl/~gent0113/.

CHAPTER 6
The Bodleian Library, University of Oxford.

CHAPTER 7
Courtesy of The Library of Congress.

CHAPTER 8
Courtesy of the Schoenberg Center, University of Pennsylvania Library / Courtesy of The Library of Congress.

CHAPTER 9
The British Library, London

CHAPTER 10
Photograph by Patricia Seed

CHAPTER 11
Photograph by Patricia Seed

CHAPTER 12
Bernard J. Shapero Rare Books, London

CHAPTER 13
De Agostini Picture Library

CHAPTER 14
British Museum, London, Great Britain; The Egyptian Museum, Cairo

CHAPTER 15
Courtesy James A. Harrell

CHAPTER 16
Copyright: © Gansu Provincial Research Institute of Antiquities and Archeology/ ChinaStock

CHAPTER 17
Soprintendenza Speciale per i Beni Archeologici di Roma

CHAPTER 18
Österreichische Nationalbibliothek

CHAPTER 19
The Bodleian Library, University of Oxford.

CHAPTER 20
The Bodleian Library, University of Oxford.

CHAPTER 21
Koninklijke Bibliotheek, National Library of the Netherlands

CHAPTER 22
The Bodleian Library, University of Oxford

CHAPTER 23
Erich Lessing / Art Resource, NY

CHAPTER 24
Rare Book and Special Collections Division, Library of Congress

CHAPTER 25
The Bodleian Library, University of Oxford

CHAPTER 26
Near East Section, African and Middle Eastern Division, Library of Congress

CHAPTER 27
Library of Congress, African and Middle Eastern Division

CHAPTER 28
Hereford Cathedral, Herefordshire, UK / The Bridgeman Art Library

CHAPTER 29
The Bodleian Library, University of Oxford

CHAPTER 30
The British Library

CHAPTER 31
Biblioteca Marciana, Venice, Italy

CHAPTER 32
Namba Collection, Kobe City Museum

CHAPTER 33
Southern Asian Section, Asian Division, Library of Congress

CHAPTER 34
Bibliothèque national de France

CHAPTER 35
Veneranda Biblioteca Ambrosiana

CHAPTER 36
Bibliothèque national de France

CHAPTER 37
Drawings by author and Tsvetelina Zdraveva from compass roses on maps in chapters 31, 36, 40, and the author's website "Latitude: The Art and Science of Fifteenth Century Navigation"

CHAPTER 77
Ethnologisches Museum, SMB, Berlin

CHAPTER 78
Library of Congress Geography and Map Division, Washington, D.C.; Kort & Matrikelstyrelsen, Denmark; (photograph) Patricia Seed

CHAPTER 79
Drawing by Tsvetelina Zdraveva based on depictions from the International Astronomical Union.

CHAPTER 80
Drawing by Tsvetelina Zdraveva

CHAPTER 81
Peter Skipper (Pijaju)
Arts Rights Agency

CHAPTER 82
Library of Congress, Geography and Map Division, Washington, D.C.; Bruce C. Heezen and Marie Tharp, 1981; Photograph by Bruce Gilbert

CHAPTER 83
Christopher Shuman, ICESAT/NASA; (photograph) Corbis/Bettman

CHAPTER 84
Patricia Seed, ESRI Mapbook

CHAPTER 85
Norman B. Leventhal Map Center, Boston Public Library; National Library, Lisbon

CHAPTER 86
ÖNB/Wien FKB O 18; Courtesy of Patricia Seed

CHAPTER 87
Library and Archives Canada, NMC 21462; photographs courtesy of the Library of Congress

CHAPTER 88
Geography and Map Division Library of Congress

CHAPTER 89
Courtesy Col. Charles Quilter, USMC (ret.)

CHAPTER 90
Courtesy Col. Charles Quilter, USMC (ret.)

CHAPTER 91
Courtesy of Patricia Seed

CHAPTER 92
Library of Congress Geography and Map Division Washington, D.C.

CHAPTER 93
Library of Congress Geography and Map Division Washington, D.C.

CHAPTER 94
U.S. Central Intelligence Agency, 1995

CHAPTER 95
Patricia Seed, ESRI ArcMap 10.0

CHAPTER 96
Library of Congress Geography and Map Division Washington, D.C.

CHAPTER 97
Library University of California-Berkeley; Courtesy of Patricia Seed

CHAPTER 98
London Transport Museum

CHAPTER 99
Civil Aviation Authority (UK), Crown Copyright, Courtesy Col. Charles Quilter, USMC (ret.)

CHAPTER 100
Map of the Internet, 2003, Opte Project, Retrieved September 2010

APPENDIX
© 2013 Google-Imagery; © 2013 NASA, TerraMetrics

Types of maps included in the volume

Locations for maps in the volume

This locator provides a general overview of the places that are associated with the maps that are included in the volume.
The number next to each dot corresponds to a map. Each dot either indicates the area that is depicted in the relevant map or the home or birthplace of its mapmaker.

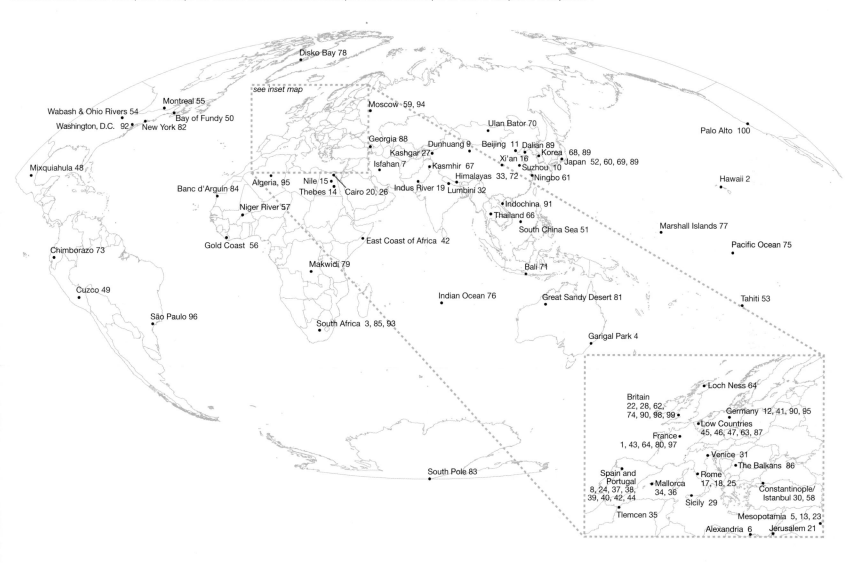

Disko Bay 78

see inset map

Moscow 59, 94

Wabash & Ohio Rivers 54
Montreal 55
Bay of Fundy 50
Washington, D.C. 92
New York 82

Ulan Bator 70

Palo Alto 100

Georgia 88
Kashgar 27
Dunhuang 9
Beijing 11
Dalian 89
Korea 68, 89
Isfahan 7
Xi'an 16
Japan 52, 60, 69, 89
Suzhou 10
Ningbo 61

Mixquiahula 48

Hawaii 2

Algeria, 95
Nile 15
Kasmhir 67
Himalayas 33, 72
Banc d'Arguin 84
Thebes 14
Cairo 20, 26
Indus River 19
Lumbini 32

Niger River 57

Indochina 91
Thailand 66
Marshall Islands 77

Chimborazo 73

South China Sea 51

Gold Coast 56
East Coast of Africa 42

Pacific Ocean 75

Cuzco 49

Makwidi 79
Bali 71

São Paulo 96

Indian Ocean 76
Great Sandy Desert 81
Tahiti 53

South Africa 3, 85, 93

Garigal Park 4

Loch Ness 64

Britain
22, 28, 62,
74, 90, 98, 99
Germany 12, 41, 90, 95
Low Countries
45, 46, 47, 63, 87
France
1, 43, 64, 80, 97
Venice 31
The Balkans 86
Spain and
Portugal
8, 24, 37, 38,
39, 40, 42, 44
Rome
17, 18, 25
Mallorca
34, 36
Constantinople/
Istanbul 30, 58
Sicily 29
Mesopotamia 5, 13, 23
Tlemcen 35
Alexandria 6
Jerusalem 21

South Pole 83

239

Technical note

Locator maps created using ESRI's Arc GIS 9.3, 10.0, and 10.1 software with data from ESRI, ArcWorld Supplement, the U.S. Geological Survey, the Food and Agriculture Organization, Geonames, National Atlas of the United States, the Jet Propulsion Laboratory, Pasadena (Shuttle Radar Topography Mission Data), and Delorme.

Index